the Tudor

HENRY VII (1457-150_
King of England (1485-150_

Arthur (1486-1502)
=(1) Catherine of
Aragon (1485-1536)

Margaret (1489-1541)
(1) = James IV (1473-1513)
of Scotland; (2) =
Archibald Douglas
(1489?-1557) Earl of Angus

Henry VIII (1491-1547)
King of England =
1509-47
(1) = (2) Catherine of
Aragon (1485-1536)

Elizabeth
(1492-95)

(2) = Anne Bole
(1507?-36_

James V (1512-42)
of Scotland (2) = (2)
Mary of Guise
(1515-60)

3 sons and
2 daughters
died young

Margaret (1515-78)
= Matthew Stewart
(1516-71) Earl of
Lennox

2 sons
and 1
daughter
died young

Mary I (1516-58)
Queen of
England
1553-58 =
Philip II
(1527-98) of
Spain

Elizabe_
(1533-1603) (
of England
(1558-1603_

2 sons
died young

Mary (1542-87) (2)
Queen of Scots
1542-67; (1) =
Francis II (1544-60)
of France; (3) =
James Hepburn (1536-78)
Earl of Bothwell

Henry Stewart (1545-67)
Lord Darnley

Charles (c. 1556-76)
Earl of Lennox =
Elizabeth Cavendish
(d. 1582)

2 sons
4 daug_
died y_

Elizabeth (1465-1503)

daughter of Edward IV

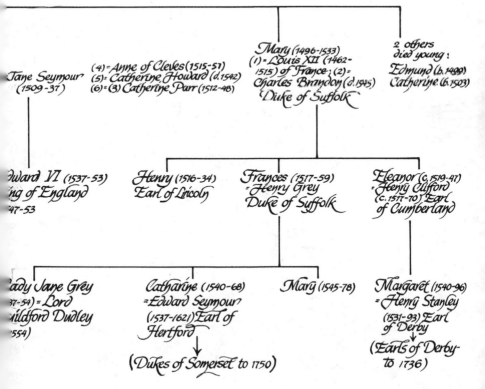

Jane Seymour
(1509-37)

(4)=Anne of Cleves(1515-57)
(5)=Catherine Howard (d.1542)
(6)=(3) Catherine Parr (1512-48)

Mary (1496-1533)
(1)=Louis XII (1462-1515) of France; (2)=
Charles Brandon (d.1545)
Duke of Suffolk

2 others
died young:
Edmund (b.1499)
Catherine (b.1503)

Edward VI (1537-53)
King of England
1547-53

Henry (1516-34)
Earl of Lincoln

Frances (1517-59)
=Henry Grey
Duke of Suffolk

Eleanor (c.1519-47)
=Henry Clifford
(c.1517-70) Earl
of Cumberland

Lady Jane Grey
(1537-54) = Lord
Guildford Dudley
(d.1554)

Catharine (1540-68)
=Edward Seymour
(1537-1621) Earl of
Hertford

(Dukes of Somerset to 1750)

Mary (1545-78)

Margaret (1540-96)
=Henry Stanley
(1531-93) Earl
of Derby

(Earls of Derby
to 1736)

The Story of
Lady Jane Grey

CORONATION
OF GLORY

The Story of
Lady Jane Grey

CORONATION
OF GLORY
Deborah Meroff

**ZONDERVAN
PUBLISHING HOUSE**
OF THE ZONDERVAN CORPORATION
GRAND RAPIDS, MICHIGAN 49506

to my mother and father—
"gentlest of critics"

CORONATION OF GLORY
© 1979 by The Zondervan Corporation
Grand Rapids, Michigan

Library of Congress Cataloging in Publication Data
Meroff, Deborah.
Coronation of glory.

Bibliography: p.
1. Dudley, Jane, Lady, known as Lady Jane Grey,
1537-1554. 2. Great Britain—History—Edward VI
and Mary, 1547-1558. 3. Great Britain—Princes and princesses—
Biography. I. Title.
DA345.1.D9M47   942.05'3'0924 [B]   79-10197
ISBN 0-310-38210-6

Printed in the United States of America

Foreword

I am afraid.

I am going to die.

They say it is not a painful death, that it hurts only for an instant. But sometimes in the night I wake, my body drenched with sweat, and I know I have dreamed again of that moment when I shall lay my bare neck in the hollow of the stone and wait for the steel to descend. . . .

Oh, God—I am seventeen! Is it time, already, to leave life behind when there is so much left untried? And yet, You have given me all the important things. The loyalty of friends, the tenderness of a man's love, and—above and through all—Your abiding Presence.

Shall I be remembered when I am gone? Will the people think of me as a schemer, a usurper, or will they understand how dearly I loved England and how with all my heart I desired to obey Your will? Forgive me my trespasses, O Lord. And help Your people to forgive.

I feel a need to set everything down as it happened. Perhaps someday, when memory has settled like dust over England, my testimony will be brought to light and will vindicate my life in some measure. I pray God it will, and that He will guide my hand to truth as I begin.

I remember perfectly that day in early spring of the year 1547. It had been only three months since our Sovereign King Henry the Eighth was laid in state beneath the stones of St. George's Chapel at Windsor; now my guardian and I were on our way to the Queen Dowager.

Her Chelsea residence was located in one of the loveliest boroughs of London, but I took little notice of my surroundings. I was in a high fever of anticipation. Although I could not endure separation from Queen Catherine any longer, I was afraid— horribly afraid—that something had occurred within the last three months to make a change between us.

"You confound me, Jane. For days—no, *weeks*, since I brought you to Seymour Place, you have teased and pleaded with me to let you see Lady Catherine. And now that the grand moment has arrived, you will not favor me with a smile. I am disconsolate."

The corners of my mouth turned up. My guardian, Lord High Admiral Thomas Seymour, was not a man to be easily disheartened. In the short time I had lived in fashionable Seymour Place on the Strand, I had found his charm nearly irresistible—and so, I had discovered, did a rather vast throng of London ladies. Although my attendants had done their best to shield my ears from the scandals that flew about the city, I had managed to learn a good deal about the tall lord riding beside me.

"It is not that I do not want to see her. It is just that—it has been so long! Three months since she sent me to Leicestershire."

"You are afraid she will not be pleased to see you?"

How could he understand? I nodded slowly. "I was only six when I first went to live with Lady Catherine. She was the new Queen at Hampton Court, and I was lost and alone among hundreds of courtiers and ladies-in-waiting. I wanted nothing more than to return to Bradgate. But it was not long before I made a discovery. The Queen was unhappy too. And she was—frightened. Sometimes when the King was in a frightful temper, he made her weep, and she would have no one but me near to comfort her."

I stopped, wondering if I should be telling him these things.

"We all knew, of course, that the King threatened Catherine's life," Lord Thomas responded. "She was entirely at his mercy. At any moment he might have chosen to do away with her as he had his other wives. She must have been in torment!"

Torment. Yes, that was what it had been. Every day for four endless years.

"We came to depend on each other. It did not seem to matter that there were so many years between us. She taught me and cared for me as though I were her child. And I loved her as my own mother."

More than my mother. The thought came unbidden, and I pushed it away. That was not true. I loved Mama.

Our horses trotted through the graceful, tree-arched entrance to Chelsea Manor. It was a lovely May morning, warm and bright with gay masses of jonquils, tulips, and celandine on both sides of the lane. Soon we would be in sight of the house. Soon I would see her.

"And you really believe her feelings toward you may have undergone some change?"

"My lord, the King is dead. Lady Catherine has left the palace and its unhappiness behind her. Why would she now have need of *me?*"

My guardian frowned, but before he could reply we reached the manor. Grooms ran forward to catch the bridles of our horses as we prepared to dismount.

"Run along in and see her," Lord Thomas instructed. "I shall follow directly. And, Jane—" he allowed himself a slight smile, "I should not be afraid if I were you."

I followed a marvelously liveried butler through a maze of halls to the double doors of the library. Here he paused to announce me while my gloved hands twisted a fold of my gown.

8

"Your Grace. The Lady Jane Grey."

As he stood aside, I could see the small, elegant woman standing on the far side of the room. During the moment of silence a thousand fears crowded into my mind. Then Lady Catherine smiled and held out her hands.

"*Jane!*"

I flew into her arms and pressed my face hard against her gown. *I am home, home at last.* And as I wept, my tears staining the fine satin of her gown beyond repair, my fears of being unwelcome dissolved.

"It has been so long, child—so long," she murmured, stroking my hair. "Here, let me look at you properly."

"I have missed you, Lady Catherine."

"And I, you, my love. But you are so thin and pale! You have not been ill?"

"Oh, no. I could never be ill at Bradgate. Papa says sickness belongs to the cities."

"Then you have spent too long at your books!" She shook her head. "You will ruin your complexion *and* your health. What is to become of you?"

I could not help smiling. "If I love learning it is only because of you, my lady. I wish to become exactly like you."

She laughed, and it was a rare, beautiful sound. "Then you must learn to set your sights a good deal higher! And I must be a more careful example. I had hoped a change from the city would be good for you, but you come back from Leicestershire as lean as my greyhounds." The keen brown eyes continued to study me, and I flushed uncomfortably.

"There is something more you are not telling me. I wonder —does it concern your father? Or Bradgate?"

"Oh, Papa could not be in better spirits, my lady. And he has transformed Bradgate! The herb and fruit gardens contain samples of every variety to be found in the northern part of the continent. I wish you could see them!"

"I should like that. It is splendid when a man such as the Marquess of Dorset takes pleasure in the earth. So many gentlemen consider it an injury to soil their hands. What a pity Frances does not share his enthusiasm."

My face must have betrayed surprise, for she laughed. "You forget that your mama and I are old acquaintances. Frances will

9

always be a town creature, however well she adapts to the country. Perhaps that is not remarkable when one remembers she is the daughter of the infamous Charles Brandon and Mary Tudor!"

Remember? I repressed a bitter smile. I was never permitted to forget Mama's royal lineage. As the daughter of King Henry the Eighth's sister Mary, Frances Brandon was the fourth heir to the Crown of England. Preceding her, of course, were King Henry's own children—Edward, Mary, and Elizabeth, in that order. And since I was Mama's eldest, I came fifth in the line of succession.

I had been permitted to see my grandfather, Charles Brandon, only once, when he was dying. But even then I could see the similarity to my mother's proud, handsome features.

"And your sisters, little Mary and Katie? Do they prosper?"

"Aye, Lady Catherine."

In truth I had seen little of them. My youngest sister, Mary, only two years old, had been born during my years at Hampton Court.

As for Katie—well, Katie was Katie: bright, winsome, and already attractive. Two years younger than I, she had established a place in my mother's affections that I envied. It seemed the two were always together, visiting local officials and nobility, hunting and hawking. They were both superb horsewomen and I had never quite reached a degree of mastery that could satisfy Mama. Perhaps that was why I tried so hard to excel at my studies—to compensate for my other failings.

"I should have insisted on sending for you," the Queen frowned, "but the Lord Admiral seemed to think I required some seclusion after the King's death."

"But the Princess Elizabeth is here, is she not?" When my guardian had imparted this information to me, it had created no small amount of jealousy.

"Yes. The poor girl was heartbroken over her father's death, though heaven knows Henry treated her unspeakably. Thomas was among those who rode to her at Hatfield with the news; he suggested she come to stay at Chelsea Manor for a time."

"I cannot see how *that* would give you any rest!"

"It is true, there is seldom an idle moment with our Eliza about! But it is the best sort of medicine for me—looking after one of 'my children.' I only wish I could have Edward here to mother as well."

10

It was still difficult for me to think of my cousin Edward as the King—King Edward VI of England and Ireland. Probably it was because we were the same age—born the same October of the year 1537—and had shared several years of study and play together at Hampton Court. From our association I had discovered a reluctance within my cousin to face the responsibility that must one day be his.

"He is still a child." The Queen sighed. "It troubles me that my release must mean his bondage. Did you know that he actually fainted during the coronation ceremonies? But he will at least be spared the full weight of dignity until he is of age. His uncle, the Duke of Somerset, will make the decisions—with, of course, the approval of the Privy Council."

I wondered how my cousin would find life under the protectorship of Edward Seymour, Duke of Somerset. And how odd that I should at the same time become the ward of his brother, Thomas Seymour. Lady Catherine seemed to read my thoughts.

"It is extraordinary, is it not, that two men can be so very alike in appearance and yet differ so in temperament. Thomas is every bit as fiery as Edward is sober and quiet. I do hope he will be gentle with the King."

"Papa says the Protector is a devout Protestant."

"He is indeed!" she replied with satisfaction. "At last we shall see the Reformation advance. The country has been torn apart too long by religious dissension. Henry made things worse by declaring himself supreme head of the Catholic church—turning both Reformers and Romanists against him. We must be united, Jane, under one strong faith."

I remembered how the Queen and those of us who believed in the Reformation had been in constant danger during King Henry's "heresy hunts." A misplaced pamphlet—a carelessly dropped word within the hearing of one of the bishop's spies—and any one of us would have gone to the stake as rapidly as the Queen's close friend, Anne Askew. A shudder ran through me.

"Those days are over, Jane," Lady Catherine said softly. "We need not fear discovery of our faith ever again."

"Oh, my lady! Everything would be perfect if only I could be with you again."

"You are not happy with the Lord Admiral and his mother? Thomas thought you were getting on very well."

11

"I am—they are most kind to me, especially Lady Margery. But it is not the same—as it was with us."

"Tell me, my dear, why did your parents consent to your becoming Thomas's ward?"

"Mama thought it a 'splendid opportunity' to introduce me to London society. She said Lord Thomas was just the person to see to it."

"Try to understand, Jane. She wishes to give you the kind of life she herself prefers. But what of your father? Did he agree?"

"Not at first. He told Mama I had already been away too long—four years at Court with you. And besides, he did not see how a man of Lord Thomas's—reputation—could make an acceptable guardian."

Lady Catherine's finely shaped brows arched with amusement. "Apparently he changed his mind."

"He—had to, my lady. Papa has had—financial difficulties of late. When the Lord Admiral offered to help him, it seemed a godsend."

"I see." There was a hard edge to her voice.

"Papa would not have allowed me to go, even for the money, if he was not quite satisfied that I would be safe and happy with Lord Thomas."

"Of course not." She reached over and laid her hand on mine. "And it does not really matter why you are here, does it? As long as you have come. Jane—I would like you to stay."

"Here?—Now?"

"You did not suppose I would let you go again? But perhaps it is too sudden—"

"Oh—Lady Catherine!"

"Then it is settled." She smiled, and her glow of happiness matched my own. "We shall send word to your attendants at Seymour Place and collect your things. Thomas has already given his consent; it was to be a surprise."

I flung my arms about her neck and hugged her. "It is the most lovely surprise, my lady! May I find Elizabeth and tell her?"

"Of course. She will be in the schoolroom with her tutor and will no doubt welcome the interruption!"

She broke off then, and I wondered at her sudden look of radiance. I turned and saw that my guardian had entered the room.

"I shall see you settled in later, darling."

12

As Lady Catherine had predicted, Cousin Elizabeth pounced on my appearance with joy.

"Why ever did you wait so long to visit? I have been absolutely perishing for want of someone to talk to! I am in mourning, you know; I am not allowed to go out much."

"I know, and I am sorry about your father, Elizabeth. We all find the King's death difficult to accept. He was so full of life—"

"Yes, he was a good king. The people are only now beginning to appreciate him."

There was a pause. Then a scholarly looking gentleman, whom I had not before noticed, stepped forward and bowed slightly.

"Lady Jane, I am Miles Coverdale, the Queen's chaplain. I deplore having to insert a painful note into this joyful reunion, but my pupil and I did have a prior engagement with the orations of Isocrates."

"Master Coverdale! You cannot seriously suggest that we continue with the lesson? My dearest cousin and I have not seen each other for months. It would be heartless—"

"Very well, Princess. Heaven forbid that I should be called heartless. However, I should be obliged to share another few moments with you tomorrow afore noon." With a nod to each of us, he gathered up his books and left the room.

"Poor Master Coverdale!" Elizabeth giggled and drew me down beside her on a window seat. "I treat him shamefully, and he is an absolute genius! You would like him, Jane. You are both so sober about things."

She had not changed, although she had grown taller and more slender. She was only four years my senior but looked much older in her black dress of mourning. Curly red-gold hair, gray eyes, fair skin sprinkled with freckles, and a long, slightly hooked nose gave her an impish air that belied her sincere bereavement for her father.

"His scholarship is well known, even in Leicestershire. I expect Master Coverdale did not foresee that he would be tutoring you when he became Lady Catherine's almoner."

"Gracious, I am sure he did not! But he seems to be holding up nicely."

"I wonder how he will fare with—two students?"

"Two? But—*Jane!*" she shrieked. "You are coming here to stay! How perfectly marvelous! But I should have guessed—you were always the Queen's favorite."

"That is nonsense, Eliza! You know how she spoiled all of us at the palace—even Princess Mary, when she was allowed."

"Ah, but we are the King's children. She had to be good to us. But it was you she especially invited to become a part of her household."

"Only to please Mama," I said, remembering that day, over four years ago, when I had first been presented to Lady Catherine, then the widow of Lord Latimer. She had come to call on Mama at our London town house and had asked to see me. When my nursemaid, Ellen, fetched me from the nursery, I was so overcome by shyness that I had handled the whole presentation clumsily. But Lady Catherine had been kind.

"She is a lovely child, Frances," she told Mama. "How I envy you."

"I am rather to be pitied that my firstborn did not live—my *son*, Catherine! I wanted him more than anything else on earth. And now I am left with a weakling girl."

The attractive widow's retort was sharp. "Give thanks to God for Jane, lest He remove her, too!" She bent down and pressed her soft cheek against mine. I think I loved her from that moment.

"Good-by, little one."

As Ellen led me away, I heard Mama speak again. "If she pleases you, why not take her into your household for the next few years? Who knows? It may be useful to have a child so near Prince Edward's age if you are at Hampton Court."

"I shall not be at Hampton Court." Was there fear in my new friend's voice?

"It is no secret that Henry looks with favor upon the widow Latimer...."

"She looks very well, does she not?"

Elizabeth's question jolted me back to the present.

"The Queen?—Oh, yes!—I have never seen her so happy."

"Not at all as though she were in mourning. I think it is painfully obvious how little she cared for my father."

"Elizabeth! She was devoted to the King."

"Because she had to be." My cousin spoke coldly. "She would

14

have lost her head if she was not. Catherine married Father out of fear, not love."

"Well, what if she did? A proposal from the King is a command. She had no choice. What woman would not be afraid to marry a man who had divorced or beheaded five other wives?"

I had said too much; Eliza's face was flushed. But why should she continue to give such allegiance to the man who had executed her own mother, Anne Boleyn, and who had declared her own self illegitimate?

"Father was hatefully abused by those women. Yes, even by Mother. She was as promiscuous as they say—like that wretched Catherine Howard—and deserved death. As for the marriage to Catherine of Aragon, it was an annulment, not a divorce, because she had never truly been Father's wife.

"He was tricked into the alliance with Anne of Cleves by his ministers before he could see how ugly she was—his 'Flanders Mare' he called her. She was as relieved as he to be divorced. And you cannot blame him for Jane Seymour's death—she was simply too weak to withstand childbirth. But Papa was always loyal to her memory for giving him a son."

I was silent.

"Perhaps Catherine was most afraid that Father would find out whom she really loved," she added slyly. "Thomas Seymour."

This was too much. "You do not know what you are saying! How can you sit in judgment upon the Queen after all she did for your father? She even nursed the ugly sores on his leg; no one else dared to go near him when he was in such pain. She did not complain even when he put the leg on her lap. You have no idea what she suffered. How dare you speak so of her?"

Elizabeth shrugged.

"I did not accuse her of unfaithfulness—at least not in deed. But the Holy Scriptures condemn those who regard iniquity in their hearts. Catherine planned to accept Thomas Seymour's offer of marriage until my father stopped them. Ask her, if you doubt me. And ask her if she does not now find him attractive."

I remembered the expression I had seen on Lady Catherine's face when Lord Thomas came into the room a few minutes ago. She was not in mourning; no, even in her black satin she had the look of a bride rather than a widow.

"What makes you so certain of her feelings?" I asked finally.

15

"I should have to have been both blind and deaf these past few months not to have guessed something. The Queen has hardly been discreet, stealing out to the garden gate in the full light of the moon. Any watcher besides myself could have seen her admitting Thomas Seymour."

"Eliza! How could you spy on them like that?"

"I have every right," she said. "She is my royal stepmother, and he is my uncle. And poor Father scarcely three months dead! How do you suppose that makes me feel?"

Again I had no answer; I was as bewildered and shaken as my cousin. Despite her well-known tendency to overdramatize, I could see she was quite serious.

"Will you tell the King?"

She laughed, a bitter laugh. "My brother and his Council will learn of it without my telling them. I have no wish to see Catherine ruined, Jane, but she will bring the hurt upon her own head if she lets herself be used by that treacherous Seymour."

"What if he really cares for her? His intentions may be quite honorable."

"*Honorable?* My dear, naïve cousin, I have apparently not been explicit enough. Your guardian and the Queen Dowager do not merely chat over the garden gate. She admits him to the house, and he does not leave until dawn. What honorable man would regard the Queen's reputation so lightly? Indeed, what honorable man would even court a woman so soon after her husband's death? Thomas Seymour has never truly cared for anyone but himself. He may be fond of the Queen, but I would wager that her wealth and position attract him more than her person!"

"You seem to know him well."

"As well as any woman—better than most. We are alike in many ways."

"Then it surprises me that he did not ask *you* to marry him!"

The barb pierced deeper than I expected. She flushed a deep crimson.

"Oh, he asked me, to be sure! But without the Council's approval I should have to give up all hope of succeeding to the throne. And that, dear cousin, would not suit either of us."

Rippling laughter at the door interrupted us.

"Who has asked to marry you now, my irresistible Princess? Tell us!" said Lady Catherine.

16

All color drained from Elizabeth's face; I sat with my eyes fixed upon the Queen, whose hand rested possessively on my guardian's sleeve.

"It was nothing," Elizabeth muttered.

"Oh, come! We would like to hear your secret, would we not, Thomas?"

"Indeed we would."

Elizabeth shot him a venomous look. "Perhaps we can make a fair exchange, then. I am most eager to learn what urgent business necessitates your frequent rendezvous at the garden gate!"

This time it was Lady Catherine who paled. She glanced quickly at Lord Thomas, who smiled.

"It is true that Catherine and I have met secretly for—some time now. You are not so naïve as to believe it concerns any matter of state. Catherine's responsibilities as Queen are ended; she has her own life to live."

"With you? My father's widow disgraced a scarce few weeks after his death?"

"Elizabeth!"

Lady Catherine crossed the room and put her hands on Elizabeth's shoulders. "Listen to me! You have mistaken our meaning. I should have confided in you, but I wished to spare you the knowledge until—until you had adjusted to your father's death. Thomas and I are married, my dear. We were wed a month after your brother's coronation.

"I know how this must seem to you—to you both. It is not something that will be easy for you to understand. Perhaps when you are older—"

"The reason for the secrecy is obvious," Lord Thomas interrupted. "The kingdom is not yet ready to accept the Queen's remarriage; for her safety we must make it appear that the wedding takes place at the same time as the public announcement next month."

"Do you think the realm will forgive you even then?"

"They must, Elizabeth. Oh, I know my behavior is not what is expected of a queen dowager; it will create a scandal. But the people must accept it. I needed to start living again, quickly, before the rest of my life slipped by. And I love Thomas—very much."

Elizabeth turned away. Impulsively I slipped my own hand

17

within Lady Catherine's. "We understand; truly we do. We want you to be happy."

"Of course." My cousin's voice was emotionless. "My congratulations to you both."

"What about the bridegroom? Does he get a kiss?"

Lord Thomas must have seen the anger that froze Eliza's features, but he appeared not to and took her in his arms.

"A cool welcome to the family, Princess! I trust you will learn more warmth toward me in the future."

"And I trust," she whispered, too low for Lady Catherine to hear, "that it becomes as warm for you as you deserve."

A servant interrupted us at that moment, and Elizabeth and I followed Lady Catherine and my guardian to the private parlor for dinner. Did the Queen sense the air of tension surrounding us as she chatted with her handsome lord? If she did, she gave no sign. Thomas Seymour had chosen her above all other women, and Elizabeth was but a houseguest, young enough to be a daughter. Why then did I watch these three together with such disquiet?

2

In the days that followed I saw the shadows of my fear dissolve and vanish. Lady Catherine was a new person, no longer the tense, closely guarded Queen I had known at Hampton Court palace. Strange, I had not wanted her to be any different, yet now I could see that the change was more a revealing of her real self. She was like a gem taken for the first time from the darkness and held up to glow in the light of the sun. The same person—but gloriously transformed.

"I was first married when I was thirteen," she told me one day, I believe in an effort to explain the change to me. "My father's death left my family in poverty, and the man who agreed to marry me—Sir Edward Borough—was extremely wealthy although four times my age. After he died, I was contracted to John Neville, Lord Latimer. I was then only fifteen. I could never quite accept being called 'little mother' by his daughters, who were all older than I. John was good to me, but when he died I could not help feeling a sense of release.

"The combined estates of my late husbands left me a wealthy woman. And I was no longer a child who could be forced into another marriage against my will. For a time I was content to live independently, deepening my interest in the Reformation then sweeping the country. My home gradually became a center for the Reformers; men like Miles Coverdale, Hugh Latimer, and John Parkhurst came often to hold meetings, and commoners and nobility alike flocked to hear them. One of these persons was the King's young brother-in-law, Thomas Seymour. He was only an officer in the Navy then, but he had already distinguished himself by filling the royal coffers with goods pirated on the high seas. This and his naturally engaging personality made him a favorite wherever he went."

I could well imagine the stir this handsome officer had created among the sober gathering of Reformers—reckless, outrageously defiant of normal codes of conduct, with a lusty enjoyment of life. Half the ladies at Court fancied themselves in love with him, Lady Catherine said, and more than one was known to be "indiscreet."

"It was absurd for me to join his circle of admirers. But I did—I could not help myself any more than the others could! And when he began to show interest in return, I told myself it meant nothing."

She smiled. "It took Thomas several exasperating months to convince me he was sincere. And when I at last agreed to listen to him, it was too late. Our sovereign had elected to make me his sixth wife.

"When Henry took me from Thomas, something happened inside—as if lightning had struck and left me burned and blackened. My life stopped for four years. And then—when I thought there was no more hope—I was given another chance—to live, perhaps even to create new life."

Lady Catherine looked at me with shining eyes.

"Thomas has done this for me, Jane. That is why you must be glad and love him as I do."

I confess it was not a difficult assignment. My guardian came often to Chelsea—ostensibly to see me, of course, but these visits provided the perfect opportunity for him to be with Lady Catherine. The hours he spent with Elizabeth and me were pure delight, for he was a master storyteller. Even my proud cousin appeared to have softened toward him considerably. How could she remain angry with a man of so much charm?

"I will be so glad when the Lord Admiral can come whenever he likes! It must be so difficult to pretend not to be in love with someone," I sighed, looking dreamily out of the schoolroom windows at a cloudless June morning. The weather was really too fine to be confined to studies. Suddenly I rebelled at my Greek translation and shut my book.

"Mmm." Elizabeth nibbled absently at the end of her quill. "I should not waste any tears over it. He is an accomplished actor."

"But how much longer do you suppose they will wait before they officially announce the marriage? Lady Catherine frets constantly that someone on the Council will learn of it before the King does and turn it into a shocking scandal."

"Well, it is a shocking scandal. It will only seem less of one if they can make everyone believe they waited until now to get married. And I am sure Thomas is clever enough to secure my brother's approval."

At that moment we heard a horse charge into the courtyard. We promptly left our books and went to the window, in time to see a rider dismount and throw his reins to a groom.

"It is Lord Thomas!" I exclaimed. "What would he be doing here this time of day?"

"Catherine? My love! Where are you?"

My guardian took the steps two at a time and flung open the front doors. Elizabeth and I exchanged astonished looks and dashed for the front hall, arriving a moment later to see our dauntless admiral enclosing the Queen in a most compromising embrace.

"Thomas! Thomas—really! You must be drunk!"

"Aye, that I am! Drunk with the wine of enchantment, madam." He covered her mouth with more kisses.

"But the servants!" She managed to disentangle herself. "This will be all over London in twenty-four hours!"

"Good. It will save us from making all those tiresome announcements."

He flung back his Adonic head and laughed; I was certain they would have no trouble at all hearing him in Whitehall.

"Do you hear me, everyone? I want you to know this fair lady is my wife! And you may tell whomever you wish that the King has given his blessing to us this glorious day of June."

Lady Catherine turned white and might have fainted if my guardian had not scooped her up against him again.

"'Tis true," he told her. "Edward rejoices in our joy. I think he is even half-convinced that it was his idea for us to marry."

"Oh, Thomas!"

Leaning very closely together they went out into the gardens, and we did not see them again for many hours.

It seemed natural after that to have Lord Thomas at the head of our previously feminine household. We were completely dominated by his presence, as were the servants who obeyed his orders as though they had done so all their lives. And Lady Catherine seemed content that it should be so.

"Why, in heaven's name, does she allow him to take control?" Elizabeth demanded with disgust as we sat down to dinner that first night.

"I expect it is the novelty of being a wife instead of a queen. Hush—" the babble from the servants' tables below the salt was deafening— "I want to hear what they are saying."

"They have been informed by now, I am sure," Thomas was exulting. "Kate, can you imagine the rage of my self-righteous brother and his duchess? They must have stumbled over themselves in their haste to report our 'wickedness and indecency.' I would give half my estate to have seen their faces when the King announced that he not only gave his consent to our marriage, but had urged it!"

"Dear Edward," Catherine sighed. Then, like a child who still fears punishment for some prank, her forehead wrinkled anxiously.

"You are sure they can do nothing?"

"The marriage is *fait accompli,* darling, with the seal of His Royal Majesty King Edward VI. Not even my powerful brother or his Council can lift a finger against us." Satisfaction was evident on his handsome face. He did not hear Elizabeth's thoughtful murmur beside me.

"Even the baited bear chained to a post will continue to fight his enemy. I would not think it wise to anger an enemy as influential as the Duke of Somerset."

"But what can he do?" I asked.

"I do not know." She toyed with her food, her eyes on Lord Thomas. "But the Duchess hates Thomas and hates Catherine even more. I rather think it will be something—humiliating. Humiliating to them both!"

It is a common saying that scandal spreads faster than the plague and is twice as hard to cure. An astonishingly short time after the Queen's remarriage was announced, a messenger arrived with a letter for Lord Thomas from my parents.

I knew what it would contain before he and Lady Catherine summoned me, but my heart sank as he read it aloud.

Following the polite salutations and congratulations there was a demand. Softly phrased, of course, but a demand: I was to be escorted back to Bradgate at the earliest possible convenience. My continued presence at Chelsea could only be an imposition to the married couple.

"Imposition!" Lord Thomas snorted and flung the crumpled letter into the fire. I watched, fascinated, as it curled and turned black at the edges.

"I fear your father and mother are annoyed because I did not inform them of my intentions, Jane. You see, I have put myself in an extremely unpopular position with my brother, the Protector. He was upset to begin with when I made you my ward; he has other plans for you. My brother and his wife are determined to interpret my marriage as an affront to the realm. I have been accused of being an opportunist, among other unsavory terms, who has defiled the dignity of the Queen Dowager."

"Thomas—" Lady Catherine laid her hand on his.

"Jane will have to know the situation as it stands, my dear, before she can make any decision."

Decision? But I had no other course than to follow my parents' wishes.

"I have legal control of you, Jane. Although I would not wish to distress your mother and father unduly, I do have the right to insist that you remain here with me—and Catherine, of course. The arrangement was never put into writing, but there are certain financial considerations which make it understood that I am to have all authority in this matter for as long as I desire."

I bit my lip. I was fully aware that he had saved my father from public embarrassment over large gambling debts.

"However, Catherine and I agree that we want only what is best for you. We want you to be happy."

I looked over at Lady Catherine. How serene, how beautiful she looked. These past few weeks had drawn us even closer than before.

"I would like to stay here, if you will have me."

"There is something else to consider. You are acquainted with my brother's son, Edward, the Earl of Hertford?"

"Yes—slightly. He and the Duke have visited Bradgate upon occasion."

"Do you like him?"

"Well," I hedged, "Edward has always been very difficult to talk to. And I think he is arrogant for one so close to my own age. Katie gets along with him better than I."

"I see. Your parents have not informed you, then, of your unofficial betrothal to Hertford?"

"To Edward? No! They did not!"

"I am afraid it is true. My Lord Protector agreed that you should marry Edward when you come of age. I am certain your father is afraid that if you remain my ward the contract will be jeopardized."

I looked wildly from him to Lady Catherine.

"But—I do not want to wed Edward Seymour! Truly! Please say I might stay here."

Lady Catherine laughed as if vastly relieved and gathered me into her arms for a hug.

"Of course you may, my dear. We just wanted to know your feelings. Thomas and I have already decided we could not bear to part with you for the world."

"You are indispensable to us," my guardian nodded. "I am afraid the Marquess and Marchioness of Dorset will have to do without the presence of their daughter for a while longer."

There were other letters, and other statements made in public about the Queen's marriage to the Lord Admiral—some of them not so kind. No one dared to be openly discourteous, but the callers whom Lady Catherine received made it exquisitely clear what they thought of the affair. During the same visits, condolences were pointedly extended to Elizabeth on the loss of her father.

Although Lady Catherine received such slights with apparent calm, I noticed that she avoided returning these calls. Even her visit to my cousin, King Edward, was postponed.

"I expect England will survive this deathblow to propriety," she commented dryly, "but it will take a proper interval of forgiveness. At least the commons do not seem to begrudge me my happiness."

And it seemed, despite Elizabeth's prediction, that forgiveness might be forthcoming without a major incident. Until a week later, when Lord Thomas strode into the sitting room where Lady Catherine and I sat embroidering.

"I will not have it, Kate!" His rugged features were dark with fury. "I will not allow my brother to insult us like this!"

Lady Catherine's embroidery dropped to her lap.

"What has happened?"

"The jewels you mislaid when you left Whitehall after the King's death—why did you not tell me about them? Why have you not demanded their return?"

"But I did! As soon as I discovered they were missing, I asked the Protector to have them sent to me directly. When he assured me he would see to it, I did not trouble you."

"That was months ago!" cried Lord Thomas. "How could you have been so naïve, Catherine? I could have done something. Now it is too late."

"What do you mean—*too late?*"

"The Protector has just declared that those jewels are the property of the Crown. He says they never belonged to you personally."

There was a stunned silence. Lady Catherine spoke almost to herself.

"I was so desperate to leave Whitehall that night—all I could think of was that Henry might somehow awaken and it would begin all over." She shuddered.

"Kate, love, I do not fault you for what has happened. The

25

jewels were a gift from the King. You had no reason to believe your ownership would be challenged. But my self-righteous brother—so wondrously eager to help every man to his rights—makes an issue of letting me have those jewels, when even the lawyers say they are mine. And all under the pretense that 'he does not want the King to lose so much'! Why should it be a loss to Edward to let me have my own?"

I spoke impulsively; both turned to me in surprise.

"I remember what you said after the King gave you the diamonds, Lady Catherine. It was just after Lord Wriothesley tried to trap you and send you to the Tower. The King said he was sorry he had given consent to the scheme and wanted to make it up to you.

"When you got back to your apartments, you put them away in a chest. 'I never want to have those about my neck again,' you said, 'for they shall remind me of my own death. I am not safe—not even now!'"

Lady Catherine's face was as still and white as the lace about her throat.

"Those jewels belong to a time I would choose to put behind me. We are not in need, Thomas. Perhaps—it would be wisest to let them go."

"Do you realize what you are saying?" he demanded, looking incredulous. "It is not just a question of their value; it is the deliberate attempt to humiliate us, to insinuate that my brother's authority is higher than yours. He would next place those diamonds around his own wife's neck!"

"The Duchess of Somerset—ah, yes. I would not be at all surprised if she were at the root of this. It would be like her."

"We must appeal to the King. It is our only hope—if he is not too intimidated by his uncle to oppose him."

"Edward has two uncles," Lady Catherine replied with unexpected determination, "and it is said that he is immensely fond of you, Thomas. Let us see who has the most influence."

I did not want to go with her. Indeed, it did not even occur to me that she would ask. So I was badly shaken when I learned I was expected to accompany Lady Catherine to Hampton Court.

It would be her first public appearance since the King's death.

and I knew how much she dreaded facing the Court's curiosity. Worse, she would again be walking those halls that were once her personal valley of the shadow of death. But if it was the only possible way to reclaim her jewels, she would go. To please Lord Thomas.

"But why must I go with her?" I wailed as Ellen, my faithful attendant since childhood, laced me into a new ice-blue satin gown. "She knows how I feel about the palace. Elizabeth should go. She would adore the chance."

"It was not Lady Catherine who decided you should go," Ellen said grimly. "It was himself—the Lord Admiral."

"What makes you say that? You have heard something! Tell me, Ellen. Please."

"Well, 'tis only below-stairs gossip, so mind you take it with a pinch of salt. But Annie was in the Queen's bedchamber, brushin' her mistress's hair, when the Lord Admiral came in and said it was time you were seen more at Court. Especially by your cousin, His Majesty."

I frowned. "What did Lady Catherine say to that?"

"She said —'Jane is too young yet, Tom. And she still suffers nightmares of her days at Hampton Court. Give her time to forget.'"

"'Time, my love, is exactly what we are up against,' he said. 'Time and my brother. Edward cherishes the hope of having his own daughter married to the King!'"

I pondered this. Why should it matter to Lord Thomas whether or not I was seen at Court? And why should it be such a disaster if the Protector's daughter married the King?

"Would you look at the lass! Her mind a thousand furlongs away, and she with not ten minutes before leavin' on the barge." As I stood before the mirror, Ellen whisked my blue French hood with its jeweled band onto my head. A single strand of coppery hair escaped and softened my features. They were unremarkable features, I thought. Eyes rather too large and too dark against pale skin, sandy brows and lashes, a small, upturned nose and too-prim mouth. But at least I could not be called plain. "Bonny," Ellen called me, but then she had looked after me ever since I could remember and treated me as her own.

"Now remember to hold your head high, lass! Your Tudor blood's as good as your cousin's, for all the pomp and ceremony

27

about him! You played together not so long ago. You know what you must do when you are with him?"

"Curtsy three times and kneel when he addresses me," I recited glibly. "Sit only when His Majesty gives permission and then only lower than His Majesty is sitting. When dismissed, walk backward—"

"All right, then, enough of your saucy tongue! Just remember everythin' when the time comes."

Unexpectedly she bent and planted a kiss on my forehead.

"God go with ye. He'll have to since I canna'."

"Why, Ellen!" I cried in mock horror. "I do believe you lack confidence in me! Do you fear I shall run off with one of those dashing courtiers?"

"Och, get on with you. A man would have to be daft to carry you off!"

My cousin Elizabeth accompanied Lady Catherine and me across the sloping lawns of the manor and down to the dock. She waved us off with ill-concealed envy.

The barge was an elegant affair, canopied richly against the weather and providing comfortable seating for the several dozen gentlemen and ladies in our retinue. It was fortunate that the river Thames provided a link to so many of the great residences of London. Travel by water was speedier and far more pleasant than by land, and I found myself enjoying the journey in spite of my fear of our destination. Children playing on the grassy banks stopped and stared, round-eyed, at our colorful progress, and when one small, grimy-faced urchin waved impudently, I risked a word of disapproval and waved back.

What kind of existence did they have, these offspring of the city's poor? Their rags and sticklike arms and legs bespoke suffering. Did their parents live? Or did these children scavenge the streets like so many hundreds of others, stealing what they could or going without? I was saddened, wondering why such things had to be.

Glancing over at Lady Catherine I saw that her face was composed. Had she seen the children and did she wish, as she had so many times before, for children of her own? Or was she thinking of the Lord Admiral and his decision that she should go alone to see her stepson? Everyone knew how devoted Edward was to her; it seemed only a matter of making him understand the injustice that had been done in keeping her jewels.

Our eyes met suddenly, and she smiled. Could it be she was encouraging *me*, as if the ordeal before her were nothing? I was more than ever aware of the selflessness of her love—for Lord Thomas, for the King, even for myself. I felt humbled at the realization.

There was a sharp command, and river men caught the ropes as they maneuvered our bulky conveyance against a flight of stone steps. We alighted, and the dank smell of low tide reached our nostrils. What an inelegant way to approach a King's residence, I thought with amusement. The ladies lifted their skirts, and we trooped up the stairs and through the gate. And there was Hampton Court spread out before us.

The sight of it never failed to impress me. Cardinal Thomas Wolsey had had the mansion built for himself, but unfortunately for him it had appealed so well to King Henry that Wolsey was obliged to present it as a gift. The King promptly made additions which resulted in its becoming one of the most magnificent dwellings in the realm. It was here that his long-awaited son, Edward, was born, and where poor Jane Seymour, sister to the Lord Admiral and the Protector, expired a few days later.

Lady Catherine started toward the main entrance. Her arrival had caused an inevitable flurry of excitement; the great doors stood open, and lords and ladies poured out, sinking into low bows and curtsies of welcome. The Queen had been popular among them; now they were curious to see if she had been affected by her remarriage. And everyone, of course, knew the reason for her present visit.

I was embarrassed by the scrutiny we received, but Lady Catherine appeared not to notice. She passed through the assembly with superb dignity and did not pause until we reached the entrance to the King's Presence Chamber.

"Your Highness, this is a pleasure."

The Duke and Duchess of Somerset stood before us, blocking any further advance. Lady Catherine surveyed them coldly and inclined her head.

"My Lord Protector—Lady Anne."

"We are delighted to see you looking so well, madam," said the Duke, bowing. "How unfortunate that the King is indisposed

29

today. He would so have enjoyed receiving you."

"Had the Queen troubled to advise the Protector and myself of her coming," the Duchess added sharply, "we could have prevented the inconvenience of this trip."

I was appalled at her rudeness. Lady Catherine flushed.

"On the contrary, if my stepson is ill, my visit is well-ordered. Please tell him I am here."

"Your Grace mistakes our meaning," said the Protector soothingly. I noticed again the likeness of Edward Seymour to his brother, Lord Thomas. Both were unusually good-looking, and both obviously shared a fondness for fine apparel, although the Protector appeared more conservative. Perhaps it was the stern expression reflected in the Duke of Somerset's gray eyes that set the men apart most. I recalled with a twinge of discomfort that his eldest son, Edward the Earl of Hertford, often bore the same expression.

"The King is not ill, simply overtired. His physicians advise that he be spared the strain of visitors."

"Why should he be overtired? Perhaps what your brother observes is true—that the boy has been forced to endure more study than his youth will allow!"

The Duchess's face mottled an angry red. She was a tall woman, attractive in a masculine sort of way, and it was rumored that she cherished a bitter resentment of Lady Catherine's superior title.

"I like not that word 'force,' my lady!" she said. "Nor, I shall add, do I care for any of the slanders your husband has used to win the favor of the King!"

I had never seen Lady Catherine so vexed; she spoke with an effort.

"You forget yourself, madam. Stand aside. I will see Edward—now."

For an instant the Duchess hesitated. Then she deliberately placed herself directly in the path of the Queen.

"Shall I give place to one who in her former estate was only Latimer's widow and has now thrown herself for support on my husband's younger brother? If Lord Thomas can teach his wife no better manners, I am she that will!"

I could not believe her effrontery. The woman was clearly beyond herself—perhaps even capable of doing Lady Catherine physical harm. One of our gentlemen stepped forward instantly with his hand on his sword; the Protector seized his wife's wrist.

"Accept my apology for the Duchess's behavior, Your Grace. The King shall be advised of your presence."

Lady Catherine swept by the pair without troubling to reply. The rest of us trailed after. It was only moments before a gentleman-at-arms appeared to escort her to an inner room, and I was left alone in an antechamber.

Apparently I was not to be included in Edward's reunion with his stepmother, and I was relieved. The foregoing scene had drained me of any vestige of poise, and I would undoubtedly have committed some unforgivable faux pas.

I leaned against the lead-paned window and looked out, regretting that the maze and orangery which had been my chief delight at Hampton Court were not visible. The Queen also had loved the gardens, filling her apartments daily with fresh bouquets. Often when the tensions of life within the palace grew intolerable she would go outside for healing.

The soft click of the door interrupted my thoughts.

"Lady Jane?"

My heart sank. It was Edward Seymour, the Protector's son, and at that moment there was no one whom I cared less to see.

He cleared his throat. "I have come to apologize for the— unfortunate—occurrence between my mother and the Queen."

"Unfortunate? I should say that is putting it mildly. By now the whole Court is agape with the scandal."

"Yes. Father is most unhappy about it."

"I find that hard to believe, since he could have avoided the matter by delivering Lady Catherine's jewels to her three months ago."

His eyebrows lifted.

"So, our Lady Jane Grey has acquired claws. A pity. She used to be such a gentle kitten."

"Perhaps she has found they are a necessary defense against the unprincipled."

"The quarrel is not yours. It is a rivalry between two women who desire preeminence."

"If you believe that, you are much deceived, for the quarrel lies between two brothers—your father and Lord Thomas."

He shrugged. "It is still none of your concern. Unless—" he

31

watched me closely, "unless you have taken the Lord Admiral's crusade as your own."

"I have no idea what you are talking about. And if I did, I would not feel obliged to share my guardian's business with you."

"Indeed. The Court finds it curious that you have accompanied Lady Catherine today. They know her errand, but what of yours?"

"I do not see why that should be a matter of curiosity. King Edward and I are cousins. We saw each other frequently before his coronation."

"So you are here by your own request?"

I hated myself for blushing so easily; he smiled.

"I thought not. It was the Lord Admiral's idea. He suggested it would be the polite, cousinly thing to do, since Edward is so very fond of you—"

I took a deep breath and let it out slowly. "Your parents obviously sent you here to extract information from me. I am sorry I cannot produce word of any plot or intrigue. Your father has wrongfully abused Lord Thomas. He is a good man. He has been most attentive to Lady Catherine and me."

"Undoubtedly. My uncle has always been known to guard his interests."

I flinched.

"Jane—do not suppose that I enjoy speaking ill of him. But surely even you realize by now that his reputation is not the most exemplary—"

"That is all in the past. He is married now and loves the Queen devotedly. He could have married anyone he chose—"

"Oh? Perhaps it is time your eyes were opened. Before Henry's body was in the ground, your Lord Thomas rode posthaste to the widowed Anne of Cleves and begged her to marry him. When she refused, he asked Princess Mary, and got the same answer. Then there was Princess Elizabeth—"

I turned my face away.

"The truth is not pleasant, is it? We can even verify the fact that your guardian contemplated taking you as his wife, before he took you as his ward. But then you are only the fifth heir to the throne, and not nearly as wealthy as Lady Catherine."

"*Stop it!* Those are lies, all of them! How dare you repeat such vicious gossip?"

He was unperturbed. "You have had fair warning. If you wish to persist in thinking him innocent, do so. But know that under the exterior charm of Thomas Seymour lies a hard core of ambition. He will use anything and any*one* to get what he wants."

"Have you quite finished?" I asked icily.

"Not quite. We are unofficially contracted to wed each other in a few years. If your guardian has informed you of that fact, he also has probably tried to influence you against it."

"He has done nothing of the kind—and he does not need to! The inadvisability of such a match is plain."

"Marriages of convenience seldom take into consideration the mutual likes or dislikes of the persons involved. Our family would stand to benefit politically by a union, and so would yours."

I stared at him with infinite distaste. "You would actually agree to it then? No matter how you felt about me as a person? I find that contemptible, my lord."

"Do you? Is it so much worse than marrying one's cousin in order to gain the throne?"

All the pieces of the puzzle suddenly locked together. I laughed unbelievingly.

"King Edward and I are fond of each other, but he would never consider asking me to marry him. Nor should I accept. The Lord Admiral would never propose such a thing!"

Edward lifted a brow, a cynical habit of his which always infuriated me. "My uncle generally does as he pleases. In this case, however, I can assure you he will not. The Privy Council has other plans for the King. A foreign princess—"

"Or your own sister perhaps?"

I was triumphant as his face registered surprise. "There are rumors that the Protector would enjoy seeing his own daughter married to the King. No wonder he would like to see me married off to you. That would put me safely out of the competition."

His lips were drawn into a tight, thin line. "You are right. We should pray to God that we never marry. I could not tolerate such a simpleton for a wife." He wheeled and left the room.

I was shaking so badly that I sank down upon the window seat and burst into tears.

Why was everyone so intent on marrying me off? Could they not leave me alone for just a few years longer—at least until I was fifteen or sixteen? It was true that many girls were wed at thirteen, but I was keenly anxious not to be one of them. Marriage to the Protector's insufferable son would be bad enough; but what if it were true that my guardian looked for a royal wedding? The proposition was not outside the realm of possibility. I was a blood relative, Edward's own age, and a Protestant. And he had always seemed pleased with my company. Many of the nobility would favor an English bride, from an established family like mine, over a foreign princess. In fact, they were far more likely to accept the Marquess of Dorset's daughter than a daughter of the Protector, who had no true claim to nobility.

It would have been so much simpler to have been born a commoner. Ellen had told me once that only the poor could marry for love. She herself had wed a tenant farmer. And though they struggled to make a living, they had been blissfully happy in their humble Scottish croft until both her husband and infant son were taken in a plague. It was then she had left Scotland and come south, seeking a position with our family, and was hired as my nursemaid. Though at first bitter, she had come to accept the past as God's will. "I was sent here to care for you," she said, "but I'll always be glad for those few years with my Andrew and my own wee bairn."

I envied her strength, her right to choose her own way. A daughter of the nobility did not have that right. She was told whom she would marry and when, and once married she was under the complete rule of her husband. She had no property to call her own and no rights. She could be beaten within an inch of her life and could not complain.

Bitterly I recalled Lady Catherine telling me about her close friend, Anne Askew. Anne's older sister had been betrothed to a wealthy landlord. When the sister died unexpectedly, thirteen-year-old Anne was forced to take her place. The man was sadistic, and when he discovered Anne's leanings toward the heretical New Learning, he had used her cruelly. She had finally been driven from his house and had appealed for divorce. When the appeal was refused, with the magistrate's admonition that she return to her husband and submit to him, she instead set up a school for the London poor. Because she publicly refused to accept the doctrine of transubstantiation—that the wine and bread of the Eucharist were changed into the actual blood and body of Christ—and because of her "spirit of rebellion," she was arrested, tortured on the rack, and

34

burned at the stake. Lady Catherine's sympathy with Anne had almost cost her own life as well.

I struggled to compose myself. Lady Catherine would be returning at any moment, and I did not want her to notice my distress. Why this hesitation to relate my interview with the arrogant young earl? I did not stop to analyze my feelings, but produced a passable smile when she entered the room a few moments later. Fortunately, she was distracted by her own thoughts.

The trip back to Chelsea was quiet, as if the enjoyment had gone out of it for us all. Even the sun stayed hidden behind the clouds. When the barge arrived at the manor, we found Lord Thomas and Elizabeth waiting for us.

"How did it go, love?"

"She was magnificent!" I assured my guardian.

Lady Catherine's face brightened, and some of her weariness fell away as she took his arm. She began at once to tell him of her visit.

"Edward looks so thin, Tom. I know the Protector is too strict, and Edward told me his masters thrash him. You must try to get him out of doors more."

"But what about the jewels, Kate? You did get him to agree to intercede with the Council?"

"Yes—but Edward has little authority over them. He is sorry about the affair. He was anxious to assure me it was not his doing."

Lord Thomas looked most unhappy. Eventually he remembered to inquire if I had had a pleasant time.

"I—I—" What should I say? "I enjoyed the river trip so much, my lord. The sun sparkling on the water, the flowers on the banks. You would have loved it, Elizabeth."

"I think Lord Thomas is more interested in your visit with my brother," she said dryly.

"Oh. Well, actually—"

"She did not see Edward," Lady Catherine interposed hastily. "He was too tired. But he sent his warmest wishes and said he was looking forward to seeing her soon."

"I see." My guardian's tone conveyed his disapproval. I was just casting about in my mind for something to say to cheer him, when Elizabeth demanded to know why my eyes were so red. I could have kicked her.

"You must be mistaken."

"You have been crying! I can always tell."

By then, of course, Lady Catherine and Lord Thomas were all concern.

"Jane, dear, you did not let our—encounter—with the Duke and Duchess upset you?"

"What encounter?" demanded Lord Thomas. Lady Catherine flashed me a look of warning.

"It was nothing, really. Just that impossible Duchess of Somerset putting on airs."

"It was outrageous!" I burst out, unable to control my indignation. "I am sorry, my lady, but everyone was talking about it by the time we left Court, and I am certain Lord Thomas will hear of it. The Duchess insulted Lady Catherine," I told him. "Then she stepped directly in front of her and refused to let her see Edward."

"What happened?" breathed a wide-eyed Elizabeth.

"The Protector had to forcibly drag her out of the way! Everyone was horrified."

Lord Thomas swore. "By heaven, Kate, he shall pay dearly for this!"

"No, Tom, please. It was not the Duke's fault. He was most apologetic."

"Do you think I will allow my wife to be publicly humiliated? You are the Queen Dowager. Your authority cannot be challenged by any other woman. If my brother cannot bridle his own wife, he can scarcely be capable of ruling this country!"

Lady Catherine took his hands in her own. "Not all marriages are as happy as ours, darling. Let us pity his condition. Let this pass."

He stared at her for a long moment, then shook his head.

"I am not capable of your Christian leniency, Kate. Forgive him if you can—as for me, I shall bide my time until my clever brother stumbles into a pit of his own device."

I do not think it surprised anyone when the jewels were never returned to the Queen; nor did the Duchess of Somerset repent of her rudeness. Whenever the two women met thereafter, there was trouble.

As for me, the summer passed pleasantly. Since the subject of my marriage was not mentioned again, the fear gradually faded from my mind, and life settled into a satisfying routine.

Often Lady Margery, Lord Thomas's mother, invited me to take tea with her at Seymour Place. I always returned from these occasions refreshed and stimulated by her witty conversation. My guardian was pleased by our friendship. Elizabeth, however, merely considered me odd.

"How can you spend so much time with that old woman? I should be dreadfully bored."

"But she is not at all boring. You ought to meet her."

"Heaven preserve me. Father said her tongue was in need of a bridle, and he would have taken care of it himself long ago if she were not his 'poor dead Jane's mother.' He would not even have her at her own grandson's christening. Think of it!"

I smiled to myself. Lady Margery's version of the affair was somewhat different. "I refused to attend" she informed me, "because of the way that pompous son-in-law of mine neglected Jane."

"The Court ignores her even now that her son Edward is Lord Protector and Thomas, Lord High Admiral." Elizabeth eyed me curiously. "Whatever do you talk about?"

"What her life was like at Wolf's Hall in Wiltshire before your father visited there and changed all of their lives by marrying Jane. And what she thinks about today's dress, and religion—the state of the realm—just about everything. She does not seem at all displeased to be ignored. I rather think she prefers it."

"Indeed?" My cousin was clearly unconvinced.

"You should see her fix me with those bright blue eyes of hers. 'Jane,' she says, 'stay as far away from the whirlpool of Court intrigue as you are able, no matter how alluring it appears. There is nothing there but corruption, vanity, and deceit. It has snatched a daughter and two sons from me. I should hate to see you lost as well.'"

"Heaven save us—a second Solomon!" mocked Elizabeth. "How can you bear such drivel, Jane? Nobody would ever have heard of the Seymours of Wolf's Hall, Wiltshire, if my father had not noticed Jane and made her queen. Without that, where would her precious sons be today, pray? Not serving as Lord Protector and Lord Admiral, I warrant you!"

"Lady Margery is not a fool," I said defensively. "She is honest and wise—and I am privileged to be her friend."

"Then you are more stupid than I supposed. She cannot help you further your interests at Court, you know. She might even hinder you."

"I have no interests at Court."

Elizabeth smiled knowingly. "You will. Wait until you grow a little older."

If anything infuriated me about Elizabeth, it was her condescending air of maturity.

"You are only four years older than I," I pointed out.

"It is not the years, dear cousin, but my greater experience that makes me so much older. But never mind. You will find other interests in time, and then I wager you will not think an old woman quite so enchanting!"

Despite her words, I thought I should be perfectly content for my life to continue as it was that summer at Chelsea. Eliza was an amusing companion when she chose to be, and we spent many long, sunny days together riding, hunting, or exploring the estate. There were always lessons, too, with Master Miles Coverdale, and sometimes he would consent to let us study on the banks of the river. He was a gifted teacher who made the hours pass swiftly, and my respect for him grew as I learned more about his astonishing past.

Miles Coverdale had once been an Augustinian friar. After years in the priesthood, he had met William Tyndale and a group of zealous Lutherans who convinced him that faith alone—rather than the ritual of the church—could justify. Like Martin Luther, he abandoned his order to preach against idols and the mass.

"Tyndale was forced out of England, but his translations were not," he explained. "The Bishop of London wished to burn all of William's New Testaments and was forced to buy the unsold copies from a man named Packington. Packington, actually William's friend, sent the money on to Germany. William then printed a better edition and shipped back into England three times as many testaments as they had burned!

"But I am not a fighter like William," Coverdale sighed ruefully. "I am too fond of the quiet pursuits, of reading and writing. When my friend asked me to join him in Germany to help with a translation of the Pentateuch, I was only too glad to go.

"I lived there several years before returning home. I was disturbed at the small progress made by the Reformation and resolved to translate the tracts of Luther and parts of the New Testament and Psalms from the Vulgate. I have always been convinced that if the people could only read the Bible for themselves, in their native tongue, there would be no confusion as to what is the truth.

"Your father believed that, too," he told Elizabeth. "His Majesty commissioned me to edit Matthew's Bible—or the Great Bible, some call it—so that it could be placed in every church throughout the realm. This was my greatest undertaking.

"Unfortunately, it was barely complete when the King issued the Six Articles, which put every married priest and any man who denied transubstantiation in great danger. In London alone, several hundred Protestants were arrested. Cromwell was beheaded, and William Tyndale and some of my dearest friends went to the stake. I knew I had to leave the country without delay."

"Because you refused to worship the Communion host as Christ's own flesh and blood?"

"Yes—and because I have a wife." He smiled. "You did not know? She, too, is named Elizabeth.

"Together we escaped to Strasbourg and were kept so busy there for a time that we could almost forget we were exiles. Studying, teaching, writing—so much to be done. And all of my work here in England was turned to ashes."

"The bonfires at St. Paul's!" cried Elizabeth. "I remember Father saying that everything you had written must be burned because you were a heretic."

Memory clutched at me, making me feel ill. A vision of young Anne Askew seemed very real.

"Not only books perished in the flames," I whispered. "There were people—brave men and women—who died because they would not deny what they believed. I was only nine, but I shall never forget—"

"You must not." The chaplain's hand closed over mine. "They are an example to us all."

I shivered, remembering that Lady Catherine had put her life in peril to defend Anne.

"When King Henry died, I resolved to return to England once again. Others had to carry on what the martyrs had begun. And, as you know, it was my good fortune to be appointed the Queen Dowager's almoner. Which brings us to the fact that I am also supposed to be educating her charges." He cleared his throat with pretended sternness. "Perhaps we had better proceed with the task!"

Neither Elizabeth nor I begrudged the time spent in lessons, which was fortunate since they took up the greatest portion of every day. Daughters of the nobility were expected to be well-educated—or at least to appear so.

At Bradgate, my sister Katie and I had suffered under the tiresome tutelage of Dr. Harding. He was learned enough—my parents saw to that, of course—but he had a most appalling aversion to children, especially giggling little girls who delighted in his discomfort. Since my performance on the sporting field did not seem likely to improve, however, I gradually discovered a respect and enjoyment for the world of books. Mother appeared relieved that I had at last found something else for diversion, and Papa encouraged me out of his own real regard for learning. Like the rest of my peers, I started instruction in Spanish, French, Italian, and Greek at age seven, while continuing lessons in music, writing, drawing, and the all-important Latin.

Writing and music soon emerged as my favorite studies; somehow they helped me release all my bottled-up emotions. When I went to live at Hampton Court the Queen undertook to increase my love for music. She and I had spent many happy hours together with the lute, harp, and cittern.

Now, at Chelsea, we took up our music once again, with the occasional addition of Elizabeth's low, clear voice for accompaniment. In fact, it was in the music room one day in August that Eliza made mention of Lord Thomas's frequent absences from the manor.

"I suppose it has to do with the trouble those impossible Scots keep causing. If you ask me, England should declare war and put an end to it!"

Lady Catherine did not reply, but I noticed the faint lines creasing her forehead. She, too, must be concerned about this danger of war.

"I do not understand," I said. "What trouble are they causing?"

My cousin looked pained. "You know so little of what goes on in this world it appalls me. You *do* recall that Scotland broke the marriage treaty between Mary, Queen of Scots, and my brother Edward when they were both infants?"

"Of course. Your father burned Edinburgh because of it."

"But they still refused to renew the marriage treaty. They made an alliance with France instead, and now France threatens to make Scotland a province. Can you imagine?"

"Then the Protector has to declare war to stop them?"

"He does if there is ever to be a hope of uniting Scotland with England!"

Lady Catherine spoke. "Peace cannot be accomplished through war, nor can Edward's betrothal be sealed by bloodshed. The Scots will only hate us all the more."

"They are like servants," Elizabeth shrugged. "One has to beat them to gain their respect."

I did not want to believe my cousin was right. War seemed to me an unpleasant thing, although she assured me it was a fine sight to see men riding off to fight for the honor of the realm.

"I wonder how the soldiers feel?"

"They are proud, of course!" she cried. "I know I would be. And excited, too."

Ellen did not agree. Although she did not say much, I knew she was deeply troubled over the possibility of an English invasion

41

into her beloved Scotland. She had described her homeland to me many times. I felt as though I had seen the ragged mountains with the jewel/blue lochs nestled below them, the gorse and heather in flower, the fierce wildness that both lowlanders and highlanders had been bred to endure. She had told me of those people—the pride of the clansmen and their unyielding nature. I knew of the resentment that had long been nourished in the heart of every Scot for his southern neighbor.

"It's no' been easy to suffer England's insults," she said. "'Twas the Duke of Somerset—then only Earl of Hertford under King Henry the Eighth—who burnt Edinburgh ten years ago. They have no' forgotten it; and they'll be ready for him."

She was right. The rumblings of war grew closer as the Protector's efforts to reach a verbal settlement proved fruitless. At last came a stormy night in mid-August when Lord Thomas reached Chelsea with the news. His clothes were still streaming from the ride from Hampton Court, but it was his face, shining with excitement, that rivited our attention.

"The Protector has declared war on Scotland!" cried Elizabeth, jumping to her feet. "I knew it would happen. I knew it! And you shall command the fleet. How splendid!"

"Elizabeth! Hush!"

Lady Catherine rose slowly and faced her husband.

"It is true, is it not? You are leaving us?"

"Sail away to foreign parts and leave my fair-haired bride undefended? I would have to be daft!"

"You are joking, Thomas! How can you treat this matter so lightly?" Her restraint broke suddenly, and she covered her face with her hands. "It is not fair! I knew something like this would happen. We have not had four months together—"

"Kate, Kate," He took her hands and kissed them gently. "For once I am completely serious. My brother did ask me to command the invasion fleet, but I refused."

"Refused?" Elizabeth cried. "You could not!"

He laughed. "You sound like Edward— 'You have your duty!' he said. 'My dear Lord Protector,' I replied. 'It is all very well for you to go tramping off to war to escape your termagant wife, but it is an altogether different proposition for me. You will just have to do without your brother.' —Needless to say, he was enraged."

"But who will go?"

42

"Vice Admiral Clinton. Do not look so disapproving, Eliza. Clinton is a good man, and I will not be altogether idle. After he calmed down a bit, Edward consented to appoint me Lieutenant General of the southlands while he is away."

"But that is wonderful! Oh, Thomas—" Lady Catherine quite forgot we were there and threw her arms about his neck. "I am so glad. You will have all of the kingdom to command!"

"All of the kingdom and all of the King." He gathered her close. "We shall have to make good use of our time."

The Protector and his army of almost ten thousand left London on 22 August 1547. A week later we learned that he had reached the border safely and was making one last effort to negotiate with the Scots.

Feeling ran high in the city, and there were many boasts that England would soon drive the "kilted barbarians" to their knees. But there were already Englishmen and Scots—like Ellen—who were on their knees, beseeching God to avert the shedding of blood. They knew what would be the outcome of a battle between those two great armies.

For me the war was remote. Chelsea was like a secure island where the waves of men's anger surged around us but left us untouched. Though the Lord Admiral now spent a great deal of time at Hampton Court, Lady Catherine was content. She expressed satisfaction that King Edward was at last seeing as much of his favorite uncle as he would like.

"He will probably have the boy spoiled by the time the Protector returns," she laughed. "Thomas never does things by halves."

And though Elizabeth cast me a peculiar look when she said this, I really did not take much notice. For some reason my thoughts were far away these days; I realized with some surprise that I missed Bradgate.

Letters had always been infrequent, but I could not help worrying as a spell of unusual heat settled over the country, causing an outbreak of disease in many areas. The stench in London's streets became intolerable; one could not pass through them without a handkerchief pressed tightly to mouth and nostrils. I found myself without appetite and lacking my customary enjoyment in the companionship of my cousin and Lady Catherine. Even lessons were a drudgery; my head seemed to ache persistently.

"What is it, Jane?" Lady Catherine came to me one night as I lay struggling to sleep. "Ellen and Master Coverdale are quite concerned. I am afraid I have been neglecting you."

"Oh, no! You have been wonderful, as always. It is just—" To my distress, two large tears escaped my eyes and rolled down my face. "I am so ashamed. You will think me an ungrateful beast. But I have not received a letter from Bradgate for so long— I do wonder if anything is the matter."

Lady Catherine smiled, smoothing the hair back from my temples.

"Of course you do. It would not be natural if you did not care. I have been selfish to keep you here so long. You must go home to Bradgate at once."

"But this is my home—truly. I want you to know that. And I shall return just as quickly as I can—"

"Ah, no," she laughed, placing her finger across my lips. "You must not come back until you have done all the things you miss— ride in that forest of yours, enjoy your father's rose gardens, breathe deeply of all that fresh Leicestershire air about which you have told me. I should have guessed that London in summer heat is no place for you!"

The ancestral home of the Greys, Bradgate Manor, stood in a valley surrounded by the oaks of Charnwood Forest (How I love the sound of that name! It even suggests the hush of the woodland and its cool, dripping glades). The house was built by my grandfather on the ruins of an abbey bought from King Henry the Eighth. I liked to believe that some of the abbey's ancient air of serenity had lingered in the valley.

As our horses wound through the five miles of rich park that separated the town of Leicester from our manor—really a village in itself with housing for over three hundred servants—I wondered if the family would be on hand to greet me. Although Lady Catherine had sent word ahead, my escort was large, and we had been forced to travel slowly on crude paths. I would be glad to get there; I was as sore and exhausted as my poor horse.

At last the huge, ornamental towers and gatehouse of Bradgate came into view. I felt a rush of pride as the old gatekeeper hurried to swing open the gates. Our horses trotted into the tiltyard; there it was—the familiar rose-colored brick walls and white stone turrets. It was good to be back.

"Jane has arrived! Mama, Papa! Come quickly!"

For an instant I glimpsed my sister at the windows above the entrance. Seconds later she was running down the steps, her face alight.

"How good to see you! And how elegant you look!"

"I am afraid I do not feel elegant at all. The journey was frightful!"

"Nevertheless, we are glad you came, daughter."

I turned and smiled at the man who had just appeared from a different direction. "Dear Papa! I have missed you so."

"And did you miss me, daughter?" A lazy laugh floated from the doorway. My mother, obviously about to go riding, was clad in a smart silk dress which accentuated her figure. Her foot tapped impatiently on the step, and she laughed again. "Your manners have not improved at all, I see. Do not stand there gaping. Come and kiss me."

I hurried up the steps, aware of how stained and rumpled I looked beside her.

"Forgive me, Mama. I am afraid the heat has slowed me somewhat."

"You always were over-delicate. Perhaps, when you are sufficiently recovered, you will have the grace to greet our guest."

I reddened; I had not seen the visitor, previously obscured by the others. "I am sorry. I—"

It could not be. Dark brows above cool, gray eyes which twinkled with amusement.

"Edward!"

"Lady Jane—what a *pleasant* surprise." Edward Seymour bowed over my hand. Mother, observing us curiously, was about to comment when Katie interrupted.

"Jane, do tell us about the Lord Admiral's marriage to the Queen! Everyone here was so startled. What do they say of it at Court?"

"As to that," I shot a meaningful glance at the Protector's son, "I am sure Lord Hertford is able to tell you more about the affair than I."

"Oh, Edward! He is impossible. I have already begged him for details, and he cannot—or will not—tell me a thing!" She pouted prettily, but the person in question failed to respond. Poor Katie, I thought; talking with Edward is like chatting with the stone cliffs of Dover.

"I suggest that questions wait until later," said Papa. "Jane would doubtless like some time to rest, and I have business at one of the tenant farms on the west side of the valley. Edward—care to come along?"

As Papa and Edward started for the stables, Mama turned to Katie. "It is time we started for Leicester, Katherine, if we are to join the mayor for tea this afternoon."

"But, Mother, Jane has only just arrived—"

"Jane will tell us everything we wish to know, I assure you, darling. But your father is right. Now is not the time. Come along."

Katie knew better than to argue with Mama. She threw me a helpless look and followed.

So, I thought, watching them go, nothing has changed. What a fool I was to hope it could be otherwise; to hope Mama would embrace me with some of the warmth and affection she reserved for Katie. Tears of anger slipped down my face, and I dashed them away.

It would not always be like this, I told myself fiercely. One day I would discover that thing which would make her proud of me. And no matter how difficult or how despised the task, I would do it. The resolve quieted me. I turned and walked into the house.

6

I should not have been so shocked to find Edward at Bradgate. He and his father had called frequently in the past. But for some reason I had assumed he had accompanied the Protector to Scotland.

"He was wild to go, but the King would not permit it," Katie explained to me as we prepared for dinner that evening. "They are close friends, and he said it was enough to risk the Protector's life. Edward was furious. When he could not get the King to change his mind, he left London and came here."

"I can imagine how he feels—to be left behind."

"Well, I am glad of it! You cannot imagine how tedious things get here in the country, Jane, with no one to visit but the mayor and the sheep. How I envy you, living in London."

She fingered a tiny pearl necklace at her throat. "He seems—changed, does he not?"

"Are we still talking about Edward?"

"I had not seen him since the coronation, and then only at a distance. What a bore that women are not allowed at a bachelor sovereign's coronation! Anyway, I think he is more serious about things. He does not laugh at me like he used to."

"Perhaps he has noticed that you are no longer a child," I observed dryly.

She brightened. "Do you really think so?"

"Katherine Grey, you are not seriously attracted to him!"

"Well, why not? I must wed someone in a few years, and he is terribly good-looking—and rich—and titled. Besides, I have the feeling Papa might welcome him as a son-in-law. He keeps dropping obvious comments to Edward about how 'accomplished' we are.''

Should I tell her about our proposed betrothal? But perhaps the agreement would no longer be honored since the Lord Admiral had refused to relinquish his guardianship of me. In that case, Papa might well look to Katie to provide an alliance between the two families. It was all too complicated, and since I was hardly ready to echo my sister's praise of Edward, I kept silent.

It was fortunate that our respective activities would keep us separated for the most part. Only during the evening hour, when the family met formally to dine, would Edward and I be called upon to present some semblance of graciousness toward each other.

I had always dreaded the elaborate banquets in the great hall. It was a magnificent chamber—some eighty feet long and extending in height from the bottom of the house to the top. On each side were wainscoted bay windows and on one end a musician's gallery. The other end was where the family dined, on a dais that looked down upon tables for over two hundred, which included guests, house servants, retainers, and wayfarers. Each meal was produced on a massive scale, as was quite routine in all the houses of the nobility.

As Katie and I slipped into our places the first night, I was conscious of being the object of frank scrutiny from the tables below. I had chosen one of my favorite gowns to bolster my courage, a water-green satin with lace cuffs and collar that flattered my light coloring. Katie was dazzling in a vivacious peacock blue. She really is growing up, I thought, and noticed the admiration kindled in our guest's eyes.

Dr. Harding, Bradgate's resident chaplain, rose and lifted his hand for silence.

"God save His Gracious Majesty Edward the Sixth. Grant to us victory over our foes who rebel against our realm and Thy righteous cause. In Christ's name, Amen."

A trumpet was sounded, and a score of servants entered from the curtains behind the dais, bowed, and proffered the first course. I selected a small portion of one or two dishes from the choice of soup, capon, stewed pheasant, and swan. Dr. Harding's prayer for the realm had provoked an earnest discussion between Edward Seymour and my parents; I longed to ask if they had received any news of the campaign, but knew I was forbidden. If only the daughters of the house were permitted to take part in conversation, I thought rebelliously, these dinners would not be so unendurable!

"My father is convinced that if England is ever to be united with Scotland, the Scots must be converted from Catholicism." Edward's lean face was intent. I strained to listen above the babble of sound from below the salt.

"Our invading armies have orders to dissolve the monasteries wherever they go and place Bibles in the churches."

"If we are not defeated," my father said grimly. "I do not wish to undervalue your father, Edward, but the Scots outnumber us two to one and fight on their own soil."

"The very odds will make them overconfident. Excessive pride—demonstrated by their refusal to negotiate peaceably—is always the leaven for military error."

Mama gave him an admiring smile. "We certainly trust that will be the case, Edward."

The second course of brawn, stuffed plover, mutton, red deer, omeletts, and more soups arrived. I sighed; the ragamuffins I had seen playing on the banks of the Thames would never see the like of this feast in all their lives.

"—and the exchequer, of course, has fallen into a wretched state. King Henry practically emptied it with his wars in France, then started minting coins with base metal. Father is doing his best to reduce household expenses. He plans to restore the economy by a purer coinage, although such coins would have to be lighter."

"He is an intelligent man, the Duke. But he has been given a heavy burden of reform. I do not envy him the task," sighed Papa.

"It would be much easier if the Council stood behind him. As you know, only seven of the twenty-six signed his patent as Protector, and they watch him jealously for any changes which threaten their own power."

I did not see how they could feel threatened. Everyone knew the Privy Council's jurisdiction was practically limitless, regulating the realm's defense, trade, and foreign affairs. It even had a Court of Star Chamber which tried criminal and ecclesiastical cases and reached into the farthest corners of the kingdom.

"Well, he can count on my support," Papa said heartily. "I am anxious for the first Parliament to sit in November. We should see much accomplished."

We had worked our way through to the third course—a repast of crayfish, warden pie, and sweetmeats. To my immense relief the servants came a short while later with napkins and silver bowls of water. We drank a toast of hot spiced wine; then Dr. Harding rose again for prayer, and the company was dismissed.

"I shall not eat another mouthful for a month," I groaned as Katie and I fled to the gallery to stroll a bit of it off. She giggled.

"You shall—tomorrow night! Did you not feast so well at Chelsea?"

"We did, but the feasts were not always public. Lady Catherine dislikes being a spectacle."

"How odd. I do not mind in the least. Especially when one's guest is so diverting," she added slyly. "Mama and Papa do not usually exchange a word at the table, but they both adore Edward. I have even caught them calling him 'son' once or twice."

"Good heavens—that should please him. He and his father are both obsessed by Mama's royal blood."

"Jane! What a beastly thing to say!"

"Only honest."

"Yes. Let us by all means be honest!"

I started at the voice close behind us; I thought Katie would faint.

"Lord Hertford! You startled us so! My sister was only speaking in jest, of course."

"Of course," Edward echoed mockingly. "Sorry to interrupt, but your parents request your presence in the parlor. If you will allow me to escort you—?"

"Most certainly."

Katie took his arm with a conciliatory smile. "I hope my lord will allow me to entertain him on the spinet. I have just learned a piece that is very popular in London now."

Edward appeared willing indeed, and while the two amused each other at the spinet, I was subjected to an inquisition which was not at all amusing. Mama and Papa wished to know everything that had transpired during my residence at Chelsea Manor: What was the King's attitude toward the Lord Admiral? How successful had been my appearance at Hampton Court? When had the Queen Dowager actually been remarried? Why had Lord Thomas refused command of the expedition fleet? . . . The questions went on and on. At last I closed my eyes in exasperation.

"That is all I can tell you, Mama. Please!"

"I shall tell you when I have finished. You have not been very observant. Pray remember in future that you are not at Chelsea merely to play games with Princess Elizabeth!"

"But I am not supposed to—*spy*—am I?"

Mother's hand, heavily ringed, caught me full across the mouth. I cried out involuntarily, and Katie stopped playing. Edward rose I think, but I did not look at him—I could not bear the thought that he had witnessed my humiliation.

"You may retire," Papa said sharply. "I trust you will meditate on that ill-bred remark and beg your mother's forgiveness in the morning."

I curtsied unsteadily and fled.

"Jane, love! Whatever did you say to provoke Mama so?"

Katie had joined me in my chamber as soon as she was excused. Ellen was still trying to stop the swelling of my lip while I sat unable to control my sobs.

"Who knows, Katie? I seem to have a talent for it. But—to strike me in front of *him*!" I cried. "He must have enjoyed himself thoroughly!"

"As a matter of fact," she said calmly, "he left the room just after you did. And I should have said he was not at all pleased."

"Then he was pretending."

"Jane! I do not understand you. Edward is a bit stuffy at times, but he is very decent on the whole. I think the Lord Admiral must have turned you against him."

"It is just the opposite—Lord Thomas has never spoken ill against Edward, but Edward himself has repeated villainous slander about his uncle. He has even tried to make me believe that Lord Thomas married Lady Catherine for her money, and that—that he is scheming to marry me to the King!"

Katie blinked. "How extraordinary! But he is the Protector's son, Jane. Maybe he knows more than you—" She stopped as she saw my reaction. She was actually ready to believe Edward's lies! She did not care a jot about the harm they could do to the Lord Admiral's career.

"Well," she said brightly, popping off my bed, "I guess I had better run along and let you get a good night's rest."

"Aye, a good idea." Ellen hustled her away before she could say any more.

Why were people so ready to believe ill of someone else? I lay awake long that night, staring into the darkness. Although my face throbbed painfully, it was my inner confusion which refused me sleep. Mama and Papa wanted me to spy for them. They may not have approved of the word, but that was what it was. And how could I? I was a guest of Lady Catherine; I was the Lord Admiral's ward. I had come to love them both deeply—I knew that now. Why should it benefit my parents to repeat the arguments between the two brothers, or between their wives? Edward had no doubt already done his work in prejudicing them against Lord Thomas. But I did owe my mother and father my first loyalty. I had been taught never to question their right to command my actions, and I had always obeyed—until now. My questions were still unanswered when I fell asleep.

After a few days at Bradgate it was almost as if I had never left. Since my lessons could not be discountinued even for a short time, I was obliged to join Katie with my old tutor, Dr. Harding, whom I ruefully discovered had not changed one iota. And to be quite honest, I must admit that we probably made his life every bit as miserable as he made ours.

To vary the lessons, Katie and I were often required to ride about the estate to visit tenant families with Mama. This I enjoyed, for the people were simple and good and always seemed glad to receive us. We also learned to make quince preserves in the kitchen and how to oversee the duties of the household servants. Mama was very strict about the latter: she told us that we would one day be required to run a great house of our own, and one could never be so confident in one's housekeeper that everything could be left to her. But the management of a house with over two hundred servants seemed to me an enormous proposition! Inside, of course, were the chief steward, valet, butler, carver, cooks, sweepers, turnspits, brewers, scullions, lackeys and pages, not to mention the needlewomen, laundresses, dairy maids, and ladies-in-waiting. The outdoor servants were almost as numerous—dozens of upper and under grooms, gamekeepers, falconers, and gardeners. Most of our people's clothing was made from Bradgate wool, which had to be shorn, carded, cleaned, spun, and dyed. And of course we were expected to distribute necessary medicines, to learn the use of herbs and how to make healing salves for various sicknesses.

An estate had to be efficiently cared for in order to survive, and for that reason I found life in the country a challenging thing. I loved it and determined to make good at it.

Occasionally, however, I slipped away by myself for a few quiet hours. I kept my promise to Lady Catherine and stored away as much as I could of my valley—breathing the pungent air of the forest and gardens or simply sitting at the edge of the pond, watching the fish dart through the waters. I wanted to hold Bradgate close. Perhaps even then I sensed the changes that were to come about in my life.

On the day before I was to return to Chelsea, I rode to my childhood hiding place, the deserted Priory of Ulverscroft. Only Joshua, the old groom who had looked after me since I was very small, was permitted to go along. The priory had always held a fascination for me; no doubt some of this was due to the tales connected with the place. The year I was born the monastery had been disbanded by King Henry during the period of his anger with the Roman Catholic church. The people of Leicestershire had been shocked; they could remember how the monks had opened their kitchens during the famine of 1528 and saved the lives of hundreds of peasants. Now most of the priests were dead, having been unable to beg enough food to stay alive. Many of the local peasants claimed that their ghosts walked in the remaining shell of the priory. The central tower was still its most dominant feature, rising stark and impressive against the blue sky as we approached.

Joshua held my horse as I dismounted and passed alone under a heavy stone arch. Weeds were growing rampant everywhere; and the very walls held an air of desolation. Never again would they echo the chants of the holy. There was only the sigh of the wind, a melancholy sound. I hurried my steps to the tower and steered my thoughts away from the ghostly tales. The steps wound around and around, higher and higher. If a mouse had chosen that moment to squeak, I should have collapsed in fright, believing it to be the voice of some dead monk. I was determined, however, to reach the top, and in spite of my horror of the dripping dampness so close around me I forced myself to go on.

At last I was at the top—fresh, glorious air! I stood with my eyes closed and drank it in, letting the wind whip my clothes. Then I opened my eyes and gasped. How could I have forgotten this—

this enchanted wedding of earth and sky? Hills, streams, wooded pastures lay below me like another world.

I laughed with wonder and on impulse tore off my hood so the breeze could play with my hair. What freedom! What delight! I wished I could remain there forever. There in my tower was no ugliness, no jealousy common among men.

But I, too, was human and of the earth. I could not set myself above my own without denying the beauty and joy that was possible, despite the ugliness. I thought of Lady Catherine, of her goodness to me, and of Papa and all the others God had given me to love. Surely there was a purpose to my life. Whatever it was, I would not find it up here among the clouds.

The afternoon was passing. I groped for my hood and sought to restrain my wildly blowing hair.

"Do not do that! Please."

For an instant I froze, then spun around angrily.

"How dare you creep up on me like that?"

"Sorry." Edward Seymour looked amused. "I did not think a sensible person like you would believe all those tales about ghosts. But I had to stop you, you see. It was too much a part of the moment."

"What was?"

"Your hair—the sun was turning it into flame. I have never seen hair that color before."

I clapped the hood over my head. "What are you doing up here? Did you not see Joshua?"

"I come to the priory quite often, in answer to your first question. And no, I did not see Joshua—unless he is one of your ghosts. I may have bumped into a good number of those. One can usually be assured of one's privacy here."

"Yes—usually," I said coldly. "I must be going."

"You will be leaving for London tomorrow." He looked out across the hills as if I had not spoken. "I, too, must return shortly. A messenger just arrived from the King. The war is over."

"Oh!—Who—?"

"Our invasion was successful. It happened just as Father thought it would. The Scots were too confident of their numbers. They left their secure position behind the river Esk to attack, and cut off their own retreat." His voice held no rejoicing. "It was a slaughter. Six thousand men slain, fifteen hundred taken prisoner—English losses were slight."

I felt sick with shock. Six *thousand* of Scotland's bravest lads! Dead for what reason? The soil would never lose the stain of their blood.

"The Protector has begun a retreat. I know what you are thinking, Jane. But this was unavoidable. If Scotland had become a province of France, England would never be safe. Father hopes now to be able to form a union with Scotland."

"A union? How can he possibly hope to make peace now? Lady Catherine was right. They will hate us—all the wives and mothers and children of those six thousand men. They will mourn them forever!"

"Perhaps. But do not forget that they refused the offer of a peaceful settlement. We were willing to compromise with our former demand for the reestablishment of the marriage contract between King Edward and Mary of Scotland; we asked only that she be allowed to choose whom she wished when she came of age. But they would have none of it."

I shrugged.

"Statesmen learn to let their minds rule over their hearts, Jane Grey. You shall have to learn that as well if you wish to become queen."

"And you," I said evenly, "will have to learn that I am not what you think I am, that I have never, and could never seek such a privilege!"

"Convince me."

"I lived for four years at Hampton Court. During that time I saw Lady Catherine surrounded by more wealth than anyone could imagine. She had gowns cut from the most exquisite silks and velvets from France, jewels with no equal anywhere. Servants waited on her every whim. Yet she was the most unhappy person I have ever known. She was forced to attend masses daily although she did not believe in them; she was spied upon and plotted against by the King's own ministers; she was verbally and physically abused by the King himself. Often she was in tears or ill after bathing that great, ulcerated leg of his. And that terrible night she learned she was to be put in the Tower under false charges, she lay on her bed all night, screaming. No one could calm her. I was there that night, Edward; do you think I will ever forget the sound of her screams?"

56

"Your cousin is nothing like King Henry."

"Not now. But people change. And our late King proved to his son how easy it is for a monarch to rid himself of an unwanted wife. I want to be safe! A queen is never safe."

"Somehow it is not easy to picture you content in a cozy, thatched croft with a fire in the grate."

I was stung by his words. For some reason I had wanted him to understand.

"I had better go. Joshua will wonder."

"Jane—Forgive me. It seems we always manage to set each other off. And I did not want to part like this."

Deliberately he took my hands and held them firmly in his. A peculiar tremor went through me; I pulled away.

"Good-by, Edward."

"Good-by, Mistress Jane. Who knows? Perhaps the next time we meet it will not be as enemies."

But it was the last I saw of Edward Seymour for a long time.

7

The army returned to London in triumph on the eighth day of October. Although the Protector refused a grand welcome, King Edward personally gave a lavish banquet in his honor. There was great celebration in all parts of the realm—except at Chelsea Manor.

"If I had only had a few more weeks—days, even—I would have secured the King's undivided loyalty!" Lord Thomas paced the floor after a frustrated call at Hampton Court. "Do you know what he calls my brother now, Catherine?— 'My *dearest* uncle!'"

"It is only the excitement over the victory," she soothed. "He is a boy, after all. As soon as things quiet down a bit, he will realize how much he needs you."

"And the pocket money you give him!" Elizabeth put in. We were both supposed to be engaged in needlework, but she could never resist a barb, especially where the Lord Admiral was concerned.

"Of course! He never gets anything from the Protector. The boy feels humiliated not to have a few shillings of his own."

"I find it surprising that the Protector withdrew from Scotland so quickly. No one expected him back this soon."

"Perhaps my astute brother feared there was a—conspiracy afoot against him, Eliza. Do you suppose he was worried about *me?*" He laughed. "As if I might prove myself a better Protector than he!

"By the by, I discovered something quite interesting when I searched the records. In the past, whenever a king in his minority had two uncles, the authority was always divided—one brother became Protector, the other Governor of the king's person."

Lady Catherine looked indignant. "Something should be done! The first Parliament begins in only a few days. You must demand your right, Tom!"

"Yes, perhaps I should." But he was not looking at his wife. His eyes held Elizabeth's, and something passed between them that I wished I had not seen.

"It is much too fine a day to stay inside. Shall we all go into the gardens?"

"I would love to, darling, but you know Lady Denny expects me to call this afternoon. Perhaps Jane and Elizabeth—"

"Oh, but we are due for our drawing lessons!" I cried brightly, catching my cousin's arm. "We had better hurry—"

"Jane, have you lost your senses? The drawing master will not be here for almost an hour!" Elizabeth, clearly annoyed, rounded on me as soon as we reached my chamber.

"I wanted to ask you something that could not wait. Eliza, you do not have any kind of—well—infatuation for Lord Thomas, do you?"

"So that is the matter! You caught him looking at me just now—as if the villain did not know his wife was in the same room with us." She laughed airily. "Nothing to worry about, I assure you."

"Nothing? What if Lady Catherine had seen you? How do you think she would feel?"

"Do not be so dramatic, Jane. Catherine knows the kind of man she married—or she ought to! Thomas Seymour cannot help appreciating other women."

"But—you are a houseguest. And young enough to be his daughter!"

"That did not concern him when he asked me to marry him eight months ago, did it? It is not my fault he is attracted to me."

"All right," I said placatingly, "perhaps you should just avoid—being alone with him, encouraging him—"

"For heaven's sake! I have enough people around here to protect my virginity without you acting as my nursemaid as well! Stop making mountains out of molehills!"

She flounced away, and I tried to rid myself of my uneasiness. It seemed incredible that my guardian would risk his marriage and reputation for a flirtation with anyone—but Princess Elizabeth! I shuddered at the possible consequences. Then I shut them out of my mind. Perhaps, as Eliza said, I was making too much of it. Except for this one instance, Lord Thomas had given every appearance of devotion to Lady Catherine, and she could certainly not be any happier. I decided that most of this "romance" lay within my cousin's colorful imagining.

When Parliament convened in November, the realm was at last unburdened of many of the oppressive measures laid upon it by King Henry. The Act of Repeal removed the old treason and heresy laws, granting religious freedom to both Reformers and Catholics. Restrictions on the printing of the Bible were lifted, sermons were read in the churches in English, and the clergy was again allowed to marry.

I watched the progress with interest, wondering if I might have to revise some of my opinion of Lord Protector Seymour. It did seem that he was concerned with alleviating the suffering of the peasants after all. Early in the sessions he introduced a bill proposing that a certain number of the poorest children in each village should be brought up at the community's expense. I thought this an excellent plan, but it did not pass the House of Commons. A month later, when he pressed for action against the arbitrary eviction of tenant farmers and lessees, he was again defeated.

But whenever I tried to discuss his efforts with the Lord Admiral, I was answered either with laughter or with the comment that even if such unrealistic legislation should pass the Commons, it would never be considered in the House of Lords.

"It would mean a breakdown of all authority. If landlords lose their right to evict whom they will, they may as well lose title to the land. And as for the orphans—it is just another way of dipping into the pockets of the nobility. Who else could afford to support them? We shall always have the poor among us—so states the Scriptures, Jane, and so must my brother come to believe if he wishes to keep some friends among the Lords."

I was disappointed; I think I had expected more of the Lord Admiral. Did he truly oppose these simple acts of mercy, or was the fact that his brother had proposed them the reason for his coldness? The Bible did say the poor would always be with us; but it also said, "If thy neighbor hunger, feed him; and if he thirst, give him to drink."

Apparently the Lord Protector was not ready to abandon his efforts for the poor. With some satisfaction I learned that he had set up a Court of Requests in his own home in order to hear their grievances. There was even talk that he was planning to move against enclosures—that greatest threat of all to the common livelihood.

For dozens of years landlords had been "enclosing" or fencing in previously open pastures for their own use—despite the fact that both Henry the Seventh and Henry the Eighth had passed laws against it. But who was to stop the nobility from taking whatever they wanted, since the nobles themselves were responsible for enforcing the law? The commoners were helpless against their tyranny.

As Christmas approached we all grew merry with anticipation within our own, snug world of the manor. Frenzied preparation of gifts went on behind closed doors; messengers came and went with mysterious packages. And for endless days tantalizing aromas wafted to us from the kitchens—pastries and puddings, confections of all kinds; beef, pork, and game birds roasting slowly on their spits. Lady Catherine went about her household looking happy and pleased. She promised Elizabeth and me that this would be the most splendid Christmas we had ever seen. And it truly was.

On the eve of Christmas we hung the house with garlands of holly and ivy. The servants gathered in the hall with much singing and laughter to crown their Lord of Misrule, who was thereafter free to work what mischief he would until Twelfth Night. Lord Thomas and Lady Catherine, Princess Elizabeth and I then met together in the parlor to watch the burning of the yule log. Master Coverdale was there ahead of us, and as we settled into our places in the firelight he began the reading of the nativity story.

It was a moment of solemn joy. When he finished, no one spoke, perhaps unwilling to disturb the hush. As I looked about at the familiar faces, I discovered unguarded emotions. There were tears gleaming on Lady Catherine's cheeks. Was she thinking of last Christmas, when she was still the Queen of a dying King—still subject to his anger and lust? Or was she thinking of the infant Jesus and of her own intense longing for a child?

Elizabeth's still face held a look of wistfulness. I was startled; it was so unlike her usual proud countenance. Was her arrogance only a mask for loneliness? Did she think of her mother—the lovely, captivating Anne Boleyn—who had both enraged and entranced the Court before she was beheaded for alleged promiscuity? More than one had wondered if the charge was only invented to allow the King's remarriage. But Elizabeth had loved King Henry, despite his refusal to recognize her as legitimate. And now he, too, was dead.

Princess Mary was far away in Newhall—more a stranger than a sister—and of course she was seldom ever allowed to see King Edward. How tragic, never to have really known a family. I told myself I must learn to be more of a friend and less a critic.

The Lord Admiral was staring into the flames with a look of intense concentration. He was like a handsome buck—sleek, alert, ready to spring up and away at the scent of danger. Of anyone there, I would have given most to know what was going on inside his mind; he puzzled me. Fierce ambition, recklessness, humor—all these were part of his lust for living. But what drove him on? Why did he never seem to achieve peace of mind? He professed no faith or religion, never attended chapel, and looked on Lady Catherine's devotion to the Reformation with amused indulgence.

I wondered what good or ill fortune we would find on the path of the New Year, so soon to begin. Would our four lives remain intertwined, or would we separate, go our own ways? I closed my eyes and prayed that God would grant us another year together—a year of harmony, of health, of greater appreciation for the happiness we had found at Chelsea Manor.

Lady Catherine smiled across at me as I looked up; I lowered my head and added one other request—a petition that at this time next year there might be five.

One is not supposed to be stunned into speechlessness when God answers one's prayer, but I *was* startled when only two months later Lady Catherine announced that she was with child (which brings home the lesson that one should never ask for anything one really is not sure about). At any rate, the whole household was overcome with joy. And the Lord Admiral was so beside himself he straightaway bought Lady Catherine the most wildly extravagant gifts he could find—jeweled necklaces, a muffler of finest sable skin, a silver and gilt clock—even a collar with gold bells for her favorite greyhound, Oedipus. Lady Catherine was, of course, aghast and begged him to be more sensible, but he only laughed. He declared it was time the world saw how he valued his wife. And as for young Thomas (there was no doubt in his mind that the child would be a son), he was already considering expanding his estate holdings in the north for him.

So it was that the light-hearted mood of the holidays extended itself through the winter months. Since the baby was not expected until August, Elizabeth and I initiated the ambitious project of embroidering fancy satin coverlets for his cradle. Although her long fingers produced better results, I was allowed to make up for my clumsier efforts by playing my lute or reading to Lady Catherine while *she* worked. The skill of her needlework was known throughout the kingdom; now she delighted in employing it to create exquisite dresses for her child.

The only thing to cast a shadow over those happy days was my increasing awareness of an attraction between Lord Thomas and my cousin. Their continuous teasing, begun in jest, now seemed to contain an element of something deeper. Elizabeth was never as sparkling or witty as when she was with him—which was altogether too frequently. In the evenings, if Lady Catherine was indisposed, she encouraged us to entertain each other at chess, tables and dice, or shuttlecock. Often she would watch us play with a slight smile on her face. She was fond of Eliza. She had tried to be a mother to her and Prince Edward when she became King Henry's sixth wife, and had managed to win their affection. I was certain Elizabeth would not hurt her deliberately. The flirtation was just another game for her, the danger for everyone involved making it all the more entrancing.

My fears took on solid form when Ellen told me Lord Thomas had been observed going into Eliza's chamber several times in the early morning. Obviously the servants had been talking, and I felt panic rise. To whom could I go for advice? Certainly not my guardian—or Lady Catherine. I determined to reason with my cousin once more.

"You admit, then that he comes here?"

"But of course!" she answered, surprised when I questioned her. "He is forever complaining that I lie too late abed in the morning, and I tell him that I shall do exactly as I please. Now he takes the cruelest delight in waking me. Once the villain walked right into my chamber, pulled the draperies apart, and kissed me! I thought he was going to pop right into bed with me, but I squirmed too far away. I was furious with him—I looked a fright! But he only laughed and said I was most beautiful when I was angry. He would not go until I promised to get up—"

"But he was in his dressing gown!"

"How do you know?"

"The servants have seen him—there has been talk. Who knows what Lady Catherine has heard, or what has been said outside the manor?"

Elizabeth looked momentarily shaken, then recovered.

"Well, what should I care about servants' gossip? I have done nothing wrong. And as Master of Chelsea, Lord Thomas can jolly well go where he likes! Lady Catherine dotes on him. Do you think she would believe anything that would soil his precious name? Wagging tongues can be stilled."

Every inch of that proudly lifted chin was King Henry's daughter, I thought bitterly.

"Then why is your governess, Mistress Ashley, so concerned? She has confided in Ellen, Eliza. She is worried about the consequences if any of the gossip should find its way to the Privy Council. You know how everything would be distorted if that happened. Lord Thomas could be executed. Have you thought of that?"

"Do you know, Cousin Jane, you are getting to be a frightful bore?"

"Elizabeth, listen! Please! I know you consider it a joke, but you must realize—"

She turned her back deliberately and began brushing her hair with smooth, even strokes.

"Do you think I need another henna rinse? I believe red hair becomes me; it makes my skin look even whiter."

Something terrible is going to happen, I thought. *Nothing I can say is going to prevent it.*

My hand was on the doorknob when she stopped me.

"It is not really me you care about at all, is it? Or the Lord Admiral. You only want to make sure Lady Catherine does not discover our little—joke—and get her feelings hurt. Well, perhaps you should know something, Jane Grey. It is not a joke—not on Thomas Seymour's part. I excite him. I always have."

"Stop it, Elizabeth! That is wicked!"

"Is it?" She smiled, and suddenly I was looking at a stranger. I was afraid of her. Afraid that what she had said was true.

"Lord Thomas adores Lady Catherine—more than ever now that she carries his child. Do not ever, ever say such a thing again!"

"All right," she said. "But we both know the truth, do we not?"

I fled, angry at Elizabeth and at myself for not standing up to her. Let her believe she was irresistible to him! She was but a schoolgirl, dazzled by a few masculine attentions. She would make a fool of herself, and Lady Catherine would show her what kind of woman it took to hold Thomas Seymour! I could almost pity Elizabeth as I pictured her humiliation.

Lady Margery sent for me that afternoon, and I was glad to escape the tensions I felt closing around me at Chelsea Manor. The old woman's sharp eyes swept over me alertly; she nodded toward a chair, then waited for me to begin, as was her custom.

"Lady Catherine sends her fond regards."

"She is better?"

"Yes, she rarely feels ill now. And she is so eager for the baby, Lady Margery. I have never seen anyone more content."

"Kate has waited long enough for it, heaven knows. Thomas is lucky to have that woman, and he has the sense to see it. Perhaps now he will settle down, take care of his wife and child like a proper father. It is what he has needed."

She noticed my hesitation.

"Something is troubling you, child. My son has not, perhaps, been as attentive to Catherine as he might?"

"It is not that! He spoils her dreadfully; I am certain he wants the baby as much as Lady Catherine. But—Elizabeth—"

"Ah, Elizabeth. I was sure our princess was involved somehow! She has all of the charm that was so fatal to her mother, Anne Boleyn, and she is still too young to know how to handle it wisely. My son finds her attractive, does he?"

"I am not sure he does, Lady Margery; that is what troubles me. Lord Thomas is kind to both of us because he knows it pleases Lady Catherine. But Elizabeth has somehow got it into her head that he is mad about her—and I know she is infatuated with him!"

It was out. I felt immensely relieved to hear my friend's wise chuckle.

"Tom's appeal to our fair sex is not unknown. I can recall when every woman at Court fancied she was the sole object of Thomas Seymour's passion. He overshadowed all of King Henry's other courtiers—wore clothes that set the fashion, turned verses, and danced the galliard to perfection. His swordsmanship was superb, and no one could surpass him at the joust. And he is still devilishly handsome to boot." She looked thoughtful. "A man seldom loses such qualities when he marries. And Elizabeth is at a highly susceptible age."

"She is lonely and bored. Is it silly of me to worry?"

"No, but I think your worry is needless. My son has not always acted wisely, but he would need to be a fool to chance all that he has with Catherine. The child that is coming will seal their love."

I searched her kind, intelligent face and was convinced she was right. When the visit ended, I returned to Chelsea with a lighter heart. I did not dream that my safely propped-up world would begin to crumble in less than a week.

It was May again, and fragrant spring settled over England with wreaths of soft showers, lush green grass, and flowers— flowers everywhere. Elizabeth and I spent every free moment out-of-doors, gathering huge armfuls of daffodils, tulips, and irises for the house. At this time of year I always thought wistfully of Bradgate; the orchards would be at their most splendid, with heavy clusters of pink and white blossoms almost too beautiful against a sapphire sky.

When it was not raining, we were often permitted to have lessons in the summer pavilion. Even studying seemed less of a trial with the songs of sparrows and thrushes within yards of us and the breeze ruffling the pages of our books. We were just finishing an exercise in French one day when we saw Lady Catherine stroll by on the Lord Thomas's arm. Elizabeth, of course, promptly lost all interest in what we were doing and failed to respond to Master Coverdale's twice-repeated question.

"I suggest, mademoiselle, that to become proficient in another language one must do one's best to give one's whole attention to it. However," he sighed, "I am aware that to demand such concentration is most unreasonable. *C'est la vie.* You are both dismissed."

Eliza was out of the pavilion in a flash, pulling me after her. "Hurry!" she commanded. "I think they have gone this way."

"But why should we—"

"Hush! There they are. Does he not look marvelous in that dark blue and white? Poor Lady Catherine. She really is getting very awkward. I wonder that she does not stay inside now."

"Why should she not take some exercise if she wants it? She loves the gardens. Look—they are telling old Peter where to put those rose bushes. I want to see if they are the ones Father promised to send."

"Wait—"

"Well, Kate, love, it seems we have two young women wandering about our gardens unescorted. Do they look familiar to you?"

"There is something about them," she conceded, smiling. "I think perhaps we should invite them to join our company."

"The shorter one looks cheerful enough. But the red-haired one—that wretched black gown makes her look like an ill-tempered crow."

"My lord is quite aware," Elizabeth said icily, "that I am still in mourning for my father, and I intend to wear black for at least two years."

"Two years!" Lord Thomas came closer; I could hear my cousin catch her breath.

"Black does not suit you at all. A princess should have colors becoming to her youth and beauty."

"Nevertheless, I shall wear black."

"You will go and change that dress immediately, Princess. As long as I am master here, you shall do as I say."

"You—*dare*—command *me?*"

"It seems our charge requires a lesson in obedience, Kate."

With a single swift movement his sword was unsheathed and upraised, glittering in the sun's rays.

"Keep perfectly still, and I promise you not one scratch will mar that fair skin."

Before any of us had time to move, his weapon fell and pierced the silk cloth of Elizabeth's skirt, then traveled soundlessly to the hem. The material was divided neatly in two. With horror I saw the blade descend again—and again—a hundred times, it seemed, in the space of seconds. The skirt was reduced to tattered ribbons. We stood staring speechlessly as Lord Thomas paused, his own blue eyes fever-bright with excitement.

"Frightened, *cherie?*" My cousin's face was deathly white, but her chin lifted proudly.

"Certainly not!"

"Then I must teach you what it is to fear."

The blue eyes narrowed. Someone—I think it must have been myself—gasped aloud as the sword slashed the air with a lightning series of cuts and thrusts. It was a performance of incredible precision and skill, the like of which I have never before or since witnessed. The man and the weapon were one. I was entranced. Repelled. Unable to tear my eyes away, scarcely daring to breathe.

And then, when I thought it was over, the point of the blade ran directly at Elizabeth's throat. I shut my eyes and covered them with my hands. *Too late—too late to stop him!* When I opened them again, I saw that the blade had stopped a mere whisper from her blood. And I think it was then I realized the extent of the Lord Admiral's daring. He would stop at nothing to prove himself.

The sword slipped lazily over the bodice of my cousin's

dress—caressingly—and left her in only the flimsy remains of her petticoat. She stood trembling, swaying a little as she stared up at him.

"Now that costume," said my guardian, sheathing his weapon with maddening deliberation, "is infinitely more becoming."

"You!—How—dare you!"

She had recovered from her initial shock, rage making her incoherent. "You might have killed me!—Me!—A princess of the blood! You will regret this recklessness, my lord, when the Privy Council hears of it!"

"Oh?" he drawled. "And just what are you going to tell them? That I provoked you, or that you—provoked me? They will require all the details of the affair, I assure you."

"Thomas is only teasing," Lady Catherine interrupted, putting an arm around Eliza's shoulders. "You know he is the best swordsman in the realm. He would never harm you. Come, child, let us find something else for you to wear before you catch your death."

"As long is it is not black!"

Lord Thomas began laughing, and Elizabeth turned her back haughtily. With as much dignity as she could muster, she gathered the scraps of her petticoat about her and marched after Lady Catherine. Only once did she look back at the man who now lounged against a tree, watching her go. It was only a glance, but it was long enough for me to see the smile curving those full Tudor lips.

With each day I became more aware of how naïve I had been in allowing Lady Margery's words to reassure me. I had believed that Elizabeth's attraction to Thomas was a schoolgirl's infatuation because I had wanted to believe it—because believing otherwise would be unendurable. Now it was time to accept the truth. Lord Thomas had returned my cousin's interest—had even, perhaps, elicited it. If the truth was evident to me, it must be evident to others. How much longer would it be, before some word or action betrayed them to Lady Catherine?

My heart ached for her. Her affection was so childlike and unreserved. She seemed not to have the slightest suspicion that anything was amiss.

How could the Lord Admiral do this to her? I asked myself this question over and over. He seemed so genuinely fond of Lady Catherine and so excited about the baby. And yet if any kind of permanent relationship with Princess Elizabeth was impossible, why did he take such risks to continue it? An explanation was suggested to me when I least expected it, and by my own Ellen.

I had not meant to eavesdrop that afternoon when I ran back to my room to collect my drawing pad. On an impulse I had decided to sketch the pavilion with some of the vines and flowers that twisted around it, as a sort of present for Lady Catherine. She had been unwell the last few days and was confined to her bed by the physician. Although we brought fresh flowers in to her daily, she sorely missed her gardens. I hoped the sketch might cheer her.

"A guid day to ye, Lady Tyrwhitt. And how is the mistress?"

Ellen's cheery voice outside my door made me pause as I was turning to leave. Lady Tyrwhitt was Lady Catherine's lady-in-waiting, a thin, angular woman known to be rather tight-lipped with the servants.

"She is well enough, thank you. She frets over the inactivity."

"Aye, 'tis hard for her. But a woman carryin' her first bairn when she's past thirty and five canna' be over careful."

"That is what I keep telling her" the woman admitted in an unaccustomed burst of candor. "But she only says she would take any risk in the world to have this child. I worry. If anything should happen to her—"

"Ah, but she's a canny one, Lady Tyrwhitt. The mistress knows what she's about, and I'm willin' to say that God is on her side."

The women's conversation died away with their footsteps; I stood with my hands gripping the edge of my drawing materials. *A woman carryin' her first bairn when she's past thirty and five canna' be over careful.* Lady Catherine was old to be having her first child— perhaps too old. That was the danger implicit in Ellen's words. I was too young and too ignorant to have been aware of this danger before, but others knew. The death rate for infants and mothers was high in the best of circumstances. What if, indeed, something should happen to Lady Catherine?

It was then I thought with horror of Lord Thomas and Elizabeth. Did he seek to provide a second course for himself in case the first should fail? *Under the exterior charm lies a hard core of ambition.*

70

He will use anything and anyone to get what he wants. Edward's words came to mind unbidden. No—the man I knew as my guardian could not be like that, so—so unfeeling toward the ones he loved.

But a few days later my world was plunged into such turmoil I could not be sure of anything.

I was dressing for dinner when one of the underservants came up from the kitchens to ask if I still planned to eat in the family dining room, since there would be no one else coming down.

"No one else!" cried Ellen. "And why on earth not? It canna' be everyone's ill!"

The maid looked frightened. "I can't say, ma'am. Cook told me not to repeat rumors. She told me just to come up 'ere an' ask what my lady plans to do, beggin' yer pardon."

Ellen was clearly about to extract more information, cook or no cook, when I laid a hand on her arm.

"I think I should like something sent up to my room, thank you. Tell cook not to bother setting up the dining room."

"Yes, my lady."

Ellen watched her bob a curtsy and disappear. "'Tis verra strange—Lord Thomas is no' away, and Lady Catherine up and around—"

"I am going along to Elizabeth's chamber," I said with decision. "Something has happened."

At first there was no answer when I tapped on the door. I knocked again more firmly. "Eliza?"

The door flew open, and she looked relieved. "Jane! Thank heavens—I thought it was—one of the others." She pulled me in and stared at me, white-faced. "It has happened, Jane. The worst possible thing."

"What are you talking about?"

Elizabeth's governess appeared at the door of the connecting dressing room with a dress in her hands.

"My lady!" She ran up to me and dropped to her knees. "What is to become of us now? There will be an inquisition—disgrace. How was I to know it would come to this?"

"To what, Mrs. Ashley?"

"It is all the Lord Admiral's doing! I warned him, I did. Many's the time I begged him to leave the Lady Elizabeth in peace, stop coming to her chamber at all hours. 'But it is all innocent fun, Mrs. Ashley.' he would say in that mocking way of his. 'Aye,' I told

71

him, 'but it will not be fun for anyone if the Privy Council hears of it! It will mean disgrace!' And he only laughed!"

"Dear Mrs. Ashley, do stop wringing your hands and go watch the women pack my things. I do not want my gowns in a jumble when we get to Hatfield."

"Hatfield! Elizabeth, tell me what has happened this instant."

"Yes, of course. Only you must hear it the right way so you do not imagine things."

She arranged herself on a window seat and patted the cushion beside her, indicating where I should sit.

"There I was—over at my writing table and deeply absorbed in a nasty Greek translation for Master Coverdale. I was alone; I could not possibly concentrate with my women in the room chattering, so I dismissed them.

"I did not hear Thomas come in; it is one of his tricks, creeping up on me and startling me out of my wits. When he cleared his throat, I must have jumped a foot, dropped my quill, and upset the ink bottle all over my papers. I was furious.

" 'Why do you insist on doing that?' I shouted at him. 'Look what you have done!'

" 'Interrupted some dreadfully boring translation, I see. You are already too frighteningly intelligent. It does not do for a woman to know too much.'

" 'Well, I shall not forgive you,' I said. 'Nor shall I ever forgive you for humiliating me in the garden in front of Catherine and Jane!' "

"Why did you not tell him to go away?" I interrupted.

"Hush, I am coming to that. He said, 'I will not apologize because you loved it, you know you did. You are the kind who thrives on danger. It excites you to see a man parading his skill to win your favor!' "

" 'Oh, is that what you were doing?' I asked him. 'It looked more to me like you were trying to impress Jane and Catherine.' He had the cheek to laugh.

" 'You are jealous! My sweet Elizabeth is jealous! Do not forget—you could have married me, and you turned me away. Having regrets?'

"I felt like slapping him. I told him to leave and never come to this room again. Then he pretended to be sorry and said he would not go until I had forgiven him. What could I do?

"I said all right, and he said I must kiss him as a sign that I meant it."

"You did not kiss him? Oh, Elizabeth!"

"Well, I do not see that I had much choice! He simply would not leave. So I gave him just a little peck—and, Jane, before I knew it he had his arms around me tight, his lips so hard against mine I could not breathe."

I closed my eyes, feeling sick.

"It was the strangest feeling, Jane. All the time I knew I should be struggling to get away, but I did not want to. I have never been held by a man that way before. As if he never wanted to let me go.

"'You are mad!' I said to him. 'What if someone should walk in? What about your wife?'

"'I cannot think of her now, my dearest love. Not now.'"

I could picture the rest: one of the house servants coming in to announce tea, finding them in an embrace. . . .

"It all happened in a second, Jane, I swear it! Suddenly he was not holding me—his arms dropped to his sides. And he was staring beyond me to the door. I twisted around to look—and there she was."

"No—oh, no," I whispered. "Not Lady Catherine!"

"I did not mean to hurt her. You know how much I love her!"

I turned away, fighting a desire to strike those vain, pretty features which so resembled King Henry.

"Then why, Elizabeth? Why have you done this thing and destroyed her happiness?"

I left without waiting for an answer. I think I knew in my heart that she had told the truth, that to her it had been only an enchanting and dangerous game which would end happily. It was Thomas Seymour who had known the enormity of the stakes from the beginning.

At dawn the next day Elizabeth and her attendants took their departure. I could not help feeling that some of my youth and innocence had gone with her. Chelsea was left strangely subdued.

9

Perhaps the most extraordinary thing about the incident was that Elizabeth's abrupt departure created so little notice at Hampton Court. There was no sign that the Privy Council suspected any misconduct, and I was sure that had the Lord Protector known the facts he would have seized the opportunity to banish his brother to the Tower. It pleased me that the servants, either out of respect for Lady Catherine or fear of Lord Thomas, had kept their suspicions to themselves. If there was gossip, we did not hear it above stairs. It was as if nothing had happened.

It was Lady Catherine who set this standard for the rest of us. Not once did we see any sign of hurt or humiliation, nor did she act any less pleasantly toward anyone, including Lord Thomas. She was alert, busy efficiently overseeing the household and receiving calls just as before. It was this that disturbed me, this—unnatural cheerfulness. She was carrying on as if a large portion of her world had not just broken apart and fallen away while we all knew that it had. I wished she would talk to me, as we had so often at Court when we eased one another's disappointment or pain.

"She canna' talk, lass. She fears to let you or anyone else see how great a wound it is."

"But I would understand. If she would just let me be with her, Ellen, instead of shutting me out. I know I could help."

"There are times when even a friend must wait. Let her be. It wouldna' be a kindness to intrude until she's ready."

So, mechanically, I went back to my lessons and aimless walks through the park, watching the earth awake to spring. I missed

Elizabeth. Sometimes I talked with Miles Coverdale, who seemed to sense my feeling of isolation and began to share some of his inner self. My admiration for this man grew daily; I wondered at his kindness to me, so much younger and less learned, and I marveled at what he had accomplished with his life. I was sure that men like Coverdale and Tyndale and Latimer would be remembered long after their deaths. I said as much to him, but he shook his head, smiling.

"The reward is not in being remembered, Lady Jane, but in knowing that while one lives one has 'fought a good fight and finished the course' God has set. Why should any of us envy another as long as we have been given a particular work to do?"

"That is the trouble—not everyone has a task. How can I do anything, when all my decisions are made for me from my first breath? A man can enter what profession he likes, given the intelligence and the will, but a woman—and a gentlewoman at that? She makes the most profitable match at the earliest possible age and is thereafter expected to cheerfully surrender her body, mind, and property. She may not—ever   resist the command of a parent or husband."

The chaplain looked sad. "God knows the limitations imposed upon us. But he can work around them—even through them, if we are willing.

"I was given a bird once, a rare and exotic creature from a distant island. But when it was put into a cage, it flew against the bars ceaselessly. It refused to accept its confinement and eventually damaged itself so badly that it died. I found another to take its place. He, too, tried to escape, but after a few attempts he settled on his perch. He was a plain fellow, I remember, an English sparrow. But my word, Lady Jane, how that bird could sing! It was a lesson to me. We can kill ourselves, hurling protests against the unfairness of life, or we can make the best of who and where we are. Perhaps we can even sing."

I gave him a slow smile. "I shall try. Really I shall."

"It is a lesson your guardian might learn. He continually rebels against his brother's authority. In doing so, he may injure himself; he has already injured others around him. I am being candid, Lady Jane, because I want you to be on your guard."

"But—why? He would not harm me."

"He would not mean to," he shrugged. "There is probably

nothing to worry about as long as you are in Lady Catherine's care. Lord Thomas is not unkind, only given to unwise impulses. And so, I might add, was your father to entrust you to his guardianship. But what is done is done. I shall commit you to your heavenly Father and to your friends. I hope you will always number me as one."

His friendship was a comfort to me during those unsettled days. Lady Catherine had become discontent with Chelsea and had moved the entire houshold to the Hanworth estate. It was her effort to forget, to start over. But I could not help thinking of the happy times we were leaving behind as well as the unfortunate. Chelsea would always be a special place to me. I hoped we might one day return.

Lord Thomas was often missing from the evening meals in our new home. More than ever he was occupied at Court, and there were rumors that his differences with the Protector were worse since the campaign in Scotland.

"So little was accomplished by that war," sighed Lady Catherine. "Young Mary was taken from Scotland to France for safekeeping. She will undoubtedly marry the Dauphin instead of our King Edward.

"Union looks as far off as it ever did. And the Protector's letter to the people of Scotland sounded so good: *We two being made one . . . and having the sea for a wall, mutual love for a garrison, and God for defence, should make so noble and well agreeing a monarchy that neither in peace we may be ashamed nor in war afraid of any worldly power. . . . If it be lawful by God's law to fight in a good quarrel, this is to make an end of all wars, to conclude an eternal and perpetual peace.*

"An end of all wars." She sighed. "I am afraid the Duke is a dreamer, Jane."

"Is it wrong to dream? I know Lord Thomas thinks his brother is a fool to defend the lot of the poor. He says it is no use."

"We need dreamers—*and* realists, like Thomas, to keep a balance. But he may be right in saying the Protectorate is not the place for his brother. He is surrounded by hard men, men who will not hesitate to practice deceit for their own gain. We must have a Protector whose feet are firmly on the ground."

The feud between Lord Thomas and his brother reached a climax in mid-June. The Protector discovered the former's plan to get King Edward to write a letter of complaint against him to the

Council. Lord Thomas was arrested; threatened with imprisonment. He was forced to apologize.

That night he and Lady Catherine stayed up far into the night, talking. The decision was reached to move our residence again, this time to Sudeley Castle, deep in Gloucestershire. We would stay there until the baby was born.

I was vastly relieved to be leaving London. The heat of summer had descended and with it the beginnings of a plague, and I fretted over the danger to Lady Catherine. Most of the nobility who were free to do so had already left town. However, I wondered if Lord Thomas's sudden withdrawal had been prompted by his wife's condition or by his own precarious state.

Lady Catherine asked, somewhat hesitantly, if I would like to rejoin my family at Bradgate for the summer. I was touched by her thoughtfulness, for I knew how much she missed Elizabeth's companionship. My own absence would create a further void. I had no desire to leave her and tried to convince her of that fact.

"How could I miss the birth of the baby? He will be my first brother, you know. I have great plans for him. It would not be right if I was not there. Please say I may go with you, Lady Catherine! Please."

She laughed. "Since you put it that way, how can I deny you? You might enjoy Sudeley. It is very quiet, and the house is one of the most splendid in England."

She was right; I did like Sudeley Castle from the moment I saw it towering above St. Kenelm Wood. Was it because it reminded me so much of Bradgate, with its wide acres of park and forest and hidden, jewel-blue lake? Perhaps. But the best thing about the castle was its remoteness. I felt as if we had come ashore upon a secret island, and no one could invade our peace.

My room reflected a tasteful simplicity, and the large, sunny windows looked down upon a view almost as breathtaking as the one from the Ulverscroft Priory. The bed was hung with delicate blue silk, matched by a deeper blue carpet covering the floor. Curiously I peered into Lady Catherine's chamber on the same floor and gasped in admiration. It was decorated as sumptuously as though she were still Queen-Consort of England. Rich tapestries, a tester and curtains in a deep shade of crimson taffeta—even a small bed for the nurse had been provided. There was a door leading to another chamber that would undoubtedly serve as the day nursery.

Lady Catherine took an immediate interest in reordering the gardens and visiting the cottages of the poor all about the estate. Often we went together to distribute food, clothing, and the medicines and salves she prepared herself. With her, I had learned, this was no charitable gesture performed from duty. She had always had a deep concern for the peasant children who often starved and died because of the neglect of the landlords. I had seen her stand beside tenant parents as they laid their infant son or daughter in a grave already holding other sons and daughters who had not survived the hardships of poverty or disease.

Lord Thomas objected to our excursions, arguing that it could not be safe for the baby. "Why can you not stay here and sew things and potter about the nursery like other pregnant women?"

She made a face. "Everything is already sewn, my love. More clothes than your son will ever have need of! And the nursery is ready, too. It is to be a surprise. Now, do not frown, my handsome lord! If we did not share some of our good fortune, God would think us ungrateful. We have so much, Tom."

His face softened. "I would still feel better if you were not traipsing about, exposing yourself to whatever is in the air. You are due next month—"

"And the doctor says I could not be more fit. Very well. I shall strike a bargain. Someone else can visit the sick in my place if you promise to go with me to chapel every day to pray for them!"

"Kate." He looked so pained that we both burst out laughing.

"Aye, I have you there! You have not yet graced one of Master Coverdale's services, if my memory serves me correctly."

"It does. I leave the piety to the saints and the hypocrites—of which you are so splendid an example of the former, my dear—" he bent down and kissed her— "and my brother, the latter."

"Oh, Thomas!"

"You must admit that an income of 4800 pounds a year hardly leaves him in a position to sympathize with the penniless!" He stalked off, his quick temper ignited as always by any mention of the Protector.

"I do wish he could be more reasonable about the Duke," Lady Catherine sighed. "He is determined to hate everything about him. I have prayed that somehow—here amidst so much beauty and away from all that turmoil at Court—he might find some contentment within himself—as I have."

"Perhaps when the baby comes," I said.

"Yes! Our son! Come, Jane, I want to show you the nursery."

She led the way eagerly, looking as young as Elizabeth. "I did not want anyone else to arrange this room. It had to be exactly right."

We reached the door, and she stood back quietly.

How can I describe what I saw that sunny afternoon in July? The vision of it is still imprinted on my mind. Gold spilled everywhere, gilding the walls, the bedstead, the small chair of state—as though no treasure was too lavish to offer the coming child. I fingered a colorful tapestry representing the twelve months of the year—a work that in itself had taken a dozen years—and approached the tiny dais. Here I saw an exquisitely carved cradle, ready with fragrant down pillows and silk counterpane.

Tears sprang to my eyes as I realized the infinite care given to each detail. It was so much more than a display of wealth. It was the expression of a woman's love and the fulfillment of many years of longing.

"I have forgiven him, you know," she said at last. "I never truly blamed Elizabeth—she is a child. And Thomas—well, he is a man, only a man, not the golden god I worshiped. He and I differ in so many ways. Perhaps I tried too hard to make him into all I wanted him to be. But I love him, Jane, no matter what he is or does. He gave me back my life. And now he has given me a new life."

She took my hand and placed it upon her swollen body. "Can you feel him? He is a very active mite."

I waited a breathless moment and then felt a hard, firm pressure against my hand.

"It *is* him! I felt him move!"

"Of course, silly," she laughed. "You do not suppose I have been pretending all this time?"

"But I just thought of something—what if it is not a boy? Will you be terribly disappointed?"

She shook her head. "I think a girl, exactly like you, would suit me beautifully."

All the same, we never really did get around to choosing a girl's name. And of course it did not help when the Duchess of Somerset, the Protectors wife, proudly gave birth to a son in late July. It was almost as if the two women were competing even in childbirth! Lord Thomas was wild with jealousy but managed to drudge up a dutiful, polite letter of congratulation. He probably felt he could afford to be generous when he would so shortly be celebrating his own son's birth. Even the fortune-tellers and palmists he insisted on consulting assured him of it.

As the time of birth drew near, Lord Thomas and Lady Catherine seemed to share a new closeness. There was a tenderness in my guardian's eyes as he looked at her that had not been there before, and I knew that on her part all bitterness had been put away.

As the hot days of August inched by, I amused myself exploring the territory about St. Kenelm Wood, writing endless letters to Katie and Elizabeth, and reading to Lady Catherine, who was now feeling very uncomfortable. I was glad she and Elizabeth were again on friendly terms; Eliza had written soon after her banishment from Chelsea begging for forgiveness, which was graciously extended. Her letters were a great source of amusement to us in our quiet country setting—full of gay descriptions of her new life, her acquaintances, her clothes, her tutors—in short, we laughed, full of Elizabeth. I wondered if my cousin would ever tire of her self-absorption as she grew older; whether any man would finally be able to distract her long enough to win her love.

The twenty-ninth day of August dawned still and bright. Lady Catherine was restless, peering wistfully from her chamber window as Lord Thomas on horseback rounded up the dogs for the day's hunt. He spied her watching and saluted.

"It is a glorious day, Catherine! You should be down here instead of looking out of your tower like some imprisoned wretch!"

To everyone's distress, she burst into tears.

"I am a prisoner!" she sobbed. He dismounted instantly and came up to where we sat.

"We cannot have this, you know. Your physician said you were not to be upset. It might hurt the child."

"The child! That is all you talk about. Do you not care about me? Day after day you ride off with your hounds and your friends and have a good time, and what do I do? Sit here like some great toad, waiting for this baby!"

"Well, you shall not today," he promised. "You are going out—just you and Jane and I—none of your ladies fussing about—and we shall have a picnic by the lake."

"Oh, Tom!" she cried eagerly; then her face fell. "The doctor says I must not go anywhere now. The lake is too far to walk, and I could not ride—"

"Nonsense! We shall have a few men carry a sedan chair for you, and Jane and I will ride alongside. Nothing could be simpler!"

"It sounds so lovely—but I would feel selfish. You had your plans all made."

"Give me a chance to spoil you, darling. It is not often you do."

They gazed at each other for a long moment. I decided I was not needed.

"I will ask cook to pack us a hamper."

"Good idea. Tell her to keep it simple—game pie, cold mutton and beef, figs or plums, ale—"

"You had better tell her two hampers!" laughed Lady Catherine. She tore her eyes away from her husband. "And do hurry, Jane! I have a feeling this day will be very special indeed."

It was. From beginning to end it was magical, like a perfect gem we could put away and bring out to admire in some distant time. I decided that happiness could never be found by pursuit, that it happened accidentally. An outing. A day in the sun. Such a far cry from the elaborate entertainments at Court!

"I should like to stay here forever," murmured Lady Catherine contentedly.

"What? Here at Sudeley?"

"Why not, Tom? We do not need to go back to London. We have been so happy here—"

"We can be happy anywhere together," he said gently.

"Promise me we will not have to leave immediately after the baby is born. Please!"

He hesitated. Then, "All right. If that is what you want."

We reached the house as the sun disappeared in a blaze of pink and crimson.

"Worse luck, I promised to finish some business in the village tonight. You do not mind, darling?"

A shadow passed over her face, then was gone. "Of course not. I shall be quite all right."

Lord Thomas kissed her and strode off; probably, I thought indignantly, to one of his gambling matches or cockfights.

"Shall I stay with you for a while? Or are you too tired?"

81

"I feel too full to sleep. Young Thomas does not seem to be pleased with all that I ate. Whoever said a woman with child has a delicate appetite? Come, read something to me in my chamber, if you like."

Never content with idleness, she took up some needlework as I began a psalm.

> O Lord, thou hast searched me and known me.
> Thou knowest my downsitting and mine uprising.
> Thou understandest my thought afar off.

Lady Catherine looked up and smiled. "Psalm 139. It is one of my favorites."

> Thou hast beset me behind and before, and laid Thine hand
>   upon me.
> Such knowledge is too wonderful for me.
> It is high. I cannot attain unto it.
> Whither shall I go from Thy spirit?
> Or whither shall I flee from Thy presence?
> If I ascend up into heaven, Thou art there.
> If I make my bed in hell, behold Thou art there.
> If I take the wings of the morning or dwell in the uttermost
>   parts of the sea,
> Even there shall Thy right hand hold me.

She finished the passage for me, from memory:

> Search me, O God, and know my heart,
> Try me and know my thoughts.
> And see if there be any wicked way in me,
> And lead me in the way everlasting.

There was a moment's silence, and then a sharp intake of breath. Lady Catherine's embroidery slipped to the floor.

"I just had—the most—peculiar sensation," she gasped. Her eyes were wide and frightened; I stood up in alarm.

"Perhaps the food. I will fetch one of your ladies."

"Not—the food!" She managed a shaky laugh. "I think it is more than indigestion this time. Quickly, Jane. My son—may decide to make his entrance without—the proper decorum."

I ran. Within seconds, it seemed, the bedchamber was crowded with people. Someone galloped off to the village to find

82

Lord Thomas. I was terrified. What if he could not be found? What if something went wrong? .

Lady Tyrwhitt shooed me out of the room and told me the baby would not come for many hours, that I was only in the way. Nervously I went to my room and curled up on the window seat, watching for my guardian's stallion. It seemed many hours before I heard the clatter of hooves upon the courtyard. I closed my eyes with relief. Weariness settled over me. . . .

When I opened my eyes again, the sun was streaming in through the windows. I jumped up, stretching my cramped and stiffened limbs.

"There, now ye're up, lass!"

Ellen appeared, a tray balanced precariously with one hand and the other groping for the door.

"I hadn't the heart to wake ye sooner, ye were so pale."

"Lady Catherine! How is she? The baby—?"

"The both of them are doin' fine. Though she had a hard time of it, bless her."

I started for the door. "I want to see her."

"But—yer breakfast! What am I to do with it?"

"Eat it, Ellen! Do not let it go to waste." I blew her a kiss and ran.

The lying-in bed was freshly hung with white satin and silver lace. Lady Catherine looked small and fragile against the pillows. Her fair hair was unbound, her eyes closed and sunken. Thinking her asleep, I tiptoed to the bed and stared down anxiously.

"Jane—have you seen the baby?"

It was barely a whisper, but it reassured me.

"Not yet, my lady."

"It is—a girl. Thomas is disappointed."

"Oh, no, Lady Catherine, I am sure he is not!"

"Yes. He had his heart set on a boy. He—tried not to show it, but I could tell. He would not even hold her." A tear slipped from the corner of her eye and down into the pillow. What should I say? What *could* I say?

"You must leave now. Lady Catherine must rest."

Lady Tyrwhitt was all efficiency. I took Lady Catherine's hand and squeezed it.

"Do not cry, Lady Catherine. Please do not. Everything will be all right."

I went in search of Ellen. She must have some answer for Lady Catherine's depression.

"I thought she would be so happy. She told me it would not matter to her if she had a girl."

"'Tis only the hard time she had in birthin', lass. Dinna' fret so. A good sleep will rid her of such fancies. Just leave her to herself for a bit,"

So I stayed away and went and gathered roses for her chamber, remembering how they had soothed her during other troubled moments. August slipped into September without my noticing it. For two days I brought flowers to the lying-in chamber and was turned away. At last I was admitted.

"Things have not gone quite as we planned, my dear. I have missed you. Why have you not come to see me?"

"They—they told me I must not." I held her hot, moist hand against my cheek. "Are you feeling better now? You look better. And I have been to see the baby. She is so lovely, Lady Catherine. Have you a name for her?"

She moved her head restlessly.

"Henry's first wife, Catherine of Spain, bore him six children—only Mary lived. The rest were stillborn or died in infancy. He—he annulled their marriage because she could not give him a son."

"It was brutally unfair. Everyone says so, now that he is dead."

"She loved him. It did not make any difference to him, but she loved him until she died."

Her voice had a faraway, singsong quality. Her eyes frightened me.

"Oh, I suppose all men would like to have their first child a male, for an heir," I said lightly. "But parents seem to learn to love all their children."

"Your mother did not, did she? She never forgave you for being a girl!"

Painful color stained my cheeks. Lady Catherine had never before spoken to me so bluntly. I bit my lip.

"I—expect she has grown used to the fact by now. And Father and I have always been close. Katie says I am his favorite."

She appeared to have lost interest and began talking about her

84

life as a child and her home in Wiltshire. Her speech was so uneven and disconnected that I had difficulty following her. At last her voice trailed off, and she fell into a deep sleep.

Something was wrong. Fear twisted within me like a knife. I had seen peasant women in their cottages, happily nursing their infants only hours after labor. But Lady Catherine did not have the strength to nurse, nor the will. She did not even wish to see her baby, the child who was the answer to years of waiting.

"Dear God, please do not let anything happen to her now."

I went into the adjoining room where the wet nurse sat rocking her charge. A tiny fist waved in the air, and I marveled over its miniature perfection. She would be petite like her mother, I thought. The nurse offered to let me hold her. Cautiously I gathered the bundle into my arms and smiled. How light she was! What father or mother could not love this gift? She would be loved. A female or not, this little one would be cherished for herself.

Another day passed, then two. Visitors who called with gifts left without being admitted to Lady Catherine's bedchamber. Lord Thomas, I was told, was with her constantly.

"What is happening, Ellen? Why is she not getting better?"

"'Tis the fever—childbed fever," she frowned. "I've seen it many a time in the crofts."

"But she will get better?"

"It's in God's hands, lass." Her face softened. "She's no' in a croft. She's a lady, surrounded by fine comforts and doctors. Sure she'll be better."

I tried to pray, but found that I was only repeating words that made no sense. How did I know God listened or even cared? I needed a friend I could see and touch, not just the deafening silence of a chapel. I was too confused to confide in Miles Coverdale. How could he, of all persons, understand this sense of desertion by God?

On the fifth day of September, Lady Catherine asked to make her will. I was shocked, angry that she did not fight the enemy that threatened her. Why did she not try? I stood numbly as witness to the terms of the will. Her eyes, bright with fever, did not leave Lord Thomas's face.

"It is my wish to give my husband, Thomas Seymour, all of my property, my estates, jewels, and household goods. They are his

85

and not to be disputed. I wish—they could be a thousand times more, so great is my love for him."

It was a nightmare from which I could not wake. Two nights later my guardian told me to slip something over my nightdress and come as quickly as possible. His disheveled appearance and worn face filled me with alarm.

"Is she—worse, then?"

"She is dying," he said simply.

As we entered her bedchamber, I was struck by the suffocating closeness. Many persons whom I could not make out by the light of the candles had withdrawn into the shadows around her bed. I went to her at once and sank to my knees. There was no recognition. She groaned horribly, as if each slight movement caused intolerable torture. I saw her tongue move over her fever-cracked lips. She called for water.

"Give her water!"

"She cannot drink, my lady." One of the women near me spoke. "It chokes her. We have tried."

"But—she is dying!" I did not recognize my voice, high-pitched, angry. "The physicians must be able to do something!"

"They have bled her repeatedly. They say that is all that can be done."

"No! They are wrong! I know—"

"Lady Jane."

It was Miles Coverdale, emerging from the shadows and laying a restraining hand on my shoulder.

"The choice lies with God, my child. Do not raise your fist against His will."

I stared at him incredulously.

"God would not have allowed this to happen if He loved her. Does He throw us down like dolls when He has finished playing with us?"

"Jane is right," interrupted Lord Thomas suddenly. "Catherine loved your God as much as any creature on earth, and this is her reward. If you have any weight with Him, ask Him to save her!"

"Lady Catherine is not a prize in a tug of war between God and man. If God wishes—for some reason unknown to us—to take her to Himself, we must yield—"

"You may yield. I shall not. Command the physicians to bleed her again," he ordered and strode from the room.

I laid my cheek against Lady Catherine's burning face, praying that somehow she could feel my love. I would not stay to see the leeches applied to her delicate skin; I could bear no more of the sound of her suffering.

"Good night, my lady," I whispered. "I shall see you in the morning."

But morning never came for her.

Lady Catherine died shortly before midnight—one year, six months, and eight days after King Henry the Eighth. She was thirty-six years old.

The odd thing about death is that no one truly believes it will happen. You and all the people who belong to you are immortal. So when death comes and takes away that smile, that step, that voice which are so much a part of your own being—and leaves only empty space—you are not prepared to accept it as final. There is even an absence of pain at first, because you know it cannot have happened. It cannot.

I remember my father once told me about a cavalry officer who lost a leg on the field of battle. He did not feel anything. He did not know what had happened until he saw his leg lying there apart from his body, and then he began screaming. He said he wanted to die. But he did not; the rest of his body was whole, and he had to go on living.

When they took me to see the remains of my beloved friend lying white and still upon her bed, I looked upon a dead part of myself. I knew I would go on living; but I felt that I could never again be whole.

Elaborate funeral preparations went on around me. King Edward sent word that his stepmother was to be buried with all of the dignity befitting the widow of a great king. So over the black-covered walls of Sudeley chapel and over altar rails and cushions hung the bright-colored banners of heraldry. I remember thinking that it was wrong. Wrong to bury her as a king's consort, when all she had wanted was to be the wife of a handsome young sailor from Wiltshire.

Protocol demanded the Lord Admiral's absence from the funeral service. After a brief farewell, he left for London, and I remained to act as the chief mourner. As in a dream I took my place under the canopy of state embroidered with the Tudor and Seymour coats of arms and began following the hooded bearers of the coffin.

They told me afterward that the service was quite impressive—the first royal funeral ever conducted with Protestant rites. The Psalms and Master Coverdale's sermon were spoken in English, which would have pleased my lady. But while the servants in the back of the chapel wept unrestrainedly, my own eyes were dry. These rituals were not for Lady Catherine. I placed my sprig of evergreen—symbol of immortality—on the coffin lid and wished it would all be over so I could go to her. She would be waiting, as she always was, and assure me that this had been a nightmare.

The procession left the chapel and reached the grave. I saw the words Master Coverdale had inscribed in Latin:

In this new tomb the royal Catherine lies:
Flower of her sex, renowned, great and wise.
A wife, by every nuptial virtue known,
A faithful partner once to Henry's throne.
To Seymour next her plighted hand she yields—
Seymour, who Neptune's trident justly wields;
From him a beauteous daughter blessed her arms,
An infant copy of her parent's charms.
When now seven days this infant flower bloomed
Heaven in its wrath the mother's soul resumed. . . .

Catherine Parr

The name was chiseled in cold stone. I wanted to hammer it out, obliterate it.

The choir began singing the *Te Deum*. A spadeful of soil swung over the gaping hole, rained hollowly on the carved lid of the coffin.

I felt I must be going mad. *What are they doing, God? What are they*—? The fog of unbelief was shredding, lifting. Madness became reality. *Oh, God! She will never come back, will she? She is gone!*

I took a step forward, my hand extended blindly. And then the singing, the chaplain's voice, the vision of that grave receded and spun away into darkness. . . . .

10

A fortnight passed before we received Lord Thomas's direction to join him at Hanworth. I had begun to make the rather startling discovery that life does go on. I was able to eat, to sleep, to perform all of the duties required of me. I even discovered that there were minutes and even whole hours when I could forget. But always, always the remembrance of Lady Catherine's death rushed over me again, and each time the grief was new.

Shortly before we were to leave Sudeley, I went once more with Ellen to the bright, golden nursery prepared for the Seymour son and heir. Our footsteps sounded loud in this too-quiet room. Softly we crossed to the cradle and looked down.

"Poor, wee bairn—no one's even given thee a name."

"What will become of her, Ellen?"

She shook her head. "Lord Seymour takes precious little interest in her. I expect she'll be dispatched to some kin."

I did not want to think of Lady Catherine's baby being brought up by someone who might not care for her. But perhaps the sight of her was too painful to Lord Thomas. After all, if she had not been born, Lady Catherine might still be alive. Ellen seemed to read my thoughts.

"This babe is innocent of her death! You'll not be blamin' her. 'Twas the fever—and God's will."

"But why?" Anger flared within me. "Why does everybody have to keep saying it was God's will? She was happy. And she had her child at last. Is it sinful to be happy?"

Ellen sighed. Was she remembering her own heavy loss, the deaths of her own husband and infant?

"Sometimes—a long time after—it's given to us to ken the 'whys' of God. More times it isn't. But I know this, lass. Ye and the Queen had a feelin' for each other that was rare. Ye must not let the hurt of partin' with her blot out all the rest—the laughter, and the sunshine—all the sharin' ye did. 'Tis not fair to remember her cold and still, lass! Not fair to either of ye."

Tears spilled over my cheeks, and I wiped them away. The infant below us stirred, then lifted fringed eyelids. For an instant I thought I saw something in those large, brown eyes that looked incredibly like Lady Catherine. I could not speak.

The Greeks had believed a man was immortal as long as his name was remembered on earth. Lady Catherine was a part of this child as, in a unique way, she was a part of me. As long as either of us lived, the woman I had known as my friend would not be lost.

The household arrived at Hanworth the fourth week of September—three months since we had left it for Sudeley Castle with so much joy and expectation. The Lord Admiral sent for me at once.

"I have thought a great deal about our situation, Jane. I hoped at first that I would be able to carry things on as they were—but it will not work. You must see that."

He began pacing restlessly. He looked tired, as if all of the long, peaceful weeks at Sudeley had never been. "I am going to take chambers in the city again in order to keep a closer watch on my affairs." He stopped and looked at me. "I am sorry, Jane. I have written to your parents that I cannot continue looking after you."

I do not know what I had expected, but it was not this. I was being shuffled out of sight like his unwanted infant daughter, and I was not ready to go. Thomas Seymour and I were not close, but we had shared a love for Lady Catherine, and I needed to hold onto this last link for a little longer.

I struggled for words to convince him as he glanced impatiently at the clock.

"There really is no point in discussing it, is there? It will be better for us both. You must excuse me, Jane. I have an appointment with William Sharington," He hesitated, then left.

I did not deceive myself that he would change his mind. The mainstay of the Admiral's life had broken, and he had put about for the nearest port. I could not have been more startled, therefore, when he called me into his study again a few days later.

"I was wrong, Jane," he said abruptly. "I have written another letter to your parents. I want you to read it."

> *My last letter I wrote at a time when, with the Queen's death, I was so stunned I had small regard to myself or my doings. Thinking that my great loss must constrain me to break up and dissolve my whole house, I offered to send my Lady Jane to your lordship. I find now that with God's help I shall be able to continue my house together . . . and am now minded to keep her. Lady Margery, my mother, shall, I doubt not, be as dear to her as though she were her own daughter, and for my part I shall continue her half-father, and more. . . .*

"Thank you," I said quietly, returning the letter to him. "I shall try to make certain you do not regret your decision. If only Mother and Father agree to it."

But they did not. A reply came by return messenger that I was to pack my things and return to the "long-neglected guidance and discipline" of my mother as soon as an escort could be arranged.

"It appears they do not trust either of us!" he laughed. "You will have to go—but I promise to have you back within the month or I have lost my influence entirely!"

The last day of September I rode through the gates of Bradgate, and shortly thereafter Mama and Papa left for London at the Lord Admiral's request.

"Now what do you suppose is afoot?" Katie was consumed with curiosity. I knew she suspected I harbored some deep secret, so I indulged a temptation to tease her.

"Obviously," I said gravely, "he is going to ask to marry me."

"Jane! Are you serious?"

"You are a goose! He is three times older than I!"

"That would not matter—he is still the best-looking man in England. But you know the terrible things they are saying. I should not want to marry a man who has done away with his wife!"

I felt the color draining from my face.

"What did you say?"

"Well, I did not make it up! It is whispered everywhere that he poisoned her."

"Then everyone is mad! How dare they spread such gossip! Lady Catherine adored him. She willed him everything she had."

"Oh, it is no secret that she loved him. But whom did he love? What actually happened at Chelsea when Elizabeth was sent away?"

"That is no one's affair. It had nothing to do with Lady Catherine's death."

"All right, then, you need not be so hot about it. I really did not believe the rumors anyway. And neither did Mama and Papa, or they would not be meeting him now, would they?"

I frowned. "They seemed so set against renewing his guardianship. I wonder what could have changed their minds."

"My dear, naïve sister! Surely you realize that Lord Thomas Seymour is one of the richest men in the realm now that he has inherited the Queen's property? He can afford to pay whatever they ask."

"Do you think that is the reason?" I was taken aback. "It sounds so degrading, Katie. As if I were being traded like Papa's prize mare."

"Do not be silly. I should feel rather flattered to have the Admiral haggle over me. Besides, the grim truth is we are desperate for money. We are over our heads in debt!"

My parents did not tarry long in London; when they returned, I could tell at once they had struck a "bargain" that pleased them. I was instructed to write a cordial note to Lord Thomas and express my gratitude for his kindness to me. Was it unreasonable, as Katie said, to feel the way I did? After all, I did wish to return to the Lord Admiral's household. Why should I resent it if my parents could turn a profit from the arrangement?

It hurt, nevertheless, when my guardian arrived and there was so little regret over my going. Papa did not look at me when the Admiral presented his five hundred pounds.

"The rest of the two thousand shall be paid in a fortnight," he promised.

"I will give you a receipt."

"That will not be necessary, Henry. Jane herself shall be my pledge." He smiled and turned to me, his eyes gleaming with triumph.

"My mother and I are looking forward to having you back at Seymour Place."

It was good to see Lady Margery again. She received me with such obvious pleasure that I felt I had found a refuge—a safe, warm place of retreat until I could heal. For Lady Catherine's absence was still like an open wound which bled at the slightest touch. How many times did I turn, hearing laughter or a footfall, hoping to see that beloved face again? And how bitter was each disappointment. It was the little things, the homely reminders, I found hardest to bear. It was a hard word to accept—*never*.

Although I had hoped that our mutual loss might draw us closer, I saw little of my guardian. During the late autumn evenings when we sat together, Lady Margery spoke often of her son; she seemed to be troubled.

"He is away again—off to see that friend in Bristol, William Sharington."

"He is treasurer of the mint, is he not?"

"Aye, and a scoundrel. Those two are up to something, Jane; I can sense it. Do you notice how distracted Thomas has been whenever I put a question to him? Not like himself at all."

"But how could he be, Lady Margery? He is trying to fill his mind with business, buying property—"

"Too much property! What does a man do with a hundred manors, I ask? And where does he get the money? Sharington is involved in this somehow, and I do not like it."

I tried to think of a way to soothe her, not really understanding her reason for alarm. The Admiral was a rich man, was he not? Who could be more capable of managing his own affairs?

"I am sure there is nothing to be concerned about," I said. "Lady Catherine's death was bound to have an effect—on all of us."

She sighed. "Aye, if Kate had lived, things might have been different. I had so hoped— Ah, well. Fetch your lute, Jane dear, and play something to cheer us."

But as the weeks passed, it became clear even to me that

something was wrong. When Parliament sat in November, Lord Thomas made no attempt to attend the sessions. He seemed always to be occupied by his estates in the north. I wondered how he was able to keep up with all the duties of the admiralty.

Outwardly my life continued as before. Reading, studying, and music consumed even more of my mind and energies. Lady Margery left me quite alone except when I sought her out, understanding my need for solitude. I could not yet talk about Lady Catherine's death to anyone. Not even to Elizabeth, who called on me once that autumn. She, too, grieved, she said; she missed Catherine's companionship, her wisdom in counsel. I envied my cousin's easy flow of tears. Hers was the kind of mourning that would end gently, without a scar.

Toward the end of December I received one other visitor. I was in the music room, rehearsing a particularly difficult passage for the harp. It was to be a Christmas present for Lady Margery and Lord Thomas. As I finished, I was startled to hear a voice congratulate me—Edward Seymour's voice.

"That was very good! I was not aware that music was one of your accomplishments."

I flushed. "It is not, really. It amuses me, and sometimes pleases others. I am sorry to have kept you waiting."

"Do not apologize, please. It is I who have intruded. But when Lady Margery told me I might find you here, I thought it would be a good opportunity to see you alone. The Lord Admiral's prize possession is not often left unattended! He has not given up his ambition to marry you to the King?"

My temper flared. "You are slow to acknowledge an error, my lord. My guardian has no such interest."

"Then why did he insist on reinstating you as his ward? Solely out of a fatherly regard for you? I think not. Much has happened since we last met, Jane. It ought to have opened your eyes."

"If you are referring to the ugly rumor concerning Lady Catherine's death, I can put your mind at rest. She died of a fever following childbirth—nothing else."

"How can you be sure? They say he was in constant attendance at her sickbed. He had the perfect opportunity to take advantage of her weakened condition."

"And the motive?" I asked bitingly.

"Money. He has begun to press again for the restoration of the

94

Queen's jewels. Did you know that? He asked Princess Mary to testify as a witness that they were a bona-fide gift from King Henry. And—he has asked Elizabeth to marry him again. She refused."

A vision of Lady Catherine, her body twisted with pain, rose before me. I closed my eyes. What if it were true? What if he had—? No. I had seen his face when she made her will. His grief was genuine.

"Why did you come here, Edward? You did not really believe you could turn me against your uncle, as your father has turned you?"

There was a peculiar expression on his face. "In spite of what you think, my father is concerned about his brother."

"Oh? And why, pray?"

"Because Thomas is in danger. My uncle entertains grandiose ideas of his destiny, Jane. Do you have any knowledge of his activities since he left Sudeley Castle?"

"He is engaged in estate business in the north."

"He has not mentioned a certain Holt Castle in Cheshire?" he asked, and waited. "According to our information, Holt Castle is a storage depot for a huge supply of artillery and ammunition. Several thousand men are quartered there that your guardian calls his army."

"His army! What would he want with an army?"

"I was hoping you could tell me. He has obviously given over his duties as Lord High Admiral, and worse, he has begun to bargain with the very pirates he is supposed to suppress. For a share of their booty he will guarantee their protection in the admiralty courts. As a result, the channels are swamped with pirates."

"It is not true! It cannot be."

"How else could he afford to feed an army? Use your wits, Jane. His inheritance from the Queen would not stretch that far."

"He has friends. Sir William Sharington, for one."

"What do you know of Sharington?" he demanded sharply. I realized I had said too much.

"I know nothing. And you could not have sufficient evidence for what you say or the Protector would have had him put in the Tower. It would be the perfect excuse to put away his rival!"

"You are wrong. If my uncle were to be executed for treason, my father would wonder for the rest of his life if he had acted from the right motive."

95

Treason? . . . *Execution?* A long shudder ran through me. It was not possible.

"Lord Thomas may be ambitious, even negligent of his duties, but he has done nothing deserving of death!"

Edward's gray eyes regarded me soberly.

"When I was a small child, I adored my uncle. I thought him the bravest and most worthy hero ever to sail the high seas. But I came to discover that a hero is better seen from afar off, that one should never be close enough to see the places where the shiny armor has worn through. Because underneath is often emptiness, Jane, and a rather sad inability to love anybody but himself.

"No one likes to see a hero topple. I do not want Thomas Seymour destroyed any more than you. Talk to him, Jane! See if you can stop him from this mad self-destruction."

He bowed abruptly and left without farewell.

I did not want to believe what Edward had told me. Nevertheless, when my guardian returned from his trip to the north, I watched him. He was in rare high spirits. He did not even evade Lady Margery's questions at dinner.

"What have I been doing? Inspecting my property, Mother. It pleases me enormously."

"I am reminded of the Scripture, 'God looked on all that He had made and saw that it was very good!'" she said dryly.

"Lord Thomas—have you been to Holt Castle?"

"Holt?" He looked at me speculatively. "As a matter of fact, I have."

"And why, my son, is Holt of such particular interest?"

"Let us say that it is the means to an end which I have sought for a very long time."

"You mean the end of the Protectorship, do you not?" she asked, with sudden fear in her voice. "I knew it had something to do with that, and it is madness, Tom! You cannot hope to defeat your brother!"

"Come, Mother, you might demonstrate a little more confidence in me. At least in front of my ward. I have ten thousand men at my command and unlimited wealth. Edward is Protector in name only; his control is gone. This Parliament has proved it."

I was startled. "I did not think you attended Parliament."

"My dear Jane, I do not need to be at Whitehall to realize how far the country is split over the enclosure issue. The landlords insist on going into sheep-raising and fencing out their farming tenants. My gallant brother has decided to defend the downtrodden farmers. He will never win, of course—the nobility always have their way."

"Oh, Thomas," said Lady Margery, "Edward is idealistic, but does he deserve your contempt?"

"A fool must reap what he sows. The Council regrets electing him—even your father, Jane, and Lord Pembroke. I shall speak soon to Wriothesley and sound him out."

"Not him!" I blurted out, suffering his frown of disapproval. "Do you not remember how he betrayed Lady Catherine when she was Queen? He is treacherous!"

The Admiral shrugged. "Perhaps. But he is shrewd enough to stand with the winning party."

There was no dissuading him. I saw it, and so did the stricken Lady Margery. I could no longer doubt that he was the leader of a complex conspiracy. What Edward had said must be true—all except the rumor about Lady Catherine's death. That I would not accept—ever.

Christmas was almost upon us. We went through the motions of making Seymour Place festive, although Lady Margery was clearly distracted. For myself I could not forget the happier memories of last Christmas. Was it only a year ago that Lord Thomas and Lady Catherine, Elizabeth and myself had shared such joy?

Perhaps realizing the direction my thoughts were taking, Lady Margery kept me busy preparing small tokens for the waiting ladies and servants and overseeing the feast preparations in the kitchens. I spent days trying to think of gifts for the Lord Admiral and his mother. At last I decided on an exquisite stickpin of jade and ivory for Lady Margery; it had belonged to the Queen, and I thought she might be pleased to share a remembrance of her. For Lord Thomas I had a small garnet set in a handsome gold ring.

On Christmas Eve, with the house freshly decorated with boughs of fir, my heart lifted. The great yule log was rolled into place and the Christmas candle lit; Lady Margery and I went together to the chapel for midnight prayers. It was a lovely night—almost windless—and walking out under the stars I suddenly felt a nearness to God that I had not felt since Lady Catherine's illness. Surely He was there, watching us. Surely, this time, He would hear our prayers and would intervene to prevent another tragedy.

I slept soundly, and next morning hurried down to join the excitement in the great hall as the servants gathered for yule cakes and ale, blackjacks, cheese, toast, and nutmeg. The family feast would be served at noon, with wassail bowl of spiced ale, boar's head, and stuffed, roasted peacock with tail outspread. First we watched a mummers' play of the nativity, then opened our gifts.

Lord Thomas and his mother both expressed delight over my selections as I looked on anxiously. Then Lady Margery brought out a delicate French hood bordered with sapphires to match my favorite blue dress—as well as several pairs of gloves and shoes. I was overwhelmed and still stumbling over my thanks when my guardian kissed me and slipped over my hands a soft sable muff. I recognized it at once. It was the one he had given Lady Catherine after she had told him she was with child.

"She was very fond of it," he said. "I thought you might like to have it now."

All the emotions I had been so careful to conceal came rushing out as I stroked that soft fur, and Lord Thomas held me close. When my sobbing quieted, he spoke again.

"I want you to know something, Jane. It is true, God help me, that I caused Catherine much grief while she lived. But what they are saying is a lie. She was a rare woman. By my soul, I would not have lifted a hand against her."

His fingers bit into my arms as he held me away, willing me to answer.

"Whatever else you have done," I said slowly, "I cannot judge. But that you were not responsible for Lady Catherine's death, I know."

He seemed satisfied.

"Let us put the past behind us, then. Catherine would not have us grieve on this day, of all days. And we have plans to make for our lives. Your life, Jane, as well as mine! The new year shall bring us both what we have long desired."

"What should I require but health and your continued kindness, my lord?"

"Marriage!" he laughed. "What does any girl want more than

a man to master her? But I do not mean just any man, my dear. As Protector I shall be in a position to wed you as Catherine would have chosen. To the King himself!"

I gasped. "You do not mean that!"

"How else do you suppose I convinced your parents that you were best off in my 'disreputable' hands? Besides the money, of course."

"Thomas. I do not think Jane is ready for this. There will be time enough when and if you are made Protector. There is no use in terrifying the child."

"Nonsense! She had better get used to the fact, and quickly. I am not feeding her to the lions. The boy is fond of her, and he could hardly be less like his father. You will be *queen*, Jane! Think of it!"

The thought made me dizzy with fear. What was there to hope for now? Success for the Lord Admiral's plans would mean unwanted royalty for me. And yet if his venture failed—it would surely mean his death.

The peace of Christmas was scattered like the ashes of the yule log. I did not wait to save the traditional remnant for next year's fire. The future seemed very bleak indeed.

11

January brought days of bitter cold, and Seymour Place shivered under the attack of ceaseless wind and rain. Lady Margery took to her bed with a chill—probably as much of the mind as of the body. She seemed to take comfort in talking about her life as a young bride and as a mother burdened too early with the rearing of children. I sense that she shared these personal insights for a reason.

"I would like you to know more about my sons," she said one day. "I think it may help you understand why Thomas has determined upon this course.

"My husband—John—was not malicious by nature; I am sure he never knew how much he hurt Thomas. But it was as though he had given all of his love to Edward, our first-born, and did not have enough left over for the other children. Edward was John's whole world."

I was reminded suddenly of Mama and her first-born child, the son who died.

"Edward was a bright lad from the start, and my husband taught him to hunt and hawk and sit a horse before he was much more than a babe. But it was soon clear that Edward's greatest achievement would lie in his intellect. And even though John himself was a soldier, he was inordinately proud of Edward. Strangely enough, it was Thomas who most took after his father: strong, full of life, outrageously good-looking—but with a will of his own! He was my problem child. He worshiped his father and was fiercely jealous of every attention that went to Edward. He tried to surpass his brother in everything—and he usually could—but my husband was blind to it all. Even when he lay on his deathbed, it was Edward he called for at the last, though Thomas stood for hours outside his chambers hoping for a summons. I think it was then something happened inside Thomas."

She turned her head and I could see her startlingly blue eyes, so like her son's. "Can you understand a little now of this obsession to defeat Edward? When King Henry was alive, Thomas made himself the court favorite by pirating French galleons, filling the royal coffers with gold, turning churches and monasteries into storehouses for herring and wine. He was a sailor among sailors, Jane, a courtier among courtiers—all part of his passion to be second to no man.

"Henry did smile on him, and all England gave him the adoration he craved. Yet it was still Edward who became Earl of Hertford, Edward who, upon the King's death, was made Lord Treasurer and Duke of Somerset. And despite all of Thomas's efforts, it is Edward who is now Lord High Protector of this realm.

"I am afraid for them, Jane! For both my sons. Thomas is going to destroy his brother, or destroy himself trying."

A shiver touched me. Was this a prophecy? I was to remember her words always.

When Lord Thomas came to see his mother that afternoon, we could tell something was amiss; his rugged features were preoccupied, and I saw a small line of worry crease his forehead as he bent to kiss her.

"It is good to see the ruddy color back in your cheeks, Mother! A few drops of your physician's potion have worked wonders. What does he make it of, I wonder?"

"No more of your idle talk, Thomas! Something is troubling you. What is it?"

He hesitated. "I suppose you might as well hear it from me. Will Sharington has been arrested. He has been shearing coins at the mint, buying up church plate and making shillings out of the cheap metal. Falsified the mint books, too, of course. They say he has made thousands by it."

"But you did not just find that out, did you? You knew it when you first went to see him at Bristol to borrow money from him."

"I had to get it somewhere," he shrugged. "Catherine's estate

101

was not enough. And my brother still refuses to give up her jewelry."

"So Sharington gave you what you needed. In exchange for silence, perhaps?"

"You need not make me out such a villain, Mother. We both benefited from the arrangement, and I promised to help him if he ran into difficulties."

"Well, it seems he is in difficulties now. Tom, what if he tells the Council about your involvement with him?"

"He will not. If he has any sense at all, he will stay close-mouthed until I can get him released."

"I do not like it."

"There is nothing to worry about. I have friends on the Privy Council who will back me against Sharington, if it comes to that. We are too close to overthrowing the Protector to let anything get in the way now."

But Lady Margery was unconvinced, and so was I. Sharington's arrest could uncover Lord Thomas's conspiracy.

"Have you sounded out Lord Wriothesley?" I ventured to ask him.

"I did. And the Earl of Rutland. Both of them are doddering old fools—too old for this game. Told me I should not attempt it! Wait until I am in my brother's chair; then they will come to heel."

A maidservant appeared and curtsied.

"A messenger is arrived from Hampton Court, my lord."

He looked pleased. "From the King?"

"No, sir, from my lord's brother. He says the Protector wishes to see you."

"Indeed? He may tell my good brother I have no wish to see him. And furthermore, I will not be summoned like one of his slaves!"

"Yes, my lord."

"Thomas!" Lady Margery laid a hand on his arm as the girl hurried off. "Do you think that was wise? Perhaps Edward knows something. Should you not at least meet with him?"

"If he knew of our plot, he would have me arrested! He is playing for time, Mother. He thinks he can get me to trap myself. But he is hunting cannier game than he expects."

"Son, please stop this incredible scheme now, before it is too late."

He laughed, and I saw on his face the same fierce exhilaration he had exhibited that day in the garden, with Elizabeth's life at the point of his sword.

"You have never gambled, Mother. The thrill of the game is greatest when you have the most at stake. Whether or not I win the Protectorship—and I have no doubt that I shall win—I shall enjoy the play intensely!"

The week passed in ominous silence. Lord Thomas did not leave the house, but remained shut up in his study while the Council made special inquiry into Sharington's affairs.

On the morning of January 17 Lady Margery and I were breakfasting when we heard the clatter of horsemen in the courtyard. I ran to look out, my heart beating rapidly. It was the King's Guard. Scabbards flashed in the sun as the men in fiery red and gold uniforms dismounted. I recognized two of them—Sir Thomas Smith and Sir John Baker.

Even as I relayed the information to Lady Margery, Lord Thomas appeared and started down the entrance steps to confront them.

"Go down there, child! Do not let him do anything foolish!"

I wondered desperately how I was to accomplish this as I sped through the front hall. I reached the courtyard just as Sir John handed the Lord Admiral a warrant.

"By the authority of His Gracious Majesty King Edward VI, you are under arrest and commanded to be delivered to the keeping of the Lieutenant of the Tower."

For a moment I was incapable of speech or movement. Then, as two guardsmen advanced in the slow-motion of a nightmare, I fell on my knees in front of them with a hoarse cry.

"No! You cannot do this!"

"Lady Grey, please—!"

"By God's precious soul, Baker, whoever lays hands on me to take me to prison shall have the thrust of my daggar!"

Sir John looked alarmed. "Come, my lord, there is no need for violence!"

"Then do not trouble me. I shall take my leave in my own time. Wait here."

Deliberately he turned on his heel and reentered Seymour Place. I remained on my knees, weeping, heedless of the uncomfortable stares of the soldiers. I knew he had gone inside to take leave of Lady Margery. I knew, without anyone having to tell me, how slim the chances were of his ever seeing either of us again.

When he emerged from the house, he raised me gently by the shoulders and bade me go in to this mother. Then, taking the reins from a groom, he swung onto his horse's back and headed him toward the Strand. He did not look back once. It was almost as if he were eager for the fight that lay ahead.

But what he did not know was the strength of the forces that were to be hurled against him. It was Lords Wriothesley and Rutland who, after hearing Sharington's confession, had decided to reveal everything they knew about Lord Thomas's conspiracy against the Protector. At this, members of the Council who had previously pledged to support the Lord Admiral now turned against him. Many of his "friends" came forward eagerly to offer "evidence" in order to demonstrate their own innocence in the affair. The accusations mounted.

It was determined beyond doubt that Thomas Seymour had indeed been in collusion with Sharington. Furthermore, he had established an illegal confederation with pirate gangs and had set up a depot for stolen goods in the Scilly Isles, goods which were later taken to London for resale. The heavily armored Holt Castle was proven to be the fortress intended to harbor the abducted King Edward during the planned takeover of the Protectorship.

But Lord Thomas's enemies were not content with the recounting of his current activities. Every conceivable blot from his past was dredged up. There was even the dubious statement of a woman who had been executed for robbery and child-murder in 1540! She had claimed her crimes were a result of being "seduced and desolated by Lord Thomas Seymour"! He was named as an atheist, and Hugh Latimer, Lady Catherine's former chaplain, attested to the fact that Lord Seymour never attended prayers said in his house. And then the insinuation was made that he had behaved immorally while married to the late Queen. An investigation was begun into his relationship with Princess Elizabeth, and a body of men were sent to Hatfield to question her closely. Mrs. Ashley was arrested and sent to the Tower, and Elizabeth wrote short, terrified letters to the Protector to protest the rumors being put about that she was with child.

Lady Tyrwhitt was called upon to give evidence which might

prove Lord Thomas's guilt in poisoning Lady Catherine. Might not the fever caused by poison, they asked, resemble the symptoms of childbed fever? Lady Tyrwhitt had never liked Thomas Seymour. Her answers were brief and incriminating.

I came to dread the sight of the messengers who daily brought Lady Margery news of the trial. She maintained an outward composure, but with each piece of evidence she looked older and more vulnerable. I longed to be able to offer her some hope—but what hope remained?

And then I learned that Mama and Papa were coming to London. They had been summoned from Bradgate to explain to the Council the transaction of my wardship. I felt deeply humiliated. Why was it necessary to air so personal a matter? Everyone would be told that Lord Thomas had "purchased" me from my parents for the price of two thousand pounds. What would they think of us? Would they accuse my guardian of dishonoring me as well as Elizabeth? Or had they discovered his plan to wed me to the King?

"I am afraid that John Dudley, the Earl of Warwick, has left no stone unturned, Jane. You see, he has determined on Thomas's ruin."

I looked at Lady Margery in astonishment.

"You think it is the Protector who wants him dead. So, of course, does Thomas. But I know Edward would not arrest his brother unless he was convinced there was no alternative. Do you remember that he sent for Thomas privately before the arrest? He would have agreed to a reconciliation even then, I feel certain. But Thomas was too sure of himself."

"I still do not understand how Warwick is involved," I replied.

"The Earl of Warwick has been advancing himself in court circles for many years. His father, Edmund Dudley, was chief minister to Henry the Seventh until he was executed for extortion and general unpopularity with the people. Henry apparently realized the sentence had been unduly harsh and attempted to make it up by appointing John Dudley, the son, his Master of the Horse and Viscount Lisle. Dudley is no sluggard. He used his opportunities shrewdly and made himself indispensable to the King. In return Henry the Eighth named him one of his executors and conferred upon him the office of Lord Admiral."

"So he held the admiralty before Lord Thomas!"

"Aye—until Henry's death, when he surrendered the title to Thomas and received the Earldom of Warwick and a seat on the Privy Council in exchange. He profited by the arrangement, of course, but he has never forgotten the fact that he was forced into it by the Protector. And he hates Thomas because he is a dangerous competitor."

"So he wishes to turn brother against brother, perhaps ruining both?"

"I have no doubt that is his ambition. He is parading Thomas's sins so flagrantly that Edward will be unable to pardon him without public condemnation. And of course the Duchess— that viper Edward married—is doing her best to see Tom overthrown. She has always been jealous of his popularity."

I remembered the indignities Lady Catherine had suffered at Court because of the Duchess's jealousy, and grew hot.

"Can you not make the Protector see that Warwick is using him?"

My old friend smiled sadly.

"My sons indulge my eccentric interest in state affairs, Jane, but they do not go so far as to listen to me."

No, I thought, the proud Seymours would not listen to any woman. Not even the one closest to them.

By the end of February, there were thirty-three articles drawn up against the Admiral. The Council met in a body and went to the Tower to hear his defense; this, we learned, he refused to give. He demanded instead to have a fair trial—to be confronted with witnesses. And he would answer no questions that might endanger himself.

"But surely he is entitled to that!" I cried when the Marquess of Northampton, Lady Catherine's brother, came himself with the news. But he shook his head unhappily.

"The Council is resolved to circumvent a trial by introducing into Parliament a Bill of Attainder against him. They went to the King this afternoon to get his consent."

"The King loves Thomas. He would not condemn him to death!"

"Lady Margery, he is but a boy, surrounded by clever men. They have convinced him that Thomas was responsible for his stepmother's death."

106

"Not even you believe he killed Catherine!"

"I, alas, am not a witness. There were none to defend him."

"Not even—his brother?"

"The Lord Protector did not speak until the others were through," he told her gently. "I could see that it took a great effort—he stumbled over his words. But he said at last that he regarded his duty to the King and the Crown of England more than his own son or brother—his allegiance more than his blood—and that he would not stand against the Lords' request. He would be obedient to whatever His Majesty willed."

"So the King gave his consent to the Bill of Attainder." Lady Margery's voice was flat.

"Aye. But there is hope. The bill has yet to pass both houses before the case is declared to be treason. And the Admiral may present his defense, though not in person, of course."

"Of course," he had said, but it seemed cruelly unfair that Lord Thomas could not be there when the witnesses rose so glibly to condemn him in the Parliament sessions which followed. Would some of those voices falter, those eyes fall if he were to confront them? Many of the articles against him were vague, certainly open to interpretation. Why did not some of his friends among the nobility protest?

The Admiral sent answer to the first three charges, stating strongly that none were supported by definite proof. He would not, he said, condescend to answer the remaining thirty.

The Protector absented himself while the House of Lords voted; the bill was approved and went to the Commons.

At last, to our fierce gratification, the Bill of Attainder met resistance. Members stood to declare that they believed the whole proceeding to be illegal, that the prisoner had every right to a formal trial before his accusers. Our hopes rose—and then, just as swiftly, plummeted. The King—influenced no doubt by the Earl of Warwick—sent a directive to the House of Commons to accept the verdict of the Lords and the witnesses' testimony as valid. The bill passed with four hundred in favor, not a dozen against. Thomas Seymour was pronounced a traitor to the Crown.

"*I will see Edward. I must!*" Her spirit rekindled by determination, Lady Margery ordered a carriage as soon as we heard the vote.

"Only the Protector and the Council have the power to pardon

107

him now. If Edward listens to Warwick, Thomas will surely be executed and he himself will be censured by the people for shedding his brother's blood!''

I waited in an agony of suspense for her coach to return. This once, I reassured myself, one of Lady Margery's sons would listen to her counsel. She was gone for hours, and when she alighted from the carriage I ran to embrace her.

"Will he be pardoned?''

"Yes! My dear Jane—'' tears of joy coursed down her cheeks, "if it were up to the others, he would be dead. But Edward did not really listen to me. It was as if he had made up his mind long ago that he could not judge Thomas; not, he said, when he had a part in making him what he is.''

So I had been wrong all along about the Protector. Perhaps I had also been wrong about his son, the younger Edward Seymour. My cheeks burned with shame as I remembered the way I had mocked him. After the Admiral's release there would be a reconciliation between the brothers. There was no reason why there should not be one between Edward and me also.

The house was polished until it shone for the master's return. There was a festive spirit among the servants that was contagious, and I caught myself listening, like the rest, for the ring of his boot upon the stair and his joyous shout. The house itself was waiting, eagerly. . . .

And then our hope was gone.

The Privy Council requested the King's authority to make them solely responsible for the Lord Admiral's life or death— seeing that the case was so "heavy and lamentable to the Lord Protector." The King consented. Five days later, oblivious to every curse he hurled at them, they ordered Thomas Seymour to prepare for execution.

On 20 March 1549, he was beheaded on Tower Hill.

He had not surrendered, not even at the end. On the scaffold he horrified everyone by refusing to listen to his minister's prayer, by condemning his judges, by physically attacking the executioner. When he would not kneel for the blade, his life was hacked from him ruthlessly—bloodily.

Seymour Place had lost its soul. The tempestuous spirit which had ruled it was stilled forever. Left behind were the pitiful remnants of his mortality—gloves, sword, littered writing table, and the shell of the person who had been his mother.

Had Lady Catherine lived, could she have prevented all this? Or had God, knowing the madness which drove the man she loved, spared her the heartbreak of his inevitable destruction? I did not know; I was only conscious, as I looked at Lady Margery, of a kind of gratitude that Lady Catherine was not alive.

I was exhausted by the force of my grief and longed for Papa to come and fetch me. At last, a week after my guardian's death, he did come. And I went home to Bradgate.

12

Spring came to Bradgate that year just as it had in years past. The earth laid aside its gray mantle of ice and bared flower-garlanded shoulders to the sun—the annual triumph of life emerging from death. I found it strange that things should go on as before, that nature should be so exacting as to continue to the next season, and the next, without making concession to one's inner winter which could not thaw. Yet I was not always locked inside looking out at the sun; sometimes I could escape from the prison of my thoughts long enough to laugh in the warmth, to press the fragrant flowers to my face and inhale their beauty—and afterwards felt ashamed of my betrayal of those who could not be with me, who would never again laugh or breathe or taste the ecstasy of spring in England.

But if nature is relentless in her healing of winter's scars, she is just as persistent in waking those inner parts of us that we think dead. And though we thrust her away, she will enter, and enter again until at last we accept her bittersweet presence.

As before, when I sought to escape from memory, I fled to my books. Here there were worlds and thoughts that were not mine, and I could safely hide among the pages without fear of discovery. Ironically, I was encouraged in my emotional cowardice by my tutor—even praised. Master John Aylmer, who to my intense relief replaced Dr. Harding for most of my instruction, became a friend with whom I spent my happiest hours.

My new tutor was a native Leicestershire man, but at thirty far more highly educated than Dr. Harding. He also had a merry sense of humor which enlivened the dullest lessons, for he enjoyed inserting a witty remark or story to catch us off guard. Katie adored him, and he often served to bridge the distance that had somehow widened between us during my absence. Sometimes he would coax all of the family out to the green for his favorite game, bowling. Whenever he lost his indignation was comical.

His serious enthusiasm, however, was reserved for theology and the classics. When I exhibited an interest in the same studies, Master Aylmer was delighted.

"I must introduce you to my friends! You know, of course, of the great Reformers, John Ulmer and Henry Bullinger, and Zwingli of Switzerland?"

"I have heard of them, Lady Catherine and Master Coverdale told me of their work. But I did not know they were in the country."

"They are not, my dear Lady Jane!" he laughed. "God is an Englishman, but unfortunately there are a few of His gifted servants who are not. They are in Geneva. I meant simply that I would introduce you by letter. I have been corresponding with them for years."

"Oh, but— whatever could I write to men like that? I mean, they are so famous—they have written books—"

"Nonsense. They will be delighted. And I shall coach you with the Latin. An excellent exercise."

So began a most unusual and fascinating acquaintance with three men whom I would probably never meet. Although I am sure they benefited little on their part, I was genuinely pleased by their kindness in answering my questions in serious detail. Eventually Papa began sending them money to support some of their efforts.

It was about this time also that I began reading St. Augustine's *Confessions*. I must mention it because it was responsible for bringing me to myself, as well as bringing me to God. For all at once the words I was reading were not the reassuringly vague expression of someone else; they were my own thoughts, my own carefully hidden doubts of the past months, my own soundless groping in the dark for answers. I felt stripped, without protection. Yet how could this man born in Africa, hundreds of miles and years away, know so much about me?

I was unhappy, and so is every soul unhappy which is tied to its love for mortal things; when it loses them, it is torn in pieces, and it is then that it comes to realize the unhappiness which was there even before it lost them.

Was it possible to have lived so long with Lady Catherine, and to have sat under teachers such as Latimer and Coverdale, and never myself to have experienced the truth? I thought I had lost my faith when Lady Catherine died. In truth, I had never owned it.

It was a load I should have brought to You, Lord, for You to lighten. I knew this but I neither would nor could—all the more so because, when I thought of You, I was not thinking of something firm and solid. For it was not You Yourself who were my God; my god was an empty fantasy, a creation of my own error. If I tried to lay down my burden there, that I might rest, it slipped through the void and came tumbling back upon me again. And myself to myself had become a place of misery, a place where I could not bear to be and from which I could not go.

So I traveled with Augustine as a companion through his long inner journeying. And when, dusty and exhausted, he threw down his burden of spiritual agony, I discovered I was no longer carrying mine. It, too, had fallen at the feet of the One who had stood there all along, waiting to bear it for me.

It was well that it had. My return to Bradgate represented disgrace and failure to my family; the Lord Admiral's plans for me were at an end, and I had disappointed my parents' expectations of a royal wedding.

Bereavement and long separation from Bradgate made it difficult for me to relate to the others. Mama declared that I was "putting on airs," a result of too much freedom in the Seymour household. Her method for curing this want of humility and obedience was frequent beatings. It was a common enough occurrence in English households; we never were a people to spoil our children. But it seemed the harder I endeavored to display a proper spirit of submission, the more enraged she became. I developed severe headaches from the ceaseless strain of trying too hard, and this, in turn, made me fumble more than ever at my tasks. Hardly a day passed that did not end in some stormy scene.

I did not see Papa nearly enough; he was away a good deal of the time trying to resolve the enclosure disputes that were cropping up everywhere. The Protector's order to knock down fences put up against tenant farmers had caused excited rebellion by both gentry and peasants. The tenants now demanded more of the rights due them, and landlords—Father one of them—were hard-pressed to keep down the rising disorders. Part of the problem stemmed from the fact that when lands were taken from the church and distributed to the nobility, the new landlords had immediately raised the rents. In addition there was a new demand for wool, both in England and on the continent. As growing numbers of landowners found it profitable to use their property for pastures, tenants were turned out of their cottages. Even the small, independent farmers were deprived of the commons on which they had traditionally grazed their cattle. Last year on Plough Sunday I had attended St. Paul's and heard the reformer Hugh Latimer denounce the landlords' greed. But when the Protector appointed commissioners to hear and redress the peasants' grievances, the nobility declared the commission illegal. The commoners, infuriated, began to rise all over the country.

When Papa returned from our kinsman's manor in Wilton, he looked grave. It had not been easy, he said, to put down the rebels in Oxford and Gloucester counties.

"But they simply would not surrender! They were poorly armed. They had no chance."

Mama looked unconcerned. "They needed to be taught a lesson, did they not? Perhaps in future they will keep to their places."

"That is just the problem. There are already more outbreaks in Sussex and Kent. I pray to God they will not have to be settled in the same way."

"Well, I shall pray that the peasants in Leicestershire have the wit not to get involved. A pretty mess this is over a few fences."

Master Aylmer cleared his throat politely. "I believe that the trouble in some areas has gone beyond enclosures, my lady. Perhaps you have heard of the Devonshire priest who is trying to make this into a holy war? He has even managed to persuade some of the nobles to side with the peasants."

Mama's indifference faded. "Impossible!"

"I am afraid it is true," Father said unhappily. "The religious issue has worsened the picture considerably in Roman Catholic counties. The people are demanding that the Six Articles and Latin mass be reinstated, and at least half of the lands seized from the church restored to it. It is no longer a matter of the nobles against

113

the rabble, but against an organized army of Catholics!"

"Why does the Protector not send someone into Devonshire to break them up?"

"He has, madam—Lord Russell. But what is a small force against thousands? My guess is he will either have to come to terms or wait for reinforcements."

Within the week we learned that Russell had relayed the demands of the Devonshire people to the Council, who had refused to listen. An order was sent for the people to disperse. Incensed, they gathered strength and marched on the city of Exeter, carrying the relics of the church before them.

Lord Russell was soon joined by Sir William Herbert—who had just successfully put down a dispute in Wiltshire—and a company of German and Italian mercenaries. Their attack scattered the rebels completely, and Russell pursued and butchered hundreds of them. Afterwards martial law was declared and dozens more of the prisoners executed. The vicar of St. Thomas, who had been one leader of the uprising, was hung from his own steeple.

"It is shocking," John Aylmer told me. "And it is all the more tragic because it is not the end. The people will keep fighting; more blood will be shed. And to what purpose?"

I remembered Thomas Seymour's bitter prophecy: *The nobility will have their way, of course . . . they always do.*

"Everyone blames the Protector for stirring up this viper's nest. Well, poor man, he will not escape unscathed for his efforts."

"You do not think he was wrong?" I asked.

"His mistake is in failing to kiss the hands that elected him; and that error, my dear, can be fatal. The Council members do not take it charitably when some of their own parklands are plowed up for common use. And men like the Earl of Warwick are dangerous foes to arouse."

Master Aylmer's words proved true. The insurrections, like small fires, were stamped out in one place only to break out somewhere else. But the spark touched off by a tanner named Ket, in the county of Norfolk that summer of 1549, threatened to set all England ablaze.

No one quite knew how it really began. As elsewhere, the smoldering hatred of farmers against rich landlords found flint with the new oppression of enclosures. Ket and his friends fanned the flame until thousands of peasants rallied to him. Setting up a

114

"court" under a gnarled tree dubbed "the Oak of Reformation," Ket sent his demands to the King: the English people desired the reestablishment of the Catholic church, a redistribution of the nobility's wealth, and a dismissal of the King's present Council and appointment of a new one.

Needless to say, the suggestions did not please the Council. The Marquess of Northampton was dispatched to take care of the rebels. But when he was beaten back and several of his men killed, the Protector sent in John Dudley, the Earl of Warwick. With six thousand men at his back he could scarcely have failed. Within hours two thousand peasants lay dead. Robert Ket and his cohorts were hung from the branches of the Oak of Reformation. Insurrectionists in other counties immediately lost heart and laid down their arms. The fires of reform flickered, then went out all over England.

It was a great victory for the nobility. Warwick was applauded for putting the poor in their place. And with the rise of his star, Protector Somerset's began to wane. The King of France decided to take advantage of England's internal disruption by trying to recapture Boulogne. The winning of it had been Henry the Eighth's fondest desire and had drained the exchequer of a million and a quarter pounds. There were few funds left to defend it against King Charles's heavy assault. When the Protector suggested a treaty might be in order, however, he was bitterly denounced.

"If you ask me, we have no choice!" Papa declared at dinner one night. The Protector's increasing unpopularity was a matter of concern to our family, who had long ago chosen to support him.

"Henry nearly ruined us with his French wars. They cannot go on forever."

"I for one do not see the importance of one small territory in France. We have no need of it."

Mr. Aylmer looked pained at Chaplain Harding's remark. "It is a matter of strategy, Dr. Harding. France is our hereditary enemy. As long as we hold even one seaport, King Charles's power will not be absolute."

"But even our late king, God rest him, must have known that it would not be possible to hold Boulogne forever."

"He did! That is just the point!!" exclaimed Papa. "Henry promised France they could have their city back in 1554. What is the object in waiting? We are only pouring more men and money into a lost cause. Somerset's treaty is the only logical course!"

"The rest of the Council do not agree."

"That, Frances, is only because they are determined to oppose the Protector no matter what solution he proposes. Whether the war is prolonged or discontinued, he will be discredited."

I was toying with a piece of warden pie, made from Papa's pears, when Mama's next statement made me look up.

"Well, I have written to Edward Seymour to remind him of our little agreement. If he loses his head like Thomas, we will never get Jane married suitably!"

Everyone avoided looking at me, but Katie's elbow nudged me so hard that I gasped.

"Have you something to say?" Mama inquired icily.

"No, Mother."

"I think you do. What is it?"

"I—" I swallowed. "I was wondering if—if you were referring to the possibility of a betrothal between Edward—I mean, the Earl of Hertford—and myself."

"And if I was? Is it any concern of yours?"

"Well—actually, I had wondered if that were being contemplated, and—"

"My word, Henry, listen to the girl stutter! And *what?*"

"And I do not believe that such an arrangement would be congenial. For either of us!"

Everybody was now looking at me openly with expressions of incredulity. Beside me I felt Katie quiver.

"Let us straighten something out at once, shall we?" Mother's voice was like silk. Something in her eyes frightened me.

"The preferences of a girl your age fail to interest me. In fact, they bore me. The faculty of being boring is deplorable in anyone—more so in a child. Sins must be beaten out of children, is that not so, Dr. Harding?"

My former tutor's tongue passed over his lips. He smiled.

"A rod spared is a child spoiled, your grace."

"Then we must do as the Good Book directs. It seems that overindulgence has created a large number of sins in my daughter. We shall do our best to correct them."

But the flogging that night was no worse than any of the others—or was it that I was getting used to them? I stared dry-eyed at the ceiling as Ellen bathed my face with cool water to keep it from swelling.

"The servants were talking about what happened at the table, lass. They're angry at the way she humiliated you in front of the gentlemen!"

I shook my head. "It was my fault, Ellen. I should have known better than to give my opinion like that. And I stuttered! She hates me to stutter."

"And who wouldn't lose their tongue altogether with those eyes fixed on them?"

"But you were not there."

"I've seen it often enough. 'Tis the same look a snake has when he's tryin' to petrify a rabbit!"

"The rabbit and I make a good comparison, but Mama would hardly care for being called a snake."

Ellen muttered something inaudible under her breath.

"What do you think of Edward Seymour, Ellen?"

"The young one? Haven't thought much on him at all, but he's a fair-seemin' lad."

"You must have noticed how stuffy he is. And arrogant! Always so perfectly sure of what is going on inside other people's minds."

She shrugged noncommittally. "Some folks have that way about them. But I'm thinkin' it's a sight better than not knowin' what's in yer own mind."

"Are you trying to say in your own devious way that I do not know what is in mine?"

"Now what would I be sayin' a thing like that for?" she said innocently and rose. "Now stop ponderin' things and go to sleep, lass."

But I could not sleep, and it was not only because of the pain. The confirmation of a betrothal between Edward and myself had come as a shock. I had not really believed he would accept the convenience of an alliance between our two families just because it was his father's wish. His feelings about me were quite clear.

On the other hand, Protector Somerset's influence was on a decline. What if his authority was lost altogether and he was forced to surrender the protectorship? It was not out of the question. Edward's father had not only lost the support of the lords, but he had succeeded in alienating most of the Catholics. This had occurred when he elected to build a palatial new mansion on the Strand. In order to make room for it, he had razed the Church of St.

Mary's and the houses of three bishops; he then proceeded to obtain building materials by desecrating a charnel house, cloister, and chapel in St. Paul's churchyard. To make matters even worse, Somerset's workmen buried the bones they found in unconsecrated ground. The people were outraged. Many began murmuring that the blood of the saints as well as the blood of his brother was on his hands.

My clever brother will one day stumble into a pit of his own device. Those had been Thomas Seymour's words; I could almost see him smiling.

And yet—if the protectorship were taken from the Duke, Mama and Papa would undoubtedly break the betrothal. And I would be free.

Late in September the Earl of Warwick, with two hundred captains who had fought with him in the Ket rebellion, approached the Protector asking for a bounty in pay for their services. He refused. When Warwick left Hampton Court that day, he had two hundred more soldiers on his side. He must have felt ready then to seize the government. Ten of the Council—including the president, Lord St. John—met at Warwick's town house. From Ely Place they began issuing orders without the approval of the Protector or the rest of the Council. Within a few days seven more members joined them. Letters went out to all the nobility in the realm announcing the changes and requesting support.

On Wednesday, October 9, Papa rode from London to Bradgate with the news that the Duke of Somerset, our Lord Protector, was proclaimed a traitor.

"But where is he?" Mother cried. "Is he making no defense?"

"He has done the worst of all possible things—taken the King and fled with him to Windsor Palace! Thinks he is better fortified there, I suppose. He is still trying to negotiate with the Council; sent Petre to Ely Place with a letter, but Petre himself decided to go over to Warwick's side."

"There is no chance he can recover his position?"

"None. The Mayor of London, the Lieutenant of the Tower—everyone is swearing support to Warwick. Somerset tried to rally the commoners—" he waved a leaflet, "and thousands flocked to him, but they are poorly armed and have not a prayer."

I took one of the handbills and read aloud:

Good people, in the name of God and King Edward, let us rise

with all our power to defend the King and Lord Protector against
certain lords who would depose the Protector and so endanger the
King's royal person! Let us fight for him, for he loveth all who are
just and true, and the poor commonality of England.

"Brave words," said Mama. "But he was always good with
words. It is his unfortunate mismanagement of things that has
ruined him."

There was a depressed silence.

"Well, Henry, we must be cautious. Vote with the majority,
see what comes to pass, and do not give offense to Warwick at any
cost. It will pay to practice prudence with this man."

I was shocked by their nonchalance over their old friend's
danger. Was loyalty so easily dismissed, then? With not even a
protest at Warwick's high-handed usurpation of power?

Yet I said nothing. Protector Somerset was not guilty of
treason; his arrest would not stand. Not even Warwick would dare
execute him.

The Duke of Somerset was released after four months of imprisonment in the Tower. He had been humiliated, even made to
confess on his knees before the Council. His offices were stripped
from him, and he was to be fined two thousand pounds a year in
revenues from his lands. But the charges—usurping authority, di-
viding the nobles and commons and leading the country into
foreign and domestic strife, losing English strongholds in France,
acquiring unlawful wealth—would not justify his death in the eyes
of the people. And it was the people whom the new government
sought to win.

It seemed a stroke of genius on the part of John Dudley, Earl of
Warwick. He had brought his enemy down. That was enough. He
was too zealous of the King's favor to press his advantage further.

13

"Jane, look! Whatever is that dreadful Adrian Stokes doing here?"

Katie, who had dropped her book and flown to the window at the sound of horses, leaned so far out that Master Aylmer blanched.

"Lady Katherine, please! Come away from there before you fall out."

"Oh, do come quickly, Jane. There are about four-dozen men in our livery with him. Do you suppose anything is wrong?"

I peered over her shoulder, frowning. More than a year had elapsed since the Protector's release, and our fortunes had risen with his. Mama and Papa were even this moment in London settling an estate they had inherited from Mama's two half-brothers, dead from sleeping sickness within four hours of each other. It was one of the worst epidemics ever to sweep the city. But my parents had been oblivious to the danger, taking a suite of rooms at Richmond Palace.

"It must be an escort. Mama would not have parted with her secretary without a good reason." Katie's lip curled with distaste. "How she abides that man is beyond me! Simpering, flattering—"

But anxiety overrode our dislike as we descended the stairs to receive him. For once I was not even self-conscious of my unbecoming black gown, now required wear for girls in Protestant households. How I hated this constant look of mourning. We of the reformed faith, I felt, should dress to reflect our happiness.

"My Lady Jane—Lady Katherine. I trust you are well?"

"We are indeed, Mr. Stokes," Katie acknowledged his bow

impatiently. "But you have not ridden so hard nor so far to inquire about our health?"

"Alas, your ladyship is correct. I bear unhappy news—"

"Is Father unwell?" I cried, fear clutching at me.

"It is Lady Frances. She lies near death. I have been ordered to conduct her daughter to her without delay."

"Jane!" Katie threw herself into my arms, bursting into hysterical sobs. "I knew she should not have gone! I told her. But she insisted we needed the money. Always *money!*" she said bitterly. "We never have enough."

I stroked her hair, trying to gather my thoughts.

"We must get your things together at once, Katie."

Suddenly I knew how Thomas Seymour had felt, waiting all those hours outside his father's sickroom, yet never summoned.

"Mr. Stokes, please see that the men with you are fed and fresh horses saddled. My sister will be ready within the hour."

I was already at the door when the secretary cleared his throat.

"I am afraid I did not make myself clear. It is you I am to escort, Lady Jane."

"*Jane?*" Katie whirled on him incredulously. "You are mistaken!"

"I assure you I am not. The Marchioness was particular to give me the instructions. I am to bring Lady Jane, not Lady Katherine."

He bowed stiffly. "If you will pardon me, I will see about a mount."

"And one for Ellen. She will go with me."

Katie's bewilderment swiftly changed to anger as he left the room.

"I cannot believe it! It is impossible that she would want—" She broke off, flushing.

"You are right. Unless—" a new thought filled me with wonder, "unless she is sorry for the unhappiness between us and wants to make it up. Do you think that is possible, Katie?"

She shrugged. "Perhaps. Who can tell with Mama? But if you are going to London, you had better start packing. I do not envy you the trip in all this heat."

In spite of her words she shed many tears at our parting, and not, I suspected, all because of her worry over Mama. Poor Katie so longed to visit the city; it did not seem fair that I was always the

121

one to be setting off for it. Yet this time I allowed myself to hope. Could it be that after so many years Mama had discovered a need to have me with her? Mr. Stokes said she was near death. It was hard to picture that determined and attractive body a helpless victim of disease. She could not die. People like Mama did not die. I found myself praying that God would not let anything happen to her; I had to tell her that I loved her and would try harder to make her love me. I wanted to care for her.

By the time I arrived at Richmond Palace, my riding dress was covered with dust and every bone ached. We had pushed our horses to their limit, not daring to pause for refreshment. Every nerve strained with anxiety as I hurried to her chamber. *Please, please, God, do not let me be too late.* I pushed my way through the knots of servants and ladies-in-waiting and knelt beside her bed.

"Mama?"

For a moment I thought she was past hearing. Heavy perspiration had rolled from her burning face and soaked her nightdress. She did not stir. And then a groan escaped her lips, and I saw her eyes open. They were filled with terror.

"Jane!" she whispered hoarsely. "Is that you?"

"Yes, Mama, it is I. I came as quickly as I could."

"Katie—is not—with you?"

"No."

"Ah—" A look of relief crossed her face. "Must not—come here! Dangerous. Too—dangerous."

I stared at her, comprehension slowly dawning.

"You do not want her to become ill, is that it?"

She nodded her head slightly, then closed her eyes. Slowly I rose from my knees and turned to one of the women.

"Watch her closely. I will return as soon as I change my clothing."

I opened the door and shut it quietly behind me. Then I went along the hall to my rooms. Without stopping to remove my hood I stretched my body across the counterpane and gave way to tears.

Mama was going to live. The physicians told Papa and me that it would take a miracle, but as one breathless day melted into the next a slow improvement was perceptible. Over half of the household was ill with the plague; I was fearful for Papa, who went into the city or to Court almost every day. To keep myself busy I undertook most of Mama's care. Sometimes, while sponging her hot face, the perspiration streamed from my own and I was so lightheaded with fatigue that I was sure neither of us would ever quite recover. But when the doctor urged me to leave her to the care of her ladies, I could not. Perhaps I kept hoping that if I was the one to make her well again, it would make a difference.

Once as I sat by her side, she woke from her sleep and asked me to read aloud. I had begun the *Phaedo* a few days earlier, and so picked up the book and read to her from Socrates's stirring address to his friends. It was one of my favorite speeches, for the man who spoke it was so evidently triumphant over the death that was soon to be his.

> *Will you not allow that I have as much of the spirit of prophecy in me as the swans? For they, when they perceive that they must die, having sung all their life long, do then sing more than ever, rejoicing in the thought that they are about to go away to the God whose ministers they are. . . . And I, too, believing myself to be the consecrated servant of the same God, and the fellow servant of the swans, and thinking that I have received from my Master gifts of prophecy which are not inferior to theirs, would not go out of life less merrily than the swans.*

"No one—should rejoice at death," said Mama. "He was a fool if he did!"

I thought of the martyrs who, like St. Paul, had gone to their deaths with the claim, "For me to live is Christ—and to die is gain."

"Mistress Anne Askew and the others could have recanted if they chose. It would have been so simple. But they *preferred* to die rather than live against their conscience. They must have been very sure of eternal life."

"They were fanatics! The important thing—is *life*, at any cost, here and now," she declared.

I wondered. Did I have any right to an opinion, never having passed through the valley of death as Mama had? Would I, too, cling desperately to the known rather than pass through that door of faith? They were sober thoughts for me, but they were reality to the thousands who were dying in the city's plague.

When a maidservant one day announced that I had a visitor waiting in the drawing room, I was startled. I could think of no one who knew me well enough to hazard the infection of our house; there was little sociability these days among the nobility, most of whom stayed, frightened, within their own walls.

"Edward! You are brave indeed to come here, without even the precaution of a pomander."

"I am afraid I do not place much faith in the ability of a ball of herbs or perfume to keep one from the plague," Edward Seymour laughed. I marveled at the transformation that laughter made on his strong but usually sober features. "Since one is not safe anywhere, one might as well go where he elects."

"That is what Papa says— 'carry on as usual.' But it worries me. If anything were to happen to him—"

"Your mother is much improved, we hear. Perhaps the worst is over now, although—" he hesitated, "I must say you yourself look overtired. You are feeling quite well?"

"Yes, thank you. Edward, I was much grieved to hear of Lady Margery's death. Your grandmother was a good friend to me at Seymour Place."

"She thought a great deal of you. I regret that I never knew her as well as I would have liked; she was a very private woman. The estrangement between my father and my uncle separated her from the rest of us. And she lost her will to live after Thomas's execution. I think she had always hoped for her two sons to be reconciled."

We were silent, each wrapped in our memories of Lady Margery and her beloved son, who had gambled so largely with life and lost.

"Mama and Papa were pleased that your father's fine was canceled and his property restored. It seems that the Council is willing to forget the past."

"So it would appear. He was appointed Lord-Lieutenant of Buckinghamshire and Berkshire. Warwick was even so gracious as to consent to the marriage of my sister Anne to his oldest son."

I did not miss the bitterness in his voice. "But you still do not trust him?"

"No. A wolf cannot be trusted simply because he is silent. My father has recovered too much of his former popularity. He is a threat to Warwick."

"You worry too much, Edward. If the Duke was unpopular, you would be unhappy."

"Perhaps." He shrugged and rose. "Have I your permission to call again, Jane? Tomorrow?"

I was surprised. "If you wish."

When I told her of his visit, Mama smiled like a cat with a saucer of cream.

"The Duke of Somerset is well on his way to the top again. Henry tells me there are rumors that he will be reinstated as Protector at the next Parliament."

"But—I thought you and Papa—" I bit my lip. "Did you not decide you were not going to have any more to do with him, that you were going to support the Earl of Warwick?"

"My dear child! That was months ago. Warwick has since been more than a trifle indiscreet as Earl Marshall—allowing our ships to rot in port, coining money with so much copper they blush for shame—even closing his eyes to the marriage of Mary of Scotland to the Dauphin of France! The nobility are appalled. They are beginning to have second thoughts about him."

She sipped the tisane I had brought her and studied me over the rim of the cup. ,

"You must know that your father and I have always had the highest regard for the Duke of Somerset, despite his past errors. Even Warwick thought it well to cement family relations with him by intermarriage. We should not do less."

"What does the Duke think?"

She laughed lazily. "He adores the idea, of course—he always has. With all of his money and position he still has no claim to royal lineage."

So that was the purpose behind Edward's call. He was an emissary from his father, sent to promote the family's interests! My lips tightened. He should not have the opportunity to do so again.

Mother caught my hand as I reached for her cup. Her nails bit into my flesh until I cried out.

"I know that expression, and I forbid any willful stubbornness on your part! You will see that the young Earl of Hertford's advances are encouraged, no matter how loathsome they are to you. Or have you so soon forgotten the penalty for disobedience?"

I had not forgotten. I took the cup, curtsied, and turned to leave.

"Really, Jane, you might try to imitate a little of your sister's charm since you do not have any of her beauty! We must not press our luck too far in assuming that Edward will be willing to marry you for your name alone."

Her mocking laughter followed me out into the corridor, turning my face to crimson. Mama's return to strength had brought her again to her old habits. I marveled that she still had the power to inflict so much hurt.

14

With Edward Seymour a regular visitor at Richmond Palace, I was forced into the role of eager recipient of his attentions. The maidservants smiled slyly when they announced him, and Mama and Papa dropped shamelessly obvious comments about his admirable qualities that I was meant to pass on. I hated the whole thing. Ellen knew it, of course, for she was the unobtrusive chaperone of our stilted, artificially cordial meetings; and, I believed, so did Edward, though he would not admit it. Instead he pretended to be vastly entertained as he lounged in his chair, talking, while I sat miserably on the edge of mine. I had the distinctly uneasy feeling that he was laughing at me.

The only useful aspect of these conversations was that I eventually became well-informed about affairs of state. Edward had a seemingly endless supply of information on this subject and appeared to have undertaken the enlightenment of my ignorance as a part of his duty. I was not at all grateful. I much preferred a blissful oblivion. However, since there was little else to talk about, I did listen—and learn; and, learning, was dismayed.

Almost all of the advances for which Protector Somerset had fought were lost. In France, Boulogne was surrendered to our enemies without reimbursement of the two million crowns in arrears due our government. In Scotland, English strongholds had been retaken by the Scots; fortifications along the borders and along the coasts were left undefended against raids. The Navy was also being neglected: as our ships decayed, none were built to replace them, and many of the troops were being disbanded.

Yet even more shocking was the Earl of Warwick's callous indifference to the lot of the common people. The Protector's acts against enclosures were repealed: fences went up, and multitudes of farmers were thrown into unspeakable poverty. Religious tolerance, which had caused many Reformers to preach against the Duke of Somerset, was a thing of the past. Warwick betrayed the Papists who had helped him achieve power and effected an ardor for Protestantism to impress King Edward. Under his direction the Prayer Book was revised to eliminate any possible interpretation in favor of Catholic doctrine. The Reformer John Hooper hailed him "a most holy and fearless instrument of the Word of God," while those who dissented were burned at the stake.

"Even Princess Mary is feeling the flick of the whip," Edward told me. "Father allowed her—knowing how devotedly Catholic she is—to use the old service book and hear a private mass. But Warwick has forbidden it. He threatens to imprison her priests if she persists."

"And she will, I am sure. Mary has the same stubbornness that got her mother, Catherine of Aragon, into trouble," I said. "But why are the Catholic lords on the Privy Council not fighting all of this?"

"Because there are precious few of them left! Lord Southampton was dismissed, Lord Southwell is in the Tower, and Arundel has been barred from Court and fined some 12,000 pounds for heaven knows what. Warwick replaced them with his own toadys. And the leading bishops—Bonner, Gardiner, Tunstall, Day—have all been removed from their bishoprics."

"While his friends have been richly rewarded, I expect."

"Do you remember that my father declared Lord Northampton's second marriage illegal? Warwick has overturned the decision. And there are plans to confer new titles on his closest supporters. He has even befriended William Sharington, who did such a fine job in implicating the Lord Admiral—"

"Surely not!"

"It was one of Warwick's first acts. He gave Sharington a full pardon and employed him as an assistant." Edward's voice was thick with contempt. "He is to be Sheriff of Wiltshire."

"Mama says that many of the lords think they were too hasty in electing Warwick. Perhaps at the Parliament this autumn your father—"

128

"Ah! So you, too, believe Father will be reinstated as Protector. I had wondered, frankly, at your unexpectedly warm response to my visits."

"I have not been in the least warm!" I snapped. "I have sat here listening to your tiresome discourses solely because Mama—"

"Yes, your mama. I was afraid that dear lady was involved somehow." He shook his head with mock disappointment.

"It is a case of the pot calling the kettle black, is it not? You are here only to comply with your father's wishes."

He regarded me carefully. "Is that what you think?"

"I may not be beautiful, Edward, but pray do grant me the benefit of intelligence! Our parents made a compact."

"That does not deprive us of our own emotions and desires. Arranged matches do occasionally turn out to be quite felicitous, I understand."

"In our case, that would be impossible," I said flatly. "Let us at least be honest with each other, Edward. Go through the charade of courtship, if you must, but please spare me any false sentiment."

He rose, making me feel, as usual, absurdly childish and inadequate.

"As you wish, Lady Jane Grey. I shall try to keep strictly to business."

"Exactly!"

I snatched my hand away and left the room, furiously aware that if I had permitted myself to look back I would have found him laughing.

September arrived. Still the plague did not loosen its deathgrip on the city. Each day the carts rumbled through the streets, collecting the bodies that had become too numerous to be given private burials. There was hardly a dwelling that did not echo with the cries of mourning. Would men ever find the means, I wondered, to protect themselves from this horror?

As Mama grew stronger, her temper became increasingly harder to bear. It was as if she resented my hardiness in the face of her weakness and was determined to make my life miserable. The tea that I brought was not hot enough, I did not come quickly enough when she called me, the books I read aloud were not to her taste, and I had no sensitivity at all where her suffering was concerned. Within a short time I was thoroughly vexed and had to bite my lip several times a day to keep myself from saying what I should not.

Perhaps it is not surprising that I found myself looking forward to Edward Seymour's afternoon visits as a sort of reprieve. He demanded nothing, this strange young man. He was content to come, to sit, to talk idly of matters that did not demand my concentration, while I allowed my taut nerves to relax under the flow of his voice. It was a gentle voice, the sort that one might use to quiet a frightened animal. But the drawl was deceptive; I knew that not one of my movements or expressions passed unnoticed. Why did he persist in coming? It was a puzzle to me.

And then one day he did not come. I was annoyed at first, convinced he had been delayed by some other appointment and had forgotten to send word. But when he failed to appear at all that afternoon, I was startled by the force of my disappointment. I told myself that he had at last tired of the role of attentive suitor. I could almost see the arrogant shrug of his shoulders.

But when Papa came home from his day at Hampton Court, looking unusually tired, he told us that the Duke of Somerset had been absent from the Council. The plague had touched the Seymour household.

"The Duke himself is ill?" Mama, now well enough to be sitting up in bed, put the question sharply.

"No, but I do not know about young Edward—" Papa shot a quick look at me. "The report was somewhat confused."

I walked over to the window and looked out. Strange, how things got turned about so quickly. Only yesterday Edward had told me the sickness was abating. Indeed, he had laughed, the poorer sections of London, unable to afford leeches or surgeons, were in better condition than the houses of the nobles. We had argued at length about the respective value of various cures; he had a deep interest in medicine, I was surprised to learn, and condemned many common practices as worthless if not actually harmful. And now perhaps he himself lay ill. I did not want him to be ill. My fingers curled tightly into my palm.

"If he dies, we will be in a fine way!" complained Mama. "Somerset has no other sons of marriageable age."

"It is the Duke's absence from Court that most worries me," Papa confided as we left the bedchamber. "It will give his enemies the opportunity they have been waiting for."

"But—everyone thinks he is in such a safe position now."

"No one involved in politics is ever safe, my dear. The hunter stalking the prey can become the hunted in a moment's changing. If one is wise, one stays out of the field altogether so as never to be mistaken for game."

"Then one should never take sides?"

He smiled and shrugged. "Let us just say one should avoid making an enemy of either hunter or prey." He paused. "You are disappointed. You think, perhaps, I should stand against the Earl of Warwick?"

"Papa, has he not done harm to England?"

"He has done some good as well. Do not forget the expeditions he has sent out to find new sources for trade. Already his navigator—Sebastian Cabot—has returned with evidence of rich lands across the seas. England needs an aggressive leader, Jane, until the King is old enough to reign. Warwick may have his faults, but he is clever enough not to transgress upon the rights of the nobility."

"And the poor, Papa? Who will defend their rights?"

"The poor are a fact of life—like the rain and the plague. They will always be with us. Is that not in the Scriptures? We must then accept it."

"Were I to rule this country," I said, "I would try to do something. We are all human beings; no one should be allowed to live or die like a beast!"

He looked at me thoughtfully. "You are an odd child. Perhaps it is well that you shall never have such an opportunity."

15

By October the tide of sickness that had so long flooded the city was gone, leaving behind the debris of stricken families. We were the lucky ones, I thought, watching Mama move about; we had not lost anyone. Even Katie had come from Bradgate to be with us now. The Seymours had not been quite as fortunate. Edward had ridden to us, as soon as it was possible, with the news that his infant brother was dead. I felt deeply for his grief, and yet at the same time a great weight of fear rolled from my heart. *He* was alive and well.

On October 11 Papa attended a special investiture ceremony in the Great Hall at Hampton Court. He was made Duke of Suffolk, and several of his friends also received new titles. Perhaps most notable was the elevation of the Earl of Warwick to Duke of Northumberland. It must have given him particular pleasure to achieve that victory in front of his rival, the Duke of Somerset.

I was happy for Papa; he had looked forward to this moment for a long time.

"You shall be too important to spend any time at all with us now," I teased him. He placed a finger on the tip of my nose.

"Have you not heard? The more a gentleman is elevated in this world, the less he is expected to do!"

"Then you will not have to spend so much time away from Bradgate?"

Papa's smile faded. "I am afraid that cannot be avoided, Jane. I have responsibilities here in London."

"But—the estate, Papa. Who will see that it is managed properly? You know Mama takes no interest in the gardens or the orchards. We need you."

"Jane, be reasonable. I cannot play the country squire forever. Leicester is as far from London as a marquisate from a dukedom."

My teeth gnawed my lower lip. "You—you do not think we shall have to *leave* Bradgate?"

He sighed, shrugging his shoulders. "I do not know yet. We shall see."

On the sixteenth, only five days after the investiture, Edward's father was arrested for the second time and taken to the Tower. His strongest supporters—the Earl of Arundel, Sir Miles Partridge, Sir Michael Stanhope, Sir John Thynne, Sir Thomas Holcroft, my uncle, Lord Grey, and the Duchess of Somerset—were also imprisoned.

We were badly shocked. The charge, treason, was made by the new Duke of Northumberland's close supporter, Sir Thomas Palmer. Palmer declared that he had uncovered a plot of Somerset's to raise the people against Northumberland and to murder both him and his supporters. The prisoners were to be tried one by one in closed sessions.

The accusation was obviously false. There could be no way it would hold up in Parliament. The Duke of Somerset had been released before, and he would be released again. Yet I was worried; Northumberland knew this was his last chance to rid himself of a formidable opponent. It was an act of treason to conspire to the death or imprisonment of a Privy Councillor, and it was punishable by death.

At about the same time we learned that the Scottish Queen Regent, Mary of Guise, was to pass through London on her way to Scotland. She was coming from France after visiting her daughter, Mary, and would, of course, have to be entertained royally during her London stay. Our family would be expected to actively participate in both the procession from Whitehall to Westminster Palace and in the reception to be held in her honor.

The household was thrown into a frenzy of preparation. Katie was nearly delirious with excitement, and a controversy broke out immediately over the issue of dress.

"I refuse to go to the ball looking like I am entering a convent!" she wailed, as we tried one after another of black and brown and dove-gray gowns. My parents, like most of the nobility when

Edward succeeded to the throne, had forsaken Catholicism for the Reform movement. All of my tutors were Reformers, as were the Princess Elizabeth's. When she began to dress in the plain, sober gowns that the Reformers told her became a modest young woman, Katie and I were made to wear them also. The trouble was, Eliza had a flair for wearing clothes: what on her looked elegant, on me was a complete failure.

"What is the good of having money and titles if we have to dress like this?" Katie cried.

I laughed. "At least everyone will be in the same predicament."

"I doubt it. Everyone is going to be too anxious to show off their finery to worry about what the Reformers think. I for one would rather die than appear in these rags!" Her chin lifted. "I shall plead sickness."

"No, you will not. Not if I know you."

She smiled and tossed her head. "You are right. I would not miss it for the world. It is going to be the event of the season, Jane. Everyone says so." She lay back on the counterpane, staring dreamily up at the ceiling.

"It will be a coming out—for both of us. Our first ball. Everyone will be there! Oh, Jane, it is going to be so *wonderful.*"

There was a knock, and Ellen opened the door bearing a large parcel which she placed carefully on the bed.

"For Lady Jane, from the Princess Mary," she announced. "I saw the messenger ride up with it meself and told the mistress I'd be pleased to bring it up."

We stared at the bundle, entranced.

"Whatever do you suppose it could be? We have not seen Mary for over a year."

"Did I not say she was taken with you? Oh, *do* open it, Jane! Hurry!"

Carefully I undid the outer wrappings, letting them fall to the floor. Then I caught my breath and lifted out a dress—a dress whose like I had never seen—and shook it out to its full, shimmering length.

"It is magnificent!" I breathed, and lifted agonized eyes to Ellen. "What shall I do with it?"

"Why, wear it, lass! What else?"

"But—"

"Try it on, Jane! See how it fits." Katie could not contain her excitement; already she was unfastening the tiny row of buttons at my back. I held the gown against me wistfully.

"You know I will not be allowed to wear this. The Reformers would be—"

"Oh, bother the Reformers! The church is not going to come crashing about our heads just because we wear a pretty gown for one night! There, now. Help me pull this ugly sack off over her head, Ellen, and we will put on the other dress."

I stood obediently motionless as Mary's priceless gift whispered down over my shoulders and floated around me, weightless as a cloud. It fitted to perfection. The fragile gold and white silk, with insets of white velvet, clung becomingly. The contrast from my heavy everyday wear made me giddy. I felt—different, somehow. Attractive.

"'Tis made for ye, lass!" Ellen cried, her eyes glowing. "'Twould be a sin to refuse it!"

"Would it?" I asked hopefully.

"Well, of course! Think how you'd grieve the Lady Mary. The Almighty wouldna' approve of insultin' her!"

"Wait here, Jane. Mama *must* see you in this gown. Just one minute—" Katie dashed out of the room.

"I do want to go to the ball, Ellen. It is odd—a little while ago I did not really care if I went or not. But—with this dress—I feel I could be someone—special. I suppose that is terribly vain of me."

"Nay, lass," she hugged me to her briefly. "I ken how it is. I'm not so old that I've forgotten."

Katie was back within her promised minute, with Mama following close behind.

"Look Mama! What did I tell you? She scarcely looks like our Jane!"

I waited while Mama surveyed me critically, then gave a nod.

"It will do. We want you to make a good impression on the King at this reception."

"Then I must have a new gown, too!" Katie was triumphant. "Please say I may, Mama!"

"But of course, *ma petite*. The seamstresses will begin at once. But I do not think we shall have so much trouble finding you a husband!"

She would not say those things if she knew how much it hurt, I told myself, as some of my pleasure at Mary's gift ebbed away. I turned to Ellen and asked her to help me undress.

"Dinna let her bother ye," she told me as soon as Katie and Mama were gone. "Just you wait until everyone sees you at this fancy affair! There'll be so many brawny lads beggin' for your hand the Duchess will be proud!"

Proud? Oh, Ellen, if only I knew how to make Mama proud.

I was surprised to see him, but glad. He had not visited since his parents' arrest.

"I will not stay. The name of Seymour is not a popular one these days."

"Your welcome here has not altered, Edward. All of us are very shocked about what has happened."

"I wonder if anyone will be shocked enough to stand up against Northumberland's man."

"Of course they will. The nobility do not like the way Northumberland has misused his power, and your father has always been a favorite with the commons."

He did not answer, only stared at me, until I squirmed uncomfortably. "Why do you stare?"

"Was I? I am sorry. You will attend the reception for the Queen Regent? Yes, of course. You belong to one of the first families now. I regret that I will not see your grand debut."

"Oh, *why* did this thing have to happen to your father? He is a good man; I know that now. I think perhaps I have always known it."

"Even though he did not prevent the Lord Admiral's death?"

I looked away, and my voice was low. "I loved Lord Thomas. But he was wrong. Your father could not have saved him from himself."

"He took no pleasure in my uncle's death. Neither did I."

My eyes met his. "I do believe you, Edward. I have been unjust, although—" I laughed, "I never thought I should hear myself admit it. I have even come to have a reluctant respect for you during these terrible months of courtship."

Something kindled in his eyes, and then it was gone.

"You will have to do better than that if we are to be married! You see, I have not given you up yet. There is still the 'business arrangement,' and I shall require you to be faithful to it."

His fingers went to a thin gold chain about his neck which he removed and slipped over my head. A pendant hung from the chain—a single, small emerald that flashed against my breast.

"It is—like the sun sparkling on the water at Bradgate! How lovely!"

"They call it the stone of constancy. According to tradition, the color fades if the wearer is ever disloyal to its giver."

"Then it will never fade." I held it firmly within my hand. "I will promise you my friendship, Edward. No matter what happens."

He rose to his feet.

"It will not be wise for me to come here again. Unless, of course, my father is released after his trial in December."

"We must believe that he will be."

Suddenly Edward looked tired. "He has long been a thorn in Northumberland's side; I fear the Duke will not be satisfied by a light sentence. He wants Father's death; and God help us all, Jane, if he succeeds!"

I was struck by his gravity and gave him my hand.

"Good-by, then, Edward. God be with you."

The days passed quickly into November. On the fourth, the evening of the reception for Queen Mary, a tight, breathless feeling gripped me. It was as if I knew something was about to happen and did not quite know if it would be good or bad. The entire household was caught up in the excitement. Maids and valets scurried about, while outside, grooms rubbed the carriage horses and polished the harnesses to a sheen. Everyone knew this was to be my parents' first public appearance as the Duke and Duchess of Suffolk.

Ellen helped me dress, making as much fuss about me as possible and complaining that everybody in the house was at sixes and sevens and there was hardly a place for a body to sit down. She for one would be glad to be going back to Bradgate, she declared, and I agreed. There was little in the city of London that attracted me. I longed for a glimpse of my valley.

"You'll need to be wearin' somethin' at the neck," Ellen said, surveying me critically. "It looks a wee bit bare, and ye need some color."

I opened my jewelry casket and studied the contents.

"What about this?"

I fastened the emerald pendant around my throat and turned to Ellen.

"Aye! Aye, lass, that's well enough! 'Tis a fine, bright ornament," she added meaningfully; I laughed.

"It was given me by a friend, Ellen, not a lover! Besides I do not believe in all those superstitions."

There was a tap at my door, and Katie burst into the room, whirling me around with both hands.

"How do I look?"

"Breathtaking!" I told her honestly, and kissed her. "Grown up and beautiful."

Her rose-colored satin, trimmed with pearls and decollet bodice, did indeed complement her fresh complexion. Most spectacular of all was the pearl and ruby necklace she wore about her neck. I recognized it as one of Mama's.

"I had to beg and beg before Mama would let me have this," she laughed. "She thought I was not old enough, but I am. I look at least sixteen!"

"Ye're a bairn," Ellen snorted, but Katie gave her a withering look.

"I intend to make a proper impression."

"I dinna' see a thing proper about that dress."

"You will be the envy of every girl there," I interposed hurriedly. "And the men will fall madly in love with you."

"Oh, marvelous! I shall accept everyone's proposal and then turn around and break all their hearts."

She sank into a curtsy and then froze. "What if not a single person asks me to dance, Jane? I shall die!"

"I do not think you need worry about that," I assured her.

"As long as the King does not ask me. I would be frightfully self-conscious; and besides, they say he is a terrible dancer. — Oh, listen!" She ran to the window and looked out. "They have brought the carriage round! We had better go down."

When the gentleman-at-arms announced us—"The Duke and

Duchess of Suffolk, Lady Jane Grey and Lady Katherine Grey!"—I thought my heart would stop beating. I had never seen anything quite so grand. The gallery was lit with hundreds of candles down its entire length. At one end a group of musicians were gathered, beginning the graceful movement of a galliard. On the opposite end, upon a dais canopied with velvet, sat King Edward in a huge carved chair. To his right was the guest of honor, Mary of Guise.

"Poor Cousin Edward," Katie whispered. "He looks quite uncomfortable."

I watched his attempts at conversation with the Queen and had to agree. He had confided to me once at Hampton Court that he hated state affairs. He was constantly aware that people were comparing him to his father, and he knew himself to be inadequate. His eyes were upon me now. I smiled, and the corners of his mouth lifted.

My sister's eyes were already busy scanning the scene. Little exclamations of delight escaped her as distinguished nobles and their ladies drifted by, their jewels flashing fire in the candlelight. Now and then members of the Privy Council stopped to converse with Mama and Papa. In spite of her recent illness, our mother was one of the finest looking women there. Her cheeks were flushed as she leaned on Papa's arm; her bright eyes missed nothing.

"Jane—do look at who is watching us across the floor! I think he—" She sucked in her breath. "Oh! He *is!* He is coming over to speak with Papa! It would be divine if he asked us to dance! We have been here a full half-hour already and *no* one—"

Katie stopped speaking as one of our uncles, Thomas Grey, came up to us and asked her if she would be his partner. She looked hesitant, weighing the chances of being asked by someone else, then accepted his arm graciously. Soon she had merged with the other dancers.

I watched them miserably. With each moment I felt more conspicuous. Why was everyone dancing except me? What was wrong? To still my rising panic I watched the musicians, pretending great interest. Which one of the fat, bald widowers was eying me even now? I wanted to weep; it was not fair! If any one of them dared approach me, I would just—just—

"Pardon me, Lady Jane. Your father has given me permission to escort you during the next set—if I may?"

139

I gaped like an idiot. It was the stranger Katie had pointed out a moment ago, smiling down at me from an awesome height and offering a white-gloved hand. I took it, madly trying to think of some dazzling repartee as he led me away. We concentrated a moment on the intricate steps before he spoke again.

"Tell me, do you always glare so fiercely at prospective partners?"

"Oh!—Oh, was I—glaring?" I swallowed. "I am terribly sorry. You see, I did not think you were going to ask me. I thought some frightful friend of Father's would." He laughed, showing a row of white, gleaming teeth. I was enchanted. How had I chanced to win his favor? He was easily one of the most attractive men at the ball—as dark as Edward Seymour was fair—and so tall! I had to bend my head back a little to look at him, and this seemed to amuse him.

"You dance very well, Lady Jane Grey. You will favor me again?"

I would. I accepted almost too eagerly.

"But you have the advantage, sir. I am afraid I do not know your name."

His black eyes sparkled. "I thought as much. But you know my father, I am sure. We are said to look much alike."

He was teasing me, making a mystery of his identity, and I finally stopped guessing. It was fun to think of him as a dark stranger. The reception had suddenly blossomed into something magical. I relaxed at his touch, abandoned wholly to the music, and did not care about the interested attention we drew. When at last he pulled me away from the throng and captured two goblets of wine from a footman, I was trembling with a kind of fevered ecstasy. I did not want to stop, fearing it might break the spell.

"You are like a nymph! Tell me, do you dance in fairy circles all night when the moon is full?"

I laughed breathlessly and sipped my wine.

"I rarely dance, sir, truly. This is the first ball I have—"

I pressed my hand to my mouth, appalled. How gauche he would think me!

But he only smiled and took my hand, then brought it to his own lips. "How very fortunate for me that I am your first partner. But I am selfish to keep you to myself."

"Oh, no. Please do not think that."

140

His smile disappeared; one of the King's courtiers was threading his way toward us.

"Devilish luck! I should have hidden you away sooner, little one. I fear I shall have to surrender you."

The gentleman came up to us and bowed. "I have the pleasure of conveying His Royal Majesty's regards to his cousin, Lady Jane Grey. He asks if you would care to join him."

I darted an anxious look toward my escort.

"I shall see you later, perhaps?"

"You shall," he promised.

"So—how is my favorite cousin?"

King Edward smiled as he waved his attendants away and motioned to a chair. "I hope you do not mind if I do not ask you to dance. My guest is elsewhere occupied, and I feel in need of a respite."

As I took the chair indicated, I studied Edward with concern. Although dressed magnificently in a slashed, cream-colored silk doublet, plumed hat, and jeweled sword, he looked pale and slight in his great chair. I forced myself to remember that he was the King, not the playfellow I had known at Hampton Court.

"I must confess that I would rather have you at my side to-night. Her Majesty is a difficult person to talk to." He broke off, laughing. "Do not look so startled. You know how fond I am of you. Unfortunately, the Privy Council has made me swear to have some stuffed and jeweled queen, even if she be plain as my father's 'Flanders Mare'!"

"I am sorry, Your Grace."

"You should not be. Otherwise I should be tempted to place the crown on your reluctant head. That was what Lord Thomas wanted, I know. Who can say? Perhaps I might have agreed had he lived long enough."

"I do not think so." I shook my head. "A queen must be extraordinary, and I am not. I am the same person I was when we were children. You are deceived by the gown, perhaps."

"I never thought you were ordinary, even as a child, Jane. You and Lady Catherine were very much alike."

A shadow crossed his face. "I still miss her, you know—"

Yes, I thought, *you do, very much.*

"We shall both have to marry before long. It will seem strange to think of you as someone's wife." My cousin's glance fell to my throat, and my fingers went to it involuntarily.

"An emerald—a gift between lovers, they say. Do you have a lover, Jane?"

"I? Why, *no*, Your Grace."

"Edward Seymour has been a frequent visitor in your home." Suddenly his voice was cold. "Does he mean anything to you?"

"He is a family friend, Your Highness. He—he comes only from obligation." *To a business agreement*, I added privately.

"It is an obligation your parents would do well to remove."

"Because of Edward's father? Are you saying you believe Palmer's accusation that the Duke is guilty of treason?"

Edward's face clouded. "The charge is serious. The law demands that it be investigated."

"But he is your uncle!"

"The Lord Admiral was my uncle, too. I must ask you not to interfere with matters of state, Jane. The case is in the Duke of Northumberland's hands. He will see that it is settled fairly."

"But—"

"Enough. We will speak no more of this. I would not have thought to see such distrust of my councillor when you are obviously so pleased with his son." A wry smile touched the King's face. "You could do worse, sweet cousin. Do not let past loyalties trespass upon your good sense."

I left him, feeling puzzled and disturbed. Katie caught my arm eagerly.

"What did he say?" she hissed. "Why did you not dance? Mother and Father are wild. They are sure something is afoot."

"Well, the King did not ask me to marry him, so you can all drive that thought out of your heads."

"Then what did you talk about?"

"Oh, a bit about the past, and about the things that lie ahead." I frowned. "Katie, he has altogether too much confidence in the Duke of Northumberland. It—frightens me somehow. And what does he mean, I am 'obviously pleased with his son'? Who is Northumberland's son?"

"Why, Guildford Dudley, of course! You must realize that everyone has been watching you, Jane. He has not paid attention to any other girl here. It really does not look right."

A coldness was spreading through me. Of course! How could I have been so dull? My dark "stranger" was the Duke of Northumberland's son!

"You look distressed. His Majesty did not upset you, did he?"

"What?—Oh!"

I looked up to discover that Katie had lost herself once again in the throng, and the voice now addressing me belonged to Guildford Dudley himself.

"I—I am afraid he did—Lord Dudley. We were discussing the imprisonment of the Duke of Somerset."

"Then you have reason for concern. Treason is no light offense."

"The Duke is no traitor!"

My voice carried further than I had intended; several heads turned in our direction. Dudley, after glancing around, took my arm and steered me into a more private alcove.

"I should not trifle with this matter if I were you. My father—whose identity you have correctly guessed—has things well in hand. His greatest concern is the King's welfare, you see; whereas Somerset always had the unfortunate habit of galloping off to the rescue of some poor downtrodden peasant while ignoring his primary responsibility. If he is not a traitor, he is at least a fool."

The magic ebbed from the evening as I watched the too-perfect, too-handsome face. I saw now the trace of arrogance I had missed before. I needed to escape, to think.

"If you are finished, my lord?" I started to turn away, but his hand restrained me.

"Your father and mine have become good friends of late, Jane. I see no reason why we, too, should not reach an understanding."

He gave a short, mocking bow, and as I watched him turn on his heel I felt a surge of apprehension. Why did he speak with such cool assurance, as if he were amused at some secret hidden to me? My fingers went to the cool stone at my throat and closed around it tightly.

16

Just after the reception we left London to return to Bradgate. It was a brief stay. Mama seemed unable to bear the stillness of our country manor and determined to leave again as soon as possible. First we were to visit Princess Mary in Clerkenwell, then spend Christmas with our cousins at Tylsey. After the holidays we would go on in a continuous round to other friends and relatives until the spring. It was an exhausting prospect. I longed for the quiet of Bradgate, but Mama only laughed at my preference.

"You are the eldest daughter of a distinguished family. We must all move about as much as possible. I shall not permit you to stay cloistered like a nun, disgracing us as well as yourself!"

Mary seemed pleased to see us, and welcomed me with especial affection. I knew she remembered the pleasant times we had shared in company with Lady Catherine when she was queen. Lady Catherine had done her best to reestablish a warmth between King Henry and his eldest daughter and had succeeded in making Mary's life more bearable. The two women had been close in age and became good friends.

"It does not seem possible that it has been three years since Catherine's death," she told me as she kissed me in greeting.

"No—" My throat closed. "The baby lives, I am told, but I have heard nothing else."

"Alas, poor child. But God's ways are best."

Mary seemed very old to me when I was a child of seven. Now that I was older, the distance between us grew narrower. I found that I liked and appreciated my cousin's sharp wit, her keen intelligence. She was a plain woman, without the attractive charms of her younger sister, Elizabeth; but there was something deeper there, a seriousness of purpose that was no doubt the result of many years of loneliness and ill health. How unjust that King Henry's annulment of his marriage with her mother should have so blighted her own life. As the King's "illegitimate" daughter she was heir only to his rejection and neglect.

"Cousin Mary—?"

We had come to such familiar terms with each other that I now felt quite free to pry gently under her aloofness. And she was fond of me. I was certain of that when she asked me to stay on for another few days when the rest of the family departed for Tylsey. Together we took up the task of finishing our various Christmas gifts. It was so cozy and cheerful sewing by the fire—I could not help remembering the times I had sat thus with Lady Catherine and Lady Margery.

"Why did you send me the gown, cousin? I loved it. It is the most beautiful thing I have ever owned."

She smiled. "You have answered your own question. I sent it because it was beautiful, and I hoped you would like it. My sister has set the fashion for an absurdly plain style of dress. It suits her, but it does not suit you. You are not so tall or boyishly slim."

"I am short!" I laughed ruefully. "Even Katie is taller. But it was very thoughtful of you to send the dress."

"Was the ball very lovely, Jane? I wish I might have gone, if only to see Edward. But I am sure it was. I have heard reports, you know. They say that you were often in the company of Guildford Dudley. Did you like him?"

"He is—very handsome," I admitted. "But as you may know, he is soon to be betrothed to my first cousin, Lady Margaret Clifford. And I am unofficially pledged to the Duke of Somerset's son, Edward Seymour."

"Oh? Then perhaps you will be released from your obligation. The Duke's future is not promising; at the very least he will lose his property and title, and so will his son."

"Do you think the Duke of Northumberland has that much power?"

"Think it?—I know he does! My brother, the King, is a puppet in his hands. Northumberland is an evil, lawless man."

Too late I remembered the enmity between Northumberland

and Princess Mary. He had set himself against all Catholics and had made Mary his special target, forbidding her exercise of the mass.

"My priests were put in prison. Think of it! The old service has been forbidden in England and our books of devotion, our holy images destroyed! But he shall not stop me." Her voice shook with emotion. "I have appealed to the Emperor Charles to intervene!

"Sometimes, Jane, sometimes I think all this has come upon me as punishment for signing the submission—that odious, degrading paper that reduced my mother to a harlot and made me a product of incest. Why did I do it? I have asked myself that again and again. Perhaps I thought, Mama is dead now; I can do her no more hurt. And perhaps—just perhaps it will restore me to my father's good will. He loved me once. They say he used to hold me, play with me as an infant. He never once spoke harshly to me. It was that wicked Anne Boleyn who turned him away from Mama and me. And I did not want to remain a prisoner at Hunsdon forever—"

She got up abruptly, her face turned away from me.

"Never compromise the truth, Jane. Nothing good ever comes of it, and you will blame yourself the rest of your life for your betrayal."

"Cousin Mary—" Tears rained down my face. "Please do not torment yourself. Your mother would have understood. I am sure of it!"

She reached for my hand quickly.

"I have distressed you; I am sorry. You are a good child."

"I do wish you could be happy. Lady Catherine said once that you would make a lovely wife and mother—"

"Yes." She managed a smile. "I should like that more than anything else in the world, I think. But I do not know if I shall have another chance. I was betrothed three times, you know, and my father broke it off each time."

"I will pray that God gives you your desire. He will. I know it."

This time she laughed and bent down to kiss me. "Then I shall be much indebted."

There was only one incident to mar my stay in Clerkenwell. It happened while I was passing by the chapel with one of Mary's ladies. When we got to the doorway, she suddenly stopped and sank into a low curtsy. Surprised, I looked into the chapel and saw no one, and nothing there except the receptacle containing the communion host. My anger flared.

"Why do you curtsy? Is the Lady Mary within?"

"No, my lady. I do reverence to God, who made us all."

"Oh? And how can He who made us all be in bread made by a baker?"

The remark was, of course, repeated to Mary, and there was a definite decrease in her warmth towards me from that moment. You who read these words will wonder, I suppose, why I did not refrain from making such a remark that would inevitably affront my hostess. If you wonder, you do not know how the whole issue of transubstantiation has torn the kingdom in two. All during King Henry's reign, the Reformers—who denied the Roman Catholic teaching that the wine and bread of Holy Communion are transformed into the actual blood and body of Christ—were tortured and burned. How many hundreds and thousands lost their lives because of this one doctrine, I do not know. I only knew about one woman named Anne Askew, and that was enough to loosen my tongue in denunciation of the doctrine forever—even if it meant endangering a friendship.

When Father came to escort me to Tylsey for Christmas, however, I believe Mary was genuinely sorry to see me go. I gave her a pair of fine silk gloves that I had embroidered with special care, and she, in turn, presented me with an expensive gold necklace, delicately set with pearls and jade. I was quite overcome, knowing that such a present was far beyond her means, and tried to protest; but she would have none of it.

"Please accept the gift, *ma chere*. It is but a token of the pleasure your visit has given me. Come again soon."

It was a happy Christmas. We even had a powdering of snow, and the Greys' large house overflowed with the merry laughter of guests, good food, and, of course, the antics of the Lord of Misrule. I often thought of Princess Mary and wished she could have had a part in it. In these halls were no dark shadows of guilt or a wasted youth.

The festive spirit lasted well through Twelfth Night. Shortly afterward we left to spend some time at Walden with Papa's sister,

Lady Audley. But since Mama could bear no more than a few days of Lady Audley's company without breaking into some violent disagreement—they both being of decided opinions—we departed for Tylsey again on the twenty-second of January.

I shall not forget that journey. It was one of those turning points in life when all of the details stand out in sharpest relief as one looks back upon them, although at the time they did not seem unusual at all.

We had traveled most of the day before stopping at an inn for refreshment. The wind was bitter cold and cut through the slight protection offered by our carriage. What it must have been like for the large band of horsemen and scouts that accompanied us, I do not like to think. To make matters worse, my head had begun aching and there was a stiffness in my neck which I attributed to the merciless jolting. I longed to lie down in quietness, but dared not mention my complaint to my parents, who were intent on pressing on. There were a great many thieves on the roads at that time of year; one could not travel at night without considerable risk.

The innkeeper hastened forward to greet us, then bustled about with orders for his overworked servants to make us more comfortable. I stepped down from the carriage and, surprised by a wave of dizziness, clung to the arm of a gentleman who offered assistance.

"Are you all right, my lady?" he asked, watching me with some concern.

"Yes. At least, I am sure I will be—when I am rested."

It seemed to take a great deal of effort to assure him of this, and his grip on my arm only tightened. We entered the inn, and I saw that a long trestle table had been cleared and was being spread with the most bountiful provisions that could be produced at such short notice. But while the others set upon the food with zest, gulping down huge quantities of cold brawn and beef, washed down with tankards of ale, I looked the other way, trying not to be sick. It was so hot in the room, I thought dizzily. A great fire roared in the hearth, and perspiration rolled down my back and face.

"Aye, there's more than one what calls this a bloody day for England!"

The owner of the tavern, hovering by our table and rubbing his hands together, tried anxiously to make conversation. Papa looked up sharply.

"What are you talking about?"

"Why, the news from London, me lord! On every fellow's tongue what comes in 'ere, 'twas so shockin' sudden. But I'm one what says the Duke of Northumberland 'ad 'is reasons for doin' it the way 'e did—."

"For doing what, man? Stop babbling and tell me!" My father rose to his feet. The clatter and boisterous laughter of the room melted away; everyone's eyes fixed upon the inkeeper's discomfitted face.

"For—for executin' the good Duke, m'lord! Took off 'is 'ead this very mornin'!"

"The Duke—?"

But I knew who it was before he answered. So did everyone there.

"Aye, the Duke of Somerset!" he said.

The pounding in my head became so frightening, so unendurable, that I put my hands over my ears. Someone far away began to scream. And then I was falling, and I could hear nothing more.

I was lost at sea—a great sea of pain that surged and ebbed but would not let me go. At times I was aware that there were others around me—physicians, my family, and Ellen . . . always Ellen. Once she was standing above me, weeping, and I longed to comfort her. But before I could, I drifted away again out of reach. Edward was there once, too. It must have been a dream, for I saw him reach down and touch my face, and in his own face there was a look of pain. He was holding something. My emerald. He laid it on my pillow and said something, but I could not hear him. I wanted so badly to hear, and yet, in a way, I did not. I began to weep; someone came and told him he must leave. Then the sea swept me away again, and I was lost in the darkness.

Ellen tells me they feared for my life for a fortnight. The only thing that remains clear in my memory is waking up one morning, turning my head, and knowing with great wonder that the pain was gone. Through the window of the bedchamber I saw an azure sky and, silhouetted against it, trees. Oak trees! I smiled and wearily closed my eyes again, content. I was home. I would not leave Bradgate again.

I often wondered about those dreams as I lay in my bed convalescing and, later, as I began moving about. But whenever I asked Ellen what had actually happened, she became evasive; and a Scotswoman who chooses to be close-mouthed can be very close-mouthed indeed. Not until much later did I learn which part of my dreams were imagined and which were real.

My illness had also wiped from my mind all remembrance of the Duke of Somerset's execution. When I did not speak of it, Ellen was afraid to mention it to me, fearing that it might provoke some kind of relapse. By the time Katie finally jogged my memory, Edward's father had lain in his grave for almost a month.

"The commons call him the 'Good Duke.' Father says they are wild against Northumberland for not giving him a proper trial before both houses of Parliament. He was privately sentenced, and Northumberland himself was a judge."

"How awful for Edward," I whispered. "How could Northumberland act as a judge when the Duke was accused of plotting his death?"

Katie shrugged. "Who was there to stop him? But the Duke was not found guilty of treason, at least. Just felony."

"Felony?"

"They said he incited the people to revolt. The only advantage of felony over treason was that they could not take away his lands. But they could still behead him."

A shudder ran through me. "And what of the Duchess?"

"She is still in prison, with little hope of pardon."

So Lady Margery had been right, I thought. She had said Northumberland would destroy both of her sons. What kind of man was this, who now had supreme control of the King?

"Jane?" Katie's voice broke into my thoughts. "I know this sounds silly, but—do you remember what Ellen said about St. Agnes' Eve?"

"That if a maid fasts, her future husband will be revealed to her? That is just one of Ellen's tales, Kate."

"It is not! I know it is true. I pretended I was ill last year and did not touch a scrap of food all day. Then I went to bed and waited. And I saw him, Jane! I swear I saw him in a dream."

"Who?"

She twisted the ring on her finger. "I ought not tell you. You might be angry."

"Katie—!"

"Very well then. It was—Edward Seymour."

"Oh!" I did not want to hurt Katie by laughing. I congratulated her solemnly.

"There! You are upset with me! I knew it!"

"Why in heaven's name should I be upset?"

"Well—you are betrothed to Edward, though you have never shown much interest in him. But I believe that Papa and Mama will change their minds about letting you marry Edward."

"You are absurd. They will never change their minds."

"The Seymour name is not what it used to be—"

"But the Seymour wealth is the same," I reminded her bitterly, "as long as Edward is entitled to his father's property."

"Yes, but—I will not let him marry you. It is not fair, when you do not care for him as I do."

"Katie—sweet—I did not know you felt this way."

"I have always been mad about Edward; you have just been too selfish to notice," she shrugged.

I was astonished.

"He cares for me, too, in his way. Some of those times when he visited Bradgate, we went riding together. You never knew that either, did you? You were always stuck away in your books somewhere. I was so certain Papa was planning our betrothal. But then Edward's father became too important for just the second eldest daughter! The Duke of Somerset wanted you for his son. Well, now it does not matter what he wants, does it! I think everyone would be happier with a change in the arrangements."

"Perhaps—perhaps you are right." I shook my head. "Odd that never occurred to me. I knew you always got on well together."

"Well, it is time you woke up. We both have to marry, and I do not intend to be settled with some poor country squire who has already been through two other wives. Edward is young and rich. And I think I can make him love me."

It was a challenge, but I had no wish to take it up. What she said was true. We could both be wed to persons we cared nothing about. If she and Edward loved each other . . . *If*. Why was it so difficult for me to accept? My enforced betrothal to the Earl of Hertford had always been galling. Only after a most bitter enmity

151

had we achieved a reluctant truce—and friendship. I should be relieved to be released from the agreement.

"Jane?—You have not said anything."

"What can I say? The decision is not ours. We must pray that Papa will be guided by God's will, and wait. Perhaps Edward will come to Bradgate shortly and decide the matter himself."

But he did not come. All that spring and summer as the valley ripened and flowered I watched, hoping to see his horse winding through the leafy forest path, but he did not come. And Papa did not mention him. When the leaves turned to fire under the autumn sun and began to drop from the oaks, Papa announced that we were leaving Bradgate. The house would be converted to a hunting lodge, he said. We would never return to live in the valley again.

A person should not come to love a place—a house—as I did. I suppose Bradgate had become a symbol of rest to me after I came home from four turbulent years of childhood at Hampton Court with the Queen and King Henry. Then, after the deaths of Lady Catherine and Lord Thomas, I had returned again to find peace through study and a surer relationship with God. There was unhappiness there, too, to be sure. But there was a healing quality about the valley—its fragrant loveliness, its great age that had triumphed over years of storm. I knew why they had built a monastery there. I had felt it when I opened my eyes after my illness and looked through my chamber window to the hills.

I will life up mine eyes unto the hills, from whence cometh my help. My help cometh from the Lord, who made heaven and earth. . . .

Well, God was still my help; He would help me enjoy Sheen as I had Bradgate. Sheen, too, had been a monastery, had it not? Even if it was close by London, it was beautifully situated, right on the Thames, and had ample land on which to ride or hunt. Only two things bothered me about it: This had been Seymour property, forfeited to the Crown after the Protector's first arrest. Northumberland had made a gift of it to my parents! And his manor, Sion House, was almost directly across the river.

Katie had told me the people hated Northumberland's highhandedness. When we became the recipients of Seymour property, their resentment was turned on us. One night when Mama and Papa were strolling in the gallery, there appeared before them a hand holding a blood-covered ax. Mama fainted, and before Papa could pursue the trespasser hidden in the shadows, he was gone. It was clearly an attempt to frighten us. But though some of the less stout-hearted of our household urged Papa to leave Sheen, they did not reckon with his determination. He made it known that the penalty for anyone attempting further trickery at Sheen would be hanging and quartering. There were no more incidents.

Perhaps not surprisingly, the ones who took the greatest fancy to our new home were Katie and Mama. Each day they set off to visit some member of the nobility, except on the days they stayed home to receive calls. The talk was all of dresses and teas and the flirtations in Court circles. Lessons were secondary now, the six languages we had learned useful only to flavor one's conversation—a witty foreign phrase thrown in discreetly now and then. It was not considered good form to appear too knowledgeable, especially for a young woman who hoped to make a good marriage. Since this excluded me, I was not averse to a frank expression of my opinion; this invariably horrified Mama and the other conservative ladies, and I was often excused from their gatherings.

I was delighted with my new freedom. I still spent hours with Master Aylmer, but there was more time spent on my music, of which my tutor disapproved. He even went to the extent of writing to Dr. Bullinger in Zurich, hoping he would dissuade me from practice. Imagine his dismay when the Reformer replied with a quotation from Plato! "Musical training is a more potent instrument than any other, because rhythm and harmony find their way into the inward places of the soul." I continued playing my lute, and sent Dr. Bullinger's wife a pair of gloves and a ring.

Unfortunately, the Reformation was now making little progress in England. Although John Knox of Scotland was exerting some influence as the King's Chaplain, the Duke of Northumberland thwarted many of his efforts. John Hales, a leading Reformer, fled to Germany after the Duke of Somerset's removal. The ignorance of the Protestant clergy was appalling. It was said that when some 311 of them were asked to repeat the Ten Commandments and the Lord's Prayer, 170 were unable to say the Commandments, ten did not know the Lord's Prayer, and some did not even know who was the author of the Lord's Prayer! Reform was needed desperately, but Northumberland was hardly the man to do it. Under his "leadership," England was slowly being destroyed. He had added twelve new men to the Privy Council—all his ardent supporters. Every law against enclosures was repealed. Household expenses at Hampton Court rose from 46,000 pounds a year to over 100,000. The metal in minted coins continued to be debased. And although he gave no support to Protestantism, Northumberland did not rest in his persecution of the Catholics. Churches were pillaged and so much linen burned in the streets that the citizens petitioned him to send it to the hospitals instead; the burnings and torturings that had ceased during the Protectorship were now resumed.

Why did Papa act so unconcerned? His silence about Northumberland's misgovernment troubled me. We had had little chance to talk together of late; he was always in London—or at Sion House across the river. I dreaded the many invitations we received to visit Sion, for I was usually required to accompany my parents. Guildford Dudley was attentive on these occasions; too attentive, for one soon to be engaged to my first cousin. I could not feel easy in the house of the man I so disliked.

On 21 February, 1553, Parliament was called into session, and King Edward was given his majority. It was three years earlier than was usual, for he was only fifteen, my own age. What was the reason for it, I wondered? Papa said that the Duke of Northumberland humored the King in everything. Had Edward insisted on assuming regal authority prematurely, or was it Northumberland's idea? My cousin was ill and, it was rumored, overtired. I did not see how he was to bear his added responsibilities.

The coming of spring did not still the restlessness I had felt since leaving Bradgate. I watched the early crocuses, hyacinths, and primroses blossom with a surge of indefinable longing . . . for what? I did not know. My impatience with the interminable round of teas, hunts, and banquets increased; I could not bear the stale chatter, the feigned show of enthusiasm for persons and things one secretly considered loathsome.

Only when I was alone, exploring the wide acres of park surrounding Sheen, did I find some measure of peace. I began spending several hours each day riding, whenever possible unaccompanied by even a groom. This was not, of course, considered proper or even safe, but I was willing to leave the decorum to others, and I did not seriously believe I would come to any harm.

One day late in March, however, I questioned the wisdom of this assumption.

I had ordered a horse saddled just after the rest of the family departed on the barge for Sion House. My plea of a headache was, for once, accepted by Mama, and I was given leave to stay behind. The headache was real enough. The mere thought of another afternoon on exhibition was enough to ensure that. But I knew that a gallop in the crisp air was all that would be needed to restore me; that and the guilty pleasure of my stolen freedom.

The sky was a sharp, clear azure awash with sunshine. My heart lifted as I turned my mare toward the river and she settled into a slow, rhythmic gait. I was not an expert horsewoman, nor did I care for the hunt, but I enjoyed the muscular strength of the animal beneath me and the rush of air against my face and clothes. Our pace slowed as we entered a copse and my mount picked her way over roots and stones. When it was that I became aware of another rider, following close behind, I do not know exactly. But when I paused to free a branch that had caught my skirt and heard the sudden sharp snap of a twig, my heart began pounding with alarm. What horseman would dare trespass on our estate after Papa's stern warning of imprisonment or death? I remembered the bloody ax brandished in the faces of my parents, the hatred of the commoners for Northumberland and his friends. There were some who would dare punishment—even death—to retaliate for the murder of the "good Duke."

Heedless of the uneven path, I urged my horse to a gallop. I had been a fool, to come so far from the manor; there was no choice now but to press on toward the river and hope for a stretch of open ground. The sound of approaching hooves grew louder; perspiration broke from my forehead. *Faster girl, faster!* We were already galloping over the ground without care for roots or stones. The rider would be upon us any moment. And then, as in a nightmare, I felt my horse stumble, lose her footing, and go down upon her knees. I was thrown hard onto the path ahead. I remember thinking as I landed, *O God, preserve me now!* Then I heard the sharp exclamation of a man and closed my eyes. The rider dismounted, bent over me; I could feel his breath warm upon my face.

"Jane!"

Was it possible? The voice, though harsh with anger and fear, caused me to open my eyes again, wide.

"Jane, *thank God* you are alive! What in heaven's name made you ride into the woods like that?"

The voice was one I knew, arrogant, infuriating.

"You—might at least—ask if I am hurt!" I gasped.

"You look too put out to be in much pain. Come, then, let me see if you have broken anything."

"Stop!—Oh!—How *dare* you handle me like that?"

His hands, deftly trying my limbs, paused; sand-colored brows arched with amusement above gray eyes.

"Do not take it too personally, my lady. I would do the same for my horse."

I struggled to sit up. "My horse—? How is she?"

"All right, I think. Just wandered off a bit. But you might have thought of her sooner before you risked breaking her neck."

"*Her* neck? You nearly killed both of us, pursuing me, frightening me out of my wits—!"

"*Pursuing* you? So that is what you thought! And well you might, riding unescorted over the estate, leaving yourself open to every cutthroat's fancy! I daresay your father knows nothing of this."

"And what if he does not?" My chin lifted. "I daresay he did not know you were trespassing on his property!"

"No? How careless of me. You see, this land belonged so long to *my* father that I rather tend to forget who has possession." There was an unmistakable note of mockery in his tone. "I pray you will forgive me. When I saw you riding from another direction—alone—I thought I would warn you of your imprudence. This is not Leicestershire, you know, and the natives here are not all entirely friendly."

I was taken aback. "I am sorry. I—I suppose it was foolish of me to leap to conclusions as I did."

He offered me a hand. "Shall I help you up?"

My dress was muddy, and there were two ragged tears in the skirt. I brushed ineffectually at the stains and then burst into rueful laughter. "Ellen will be shocked when she hears that 'young Lord Seymour' has seen me like this. She speaks quite highly of you."

"And her mistress? What does she say of me?"

I looked away. "It has been a long time, Edward—well over a year. At first I kept thinking, he is grieving for his father, he has his business to see to. But I heard nothing, Edward. No letters—" I shook my head. "What was I to think?"

"You have no memory of my visit to you when you were ill?"

"I thought it was a dream! I questioned Ellen, but she would not tell me."

"She was forbidden to, by your parents. And I was forbidden to see you again—or write—until they gave me leave."

"But that makes no sense! They would never do that just because your father was—"

"Beheaded? Yes," he said quietly, "that was partly the reason. Feelings were high in London. I, too, might have been taken prisoner by Northumberland's conspirators. And then there was the question of my father's estate. Your parents thought it best to wait until things settled."

"And you agreed?"

He ran his hand through his thick blond hair. "I had little choice, Jane. They do, after all, have the upper hand in our marriage contract; they have you. And from previous indications I did not think that a year's lapse in our acquaintance would disturb you too greatly."

This last was said with an edge of bitterness, and I felt the heat rise in my face.

"You do me wrong, my lord. Did I not swear, when we last met, that I would remain faithful to our friendship?"

"You did. And I have wondered not a little at how lightly that pledge was broken."

I stared at him in amazement as he continued. "Your family name is closely intertwined these days with that of Northumberland. The ferrymen are kept busy plying their way between Sheen and Sion House. And I hear you are often prevailed upon to entertain the company with your lute and singing—I am well-informed, you see. I even know Guildford Dudley no longer looks for a betrothal with your cousin! Ah, you blush prettily at that, my lady."

"I know nothing of Lord Guildford's affairs, nor do they concern me!"

"I wonder. . . . You have not, by the way, chanced to keep that small stone I gave you? I should like to see it again. But of course, it is very easy to lose a thing like that in London—there is so much else to distract one."

158

I drew in my breath. "I will thank you to fetch my mount for me, Lord Seymour. I must be returning to Sheen."

Curtly he did as I asked, but only after examining the horse for injuries. "She is unharmed, I think, but badly lathered. You would do well to take her gently."

"You will not come with me? I—I would feel safer."

"If you wish."

His hands went around my waist to lift me into the saddle. He was very near. I felt his hands tighten, and a tremor ran through my body. We stared at each other for a long moment.

When he drew me against him, I made no move to resist. It was right, natural. I sighed as the warm closeness of his arms enveloped me, and then his lips touched mine. Lightly, at first, and then demanding. Something woke within me that had nothing to do with friendship.

"We should not, Edward!" I whispered, drawing away.

"Why not? We are still betrothed. And I have waited long enough, heaven knows!"

"You have—felt this way—for a long time?"

He laughed, and I saw in his eyes the same look of abandoned joy that I had seen in Thomas Seymour's. Something caught at my throat.

"For a girl as reputedly knowledgeable as you are, Jane Grey, you are remarkably slow at reading the lines on a man's heart."

"But you thought me a simpleton! You called on me only in obedience to your father!"

"At first, yes. Before I discovered what you were like underneath all the polish and accomplishment. You cared about things—and people. There was nothing half-hearted about the way you loved Lady Catherine or Lord Thomas—right *or* wrong. I began to realize what a great thing it would be to win that kind of love for myself. If I could only persuade you to stop hating me."

"But I never hated you—not really, Edward. I just could not accept the things you were saying. I wanted you to be wrong. But that did not stop the things from happening, did it?"

He took my hands. "They happened; they are a part of us. But we cannot let those tragedies—no matter how unfair—destroy the rest of our lives."

"It seems like such a long time ago that we stood on the tower of the priory, near Bradgate. I wished for a moment then that I could stay there, apart from everything below; it was so lovely. . . . We have both lost people we love since then. But I am glad I left my tower—I would have missed so much!"

We were silent for a moment, thoughtful, and then it was time to go. We mounted and turned our horses toward Sheen. Edward rode as far as the outlying cottages and told me he would call on my parents the next day to obtain permission to visit. But I was not to let them know that we had met today. We parted, and I ran straight up to my chambers. When Ellen saw me she gave a cry of consternation.

"Would ye look at the lass! Ye've gone and near killed yerself!"

"It is nothing, Ellen, truly. Just a few stains and rents."

"And a grand lot of bruises, I'll warrant! 'Tis a holy miracle ye're not dead. Aye, I've seen ye, ridin' off like the devil was after ye, and by yerself, more times thin not!" She shook her head. "Your Father will have to put a stop to it."

"Oh, no, Ellen, please!" I stopped in the midst of unbuttoning my dress and flung my arms around her. "Please do not tell Papa or Mama! I could not bear it if they stopped me from riding, and they will if you tell them what happened."

"Well—ye must promise not to go alone any more. It 'tisn't safe, lass! What if ye'd broken somethin'?"

"Very well then, Ellen," I said meekly. "I shall not ride alone."

She sighed and turned toward the door. "I'll get some water sent up hot from the kitchen; ye'll be needin' a scrub. And ye'd best burn the dress. It won't bear mendin'."

"Yes, Ellen. Thank you."

She stopped short, arms akimbo, and without turning around spoke again, suspiciously. "Ye're sure nothin' else happened that ye want to tell me about, lass? Ye seem in rare fine spirits for someone who's just been thrown from a horse."

"Do I?—How very strange," I said. "Perhaps I needed to be shaken up a bit. We all take so much for granted, Ellen—things all around us that we love the most. You are right; I shall not go riding alone ever again."

18

Love had burst upon me without warning, like a flash of sun through a rift in dark clouds, and I was unprepared for its beauty. They say love is blind, but I cannot agree. It is seeing for the first time—tasting, touching, sensing things as never before. I was keenly aware of everything around me; I could not hold the world close enough.

Throughout that magical April, Edward rode from London to see me. Although no date for our marriage was fixed—he wanted to wait until his estate was settled before asking—my parents accepted him on much the same footing as before the Duke of Somerset's death.

I was impatient with the hours of separation. The courtesy calls I was expected to pay, the social functions, became more of a trial than ever. Mama rebuked me constantly for inattention, and Katie . . . Katie watched me, slightly puzzled and, I think, unhappy. She knew without my telling her of the changed relationship between Edward and me. But whenever I tried talking with her she withdrew into silence.

The visits back and forth across the river continued as before. Papa and the Duke of Northumberland played endless games of chess while the rest of us engaged in bowling or tennis, shuttlecock or cards. Sometimes Guildford joined our company, sometimes not. I began to relax. Political affairs were rarely discussed, except for the state of the King's health. His persistent weakness was a matter of concern to everyone. Frequent bleedings and purges had not served to restore him as the royal physicians had hoped.

Edward, after an audience with him, was grave. "It is not just a weariness of his office, although he has taken too much upon himself too soon. He is not the same person I used to know, Jane. We studied together as children, but now it is as if we were strangers."

"Perhaps he feels guilt about your father and the Lord Admiral. He loved both his uncles, in different ways."

"If he has guilt—or grief—he does not show it. I saw the journal he keeps. My father's execution was noted the same way one might describe a change in the weather."

I laid my hand on his. "He is so lonely. Let us pity him, Edward, and pray for him."

He smiled. "I will pity him, for he cannot look forward to having you, can he? The Council has a princess all picked out for His Highness."

"I hope that he will find more contentment in marriage than his father did."

"If the Lord Admiral had lived," Edward teased, "*you* might have been Edward's queen. Are you sorry about what you have missed?"

"I think, my lord, that you are fishing for compliments!"

"Most girls would sell their souls to be a queen."

"I suffer from a deplorable lack of ambition—except to be the wife of a certain nobleman of my acquaintance."

His expression became more serious. "If that nobleman became impoverished—would that matter?"

"I do not understand."

"The Parliament is now discussing an act that would claim my father's lands for the Crown."

"But they cannot!" I cried. "Only on a conviction of treason would his lands be forfeit!"

"Laws can always be bent, Jane. The Lords are like vultures, hovering greedily over the remains of the slain. It matters not that the slain one was once a friend."

I was shocked. The Duke of Somerset's last plea on the scaffold had been for kind treatment toward his family. Yet a year later the Duchess was still in the Tower, and the property that belonged rightfully to his son was in jeopardy. How would Mama and Papa react if Edward were to lose the Seymour riches?

"Do not look so worried, my love. The bill will not pass. It will have to be voted by both houses, and I do not believe the Commons will consent."

We had been strolling in the garden, and now paused as we saw Katie approach. Daily she was growing more graceful and pleasing to the eye, and I could not help noticing how Edward's attention was attracted. She had blossomed since our move from Bradgate. She was no longer a child, nor yet a woman. More than one lord's fancy had been taken by her fresh charm; there would be no lack of suitors when the time came.

"We are pleased that you join our company, Lady Katherine."

"'Lady Katherine' is it?" she pouted. "How very formal! I would much rather be called your Katie, as before."

He smiled. "Katie, then."

"I have not come to join you. Walking bores me. But Mama sent me to ask if you will stay to sup with us this evening."

"Please tell the Duchess I accept her kind invitation, on condition that her daughter will consent to entertain me afterward. I have not heard your voice in song since I last left Bradgate."

She glowed, but lowered her eyelids demurely. "You flatter me. But it will be my pleasure to sing, if you like. Until later, then—?" She curtsied and withdrew.

"A pretty vixen, your sister. I heard Lord Pembroke's heir—Herbert—is quite taken with her."

"He is not the only one," I observed stiffly. His brows rose.

"Jane. You are not—*jealous* of Katie, are you?— Not you!"

"Well, why not? She is pretty, and sings well, and—and you have always seemed well disposed toward her. You went riding often with her at Bradgate."

"Because she liked to hunt, and you did not! Jane—my sweet—" and the laughter died from his face, "I like your sister well enough, but I do not love her. It is you I love, Jane Grey, and no other!"

He kissed me then, and any lingering doubts vanished. Edward Seymour was mine. He would always be mine.

"We have been waiting for hours, Ellen! Why must they talk so long?"

I put down the book I had been trying to read and went to warm my hands at the fire. It was early May, and the nights were still cool in the draughty stone mansion. But even if it had been Midsummer Eve I doubt that I could have stopped shivering. Mama and Papa were below deciding my future; I would know this night whom I was to marry.

"Ellen, how can you sit there knitting?"

"There's one of us should be makin' use of this evenin'," she said complacently. "I wouldna' be settin' this easy if the matter weren't already settled."

"Then you think it *is* Edward?"

"Aye. They sent for him special to sup with ye tonight, did they not?"

"Yes." And all through the long, many-coursed dinner I had watched Mama and Papa converse with Edward, unable to tell anything from their expressions. When they withdrew to the library afterward, I was excused, to await them in my chambers. "But he did not stay long; that is what worries me. Something must have gone wrong."

"Nay, lass! 'Tis a good sign. Likely they're only settin' the day now. Marriage is no' a thing to be entered into with haste—all things must be considered."

"You do like Edward, Ellen? I should be miserable if you did not."

Her busy hands ceased their work as she looked at me and smiled.

"I do like him. He puts me in mind of his father. A wee bit too serious now and again, stubborn, a mind of his own. But there's gentleness there, too. I've seen it in the way he handles his servants, and his horse. He'll make ye a proper husband, aye."

There was a muffled sound of voices from the hall below. Ellen stiffened, then went to the door and listened.

"They'll be comin' up soon, lass. I best not be found here."

"Please—" I felt unreasoning fear clutch at me. "Please stay."

"I canna', lass. Ye know that." On an unaccustomed impulse she put her arms around me. "'Tis a fine, proud moment. Ye'll be a woman grown now, an' I'm happy for ye! God be with ye." And she was gone.

I had no time for further trepidation. My door opened abruptly, admitting my parents; I sank into a low curtsy.

"Mama, Papa—good evening to you both."

Mama nodded brusquely and took the chair just vacated by

Ellen. Papa stood beside her looking uneasy. It occurred to me that this was the first time they had ever come together to my chambers. Why had they not summoned me? Perhaps they felt, as I did, the personal closeness of this occasion, this decision of intertwining my life forever with another's. Their unexpected thoughtfulness touched me.

"You are sixteen," Mama began, and her voice was not ungentle. "As our eldest daughter, it is full time you were wed; delay would be unprofitable."

"A marriage such as yours can have the profoundest effect upon the family," interposed Papa. "You understand, of course, that is the reason we have given it such grave consideration. There must be no possibility of error."

"I understand, Papa."

"Good. I trust our choice of your spouse will not be disagreeable. The Duke of Northumberland has been most gracious to allow a further strengthening of the bonds between our two families. Your betrothal to Guildford Dudley will be announced on the morrow."

"To—*whom*, Papa?"

He exchanged an impatient look with Mama.

"Lord Guildford. Northumberland's youngest son."

I do not, even now, know what possessed me in those next few moments. I knew what behavior was expected of me. Through the centuries, hundreds—no, thousands—of young girls had stood thus before their parents, listening as the hateful plans for their future were laid before them, and had bowed in silent submission to those plans. But it was as if another person took hold of me. A person who would not be restrained.

"No, Papa," I said in a low, clear voice. "I will not marry him."

"What did you say?" He was staring at me as if I had gone mad.

I ran my tongue over my lips. "I said I—I cannot—will not marry Guildford Dudley, Papa. I—"

The blow came so swiftly I could not prepare for it. I reeled backward, feeling the bedpost dig into my back.

"Please, Papa! I am already contracted—to Edward Seymour."

"There was never a written contract."

165

"But you promised!" I sobbed. "You gave his father—the Duke of Somerset—your word!"

The second blow came. I fell to my knees, tasting blood on my lips.

"You dare correct us? You *dare?*"

Through a haze I saw my mother rise from her chair and come toward me. Hatred distorted her features, making them ugly. I shrank back.

"Edward Seymour's father is dead. The Duchess is in prison, and all Seymour lands have been confiscated by the Crown. Do you suppose we would allow our daughter to be married to a pauper?"

It was madness to speak again. With terrible certainty I knew that it was Parliament's seizure of Edward's estate that had turned my parents against him. I shook my head, dazed with pain and disbelief, hardly knowing that I whispered aloud.

"You called him son," I said.

"Hold your tongue! Hold your tongue, or by heaven I shall teach you silence!" I raised my arms in a vain effort to ward off the blows that smashed against my mouth, then rained down upon my head and shoulders. My words had unwittingly goaded her into a fearful rage.

"You shall forget Edward Seymour. You shall never speak his name again, do you hear?"

Oh, God—The pain. Why is this happening, God? Where are You?

She laughed, a hideous sound, and brought her hand down again even as I screamed.

"Aye! Pain is a sure master, and the lesson will not soon be forgotten! Cry out again! Your God will not listen, nor will He care. Learn your lesson well, my clever daughter!"

From the edge of my vision I saw Papa turn away, and, groaning, I sank upon the floor. No longer did I attempt to resist her blows.

The room was very quiet. Slowly I moved my head and gasped as a knifelike pain shot through my body. I lay very still. It was cold, so cold. . . . Where was Ellen? . . . Why did she not come? I must try again to pull myself up. . . .

"Lass?—Ach, me puir, puir wee lassie!" It was Ellen's voice, filled with disbelieving horror.

"They sent me down to the kitchens, told me to fetch ye a bit of water. Ach, me poor bairn! Look what they've done to ye!"

"I am so cold. . . . Will you—hold me a moment—Ellen?"

Without a word she dropped to her knees and gathered me against her strong, solid body. She began to sing, a wild sweet Scottish melody that I had not heard since I was a child. Something warm splashed upon my face—warm and wet, like tears, only that was not possible. Ellen never cried.

"They—they told me that—" It was so difficult to talk, but it was necessary to tell her. "—I must marry Guildford—Dudley."

"I know. I know, lass. Ye mustna' think on it now."

"But—I love Edward. I tried to tell them—"

"Hush, lass." The encircling arms lifted, laid me gently on my bed. "I'm goin' to fetch the doctor. 'Tis all over now. Dinna' fret. I'll take care of ye." And she slipped out.

Over, Ellen had said. I closed my eyes, but the pain did not go away. Oh, Ellen! It will never be over. It is only just beginning. Tears slipped from my eyes, and I thought I heard again the sound of my Mother's laughter.

19

I was married three weeks later. In the intervening time I kept to my room, and it was reported that I had suffered a bad fall. Katie came to see me soon after my "accident," and if she suspected the truth she did not mention it, nor did I.

"You look quite frightful, you know. What a pity it had to happen just before the wedding. I do hope you will mend in time."

"Yes. Everyone tells me I shall mend. Even Dr. Harding."

He had come only the day before to read an exposition on the third chapter of Colossians, verse twenty: "Children, obey your parents in all things." He had delivered it with an air of self-righteousness, his eyes glittering with malice, and I knew that if I had ever disliked any man thoroughly, it was he. A "whited sepulcher," as our Lord might have said.

"We have ever so much to do, Jane," Katie bubbled on, oblivious to the irony of my tone. "Packing, fittings, the trousseau—heaven knows how we shall manage! But when Papa told me it was to be Lord Herbert, one of the richest men in the realm, I was—"

"Lord Herbert?" I interrupted, puzzled. "I am to wed Guildford Dudley, Northumberland's son.'

"But I am not talking about you, silly. Good heavens, you are not the only one who is to be—" She faltered at my stunned expression. "They have not told you? I just supposed they—had."

"Oh, Katie." I turned my head away. "Not you, too!"

"Well, why on earth not! I *am* thirteen. Lots of girls my age are married."

"That does not make it right! Not for you or—anyone."

She gave a little laugh. "If I am too young, what about poor

168

little Mary? She is going to be contracted to our cousin Arthur Grey, and she is only eight."

I wondered bitterly that Mama had drawn the line at a contract. It would have been so convenient, a triple alliance.

"Jane, I am surprised you are taking this so badly. Marriage has to come sooner or later, and I think it will be jolly fun to be my own mistress and give entertainments. I adore London society. And Pembroke Castle—Jane, think of it!—I shall be rich!"

I smiled sadly. What woman was ever rich, bound to a man not obligated to share a farthing of his wealth or even a common act of kindness, if the mood took him? "You used to speak of other things, of marrying someone you cared for—"

"That was simple of me. Mama says that what we want is not always what is best for us." Her eyes met mine defiantly. "We cannot expect to mate like peasants, after all."

"That sounds like Mama."

"Jane! You are rather hard on her." She cocked her head to one side as though listening. "I had better go. Ellen will be cross with me for disturbing you, and besides, I have a fitting. Do cheer up. You might have done much worse than the handsome Guildford Dudley."

I sat motionless after my sister left. Was that how we were to content ourselves, then, we who were matched apart from our heart's inclination? Was the comparative wretchedness of other marriages supposed to make our own more tolerable?

My fingers went to the filagree chain that still hung around my neck. I drew out the small emerald, and it lay glittering on my palm. The color was still clear—as clear as the day Edward had given it to me at Richmond Palace, a test of my loyalty. Would it ever dull in all the years to follow? I held the stone tightly, and it seemed, even while I stared, that the fierce green fire within it grew brighter. . . .

25 May 1553, Whit Sunday. My wedding day.

I was awake long before the dawn that morning —thinking. The thoughts that passed through my mind are best not recorded here. God must forgive me, and I think He has, for that last dwelling on my beloved. The nuptial vows to another were not yet spoken; my body and soul were still inviolate, my own.

169

Ellen came in so quietly, just after the sun rose, that I did not know she was there until she spoke.

"'Tis a fine morn, clear and gentle, without a hint of rain."

I smiled. "That is supposed to be a good omen."

"Aye, so it is." Her movements stilled, watching me. "How is it with ye, then, lass?"

"I—have tried to yield myself to God's will, Ellen. It is not easy, but I must believe there is a purpose in this."

"There is, lass. I'm sure of it."

There was a pause. I heard laughter and whispering outside the door.

"The maids are without," Ellen explained, "with yer bath. I bid them wait till I gave them leave."

"Tell them to come in, then. The day has begun, and there is no profit in delay."

It was soothing to give myself over to the ministrations of the ladies-in-waiting. I stood passivly in a wooden tub before the fire while my body was scrubbed, then rubbed all over with fragrant oils of rose and jasmine. Then, clad in silk undergarments, I sat before the glass while Mrs. Tylney, one of my gentlewomen, fussed over my hair, arranging it several different ways. Finally she plaited a small coronet, intertwined with pearls, on top of my head and allowed the rest of the hair to fall simply to my waist. Although not a la mode, the effect was flattering.

When all else was ready, my attendants lifted the gown over my head and reverently watched it settle around me, a gold-embroidered cloud alight with a rainbow of diamonds and emeralds.

There was an audible sigh. *"C'est magnifique, mademoiselle!"* "Exquisite!"

"Ach," said Ellen, "ye look—bonnie, lass."

I stared at myself in the glass. "Do you know where the brocade for this dress came from, Ellen?"

"Aye. The Duke of Northumberland sent it to ye as a gift."

"And do you know where *he* got it, Ellen?"

She was looking at me, troubled.

"It was part of the estate of the late Duke of Somerset. Rightfully Edward's estate, Ellen! Do you not see anything—ironic—in that?"

I began to laugh. "It is my father-in-law's idea of a jest! It

170

amuses him that I should wear this dress to his son's wedding! Do you know—I think I hate this dress."

I felt Ellen's hands on my shoulders, shaking me, but I could not stop laughing; and then the laughter changed to tears. I leaned against her.

"How shall I bear it, Ellen?—I cannot!"

"Ye can, lass, by God's grace. Ye must!"

Gradually my sobs quieted. I saw that my attendants had discreetly withdrawn, and Ellen set about repairing the damages. I must not lose control again, I told myself.

"Jane! Are you almost ready?"

Katie appeared at the door, glowing, excited. *She is so young,* I thought with a pang, and held out both my hands.

"Yes, my lovely sister. As ready as I shall ever be."

"I am *glad* we are both being wed today. It will be so much easier with you close by. Are you frightened at all, Jane? You seem so calm!"

The hands I clasped were cold. How else could a maid of thirteen—or even sixteen—face marriage, except in fear? All through childhood she was taught to sing, to embroider, to oversee a household, to ride, to converse in foreign languages—but never anything about the relations between a man and a woman. Only last night had Ellen tried to prepare me, and I had turned away, sick with dread.

Now, however, I forced a smile. "God promised He would be with us always, even unto the end of the world. We must not forget that, Katie, whatever happens."

"I do hope everything will go well," she said, nervously going to the window to look down at the courtyard where a huge number of men and horses were assembled. "The Duke of Northumberland has spared no expense redecorating the chapel at Durham House—imported carpets and gold and crimson wall hangings, and jewels incrusting the altar cloths. Everyone says this will be the most splendid wedding London has ever beheld. If only the King were not too ill to attend! Mama and Papa are quite put out. But at least he sent you the jewels."

Yes, the jewels—now set in dazzling prominence on my gown—had been a surprise to us all. But I had been most touched by the accompanying note of regret. I wondered how ill my cousin really was.

"I expect we ought to go down now," said Katie, and we looked at each other, suddenly reluctant to leave the familiarity of the chamber.

"You will come to visit me often?"

"Yes, God willing."

"It has just come over me. How strange it is! After we leave here, Jane, we shall never again be the same. Never!"

Oh, God. What lies ahead for us? Grant that we will know happiness in doing Your will.

I smiled and took her hand. Together we walked down the broad, winding stairway to the grand hall.

The procession from our residence to the chapel on the Strand was not long, but I remember feeling curiously detached from it all, as though I were not a participant but a bystander in the crowds, watching Lady Jane Grey on her way to her wedding. A gaily-dressed troop of musicians led the train, followed by sixteen maids in white carrying garlands upon their shoulders. These symbolized the innocence and purity of the bride, who followed immediately behind. I walked under a canopy of Tudor green and white, escorted on each side by young pages wearing the traditional bridal lace and rosemary on their sleeves. They were attractive youths and took with vast seriousness their responsibility of keeping me from treading on the folds of my gown or stumbling on the flowers tossed continuously in my path. Another group of virgins preceded Katie.

All about was a pandemonium of clanging church bells, the roars and coarse cheering of the crowds that pressed in on all sides. A wedding touched even the poorest hearts with gladness, for free beef and ale would be theirs in abundance for the next three days.

Horsemen in Suffolk livery swore as they beat back the mob spilling onto the path. I looked up as Papa rode by, sitting tall and straight on a handsome stallion, and saw him smile. The knowledge that I had pleased him warmed the coldness that had taken hold of me; when we reached the chapel, I passed through the great, open doors without wavering and walked down the long stone transept toward the man I was to marry.

"What God hath joined together, let no man put asunder. . . ." *Dear God, resign my will to Thine.* "In the sight of all these present, I now declare you to be man and wife. Drink now of the wine of prosperity."

The ceremony was over. The maids broke pieces of the spiced bridal cakes and circulated them among the guests. Guildford drank from a silver goblet, then held the cup to my lips. It was then I saw it: a huge, square-cut ruby on his finger. It was the ring the Protector always used to wear; I had never seen him without it. Sickness washed over me. I could picture Guildford bending over the mutilated body of his father's enemy, forcing the ring over his knuckles. I must have swayed, for suddenly I felt Guildford's breath upon my neck.

"Do not humiliate me. Do not, I tell you! Or you shall be made to regret it!"

Disgust at his touch and cold anger made me straighten, sustained me through the unendurable moments—and hours. The feasting, jousting, and pageantry wore on endlessly through the morning and afternoon and deep into the night. I touched little of the food, and, smiling fixedly, repeated trite, polite phrases whenever called upon. At long last my new husband rose and bid my attendants lead me from the hall.

I went amid a loud chorus of bawdy laughter, my cheeks stained scarlet by the meaningful looks that followed me. Ellen had warned me to expect this, and I knew what to follow: the ritual undressing by my maids, the coarsely given advice, the careful unbraiding of my hair so that there would be no knots, the waiting—in bed—for my groom. And at last he would come, accompanied by his drunken fellows, and then—oh, God help me!—we would be bedded in the sight of all.

But it did not come about like that. It was Ellen who awaited me in my bedchamber—dear, good Ellen—who embraced me and then waved the others off. She had done everything to make my new surroundings less forbidding—a warm fire in the grate, great bouquets of colorful blooms massed everywhere, perfuming the air. The center of the room was dominated by an ancient canopied bed, its counterpane now turned back invitingly. It was this object that riveted my attention. I ran my tongue over my dry lips.

"Ellen—the draperies. Why—?"

"Why green and silver slavered from floor to ceilin'?" she shrugged grimly. "'Twould seem an overfondness for the Tudor colors!"

173

"But a bridal chamber is supposed to be white. This room is for—for royalty!"

"Aye, but dinna' fash yerself, lass. The sheets are white enough, and I'm thinkin' ye'll soon be puttin' other things in yer fine lad's heart!"

I stood numbly as she set about unfastening my gown. "Ye look that weary, lass, I could be wishin' ye'd have a good night's sleep tonight."

"Ellen—I—"

"Nay, ye must not speak it! Not even think it. Ye be wed now. 'Tis no use in looking back."

But I wondered at the way her hands trembled when she lifted the soft muslin nightdress from the bed and slipped it over my shoulders. I sat down so she could brush my hair, and felt comfort in the smooth, even strokes.

"If only—it did not have to be a public spectacle, Ellen. I shall hate everyone gawking at us."

"It will be over soon," she soothed. "Think on that."

There was a sudden rattle at the door, and it swung open. My husband stood there, smiling slightly, but alone. Ellen put the brush down swiftly and curtsied.

"If that's all ye'll be needin' me for, my lady?"

She did not wait for an answer. Indeed, I could not have given her one had my life depended on it. She flung me one last look—full of love and encouragement—and went out. The door shut behind her. I was alone with my husband.

"I—I had not looked for you so soon, my lord."

"Indeed?"

"Your—friends—are not with you. I am glad. It—was thoughtful of you."

He shrugged. "I had little to do with the arrangements, I assure you."

"Oh."

Why was he making it so difficult? I rose now and faced him. "Then I must thank your father. Did the Duke also furnish this bedchamber for us?"

"And if he did? Do the colors not suit you?"

"Oh—yes. I was just surprised." I laughed nervously. "I am, after all, only the fourth heir to the throne—not a princess."

His dark eyes continued to watch me without amusement.

"Have you quite recovered from your faintness, then?"

"Faintness?—Oh, in the chapel. Yes—it was only a turn."

"I thought it might have had something to do with this ring."
He held it up so I could see it better. "You recognized it, did you
not? It belonged to the Duke of Somerset."

I nodded, unable to speak. With fascinated horror I watched
him slip the ring from his finger and hold it out. "Come here, Jane.
I want you to put it on. It is very handsome, really."

Slowly I advanced. He took my hand and impatiently jammed
my finger through the circlet. The ruby was large—and so red—
like blood—Edward's father's blood which had dripped upon the
scaffold that day. Suddenly I could bear it no longer and flung it off.
It hit the wall and bounced to the floor. Then there was silence.

I looked at Guildford's face and saw that it was dark with
anger.

"Never do that again," he said deliberately. *"Never."* He
stepped closer to me, and I was aware of his closeness and the thinness
of my gown. "The Duke of Somerset lies in a bloody grave, and as
far as you are concerned, my Lady Jane, so does his son!"

He laughed harshly as I looked away. "Aye! You are mine
alone now, body and soul! And I shall see that you do not forget it."

His hand reached out and jerked my body, hard, against his.
As his mouth came down on mine, I struggled to get free. I was
sickened and terrified; here was nothing of the gentleness I had
known in Edward's arms. His kiss was savage, full of greed. My
nails dug into his flesh, and he let me go; I slid to the floor.

"So the cat wants taming!" he laughed down at me, his breath
ragged. "There is not a cat alive that cannot be tamed, my pretty,
and I shall enjoy trimming your claws!"

I cowered away from him, sobbing, and he shook his head.
"You need not fear it quite yet, love. Not until my father gives the
word. And if you are quite honest with yourself, I think you will not
find the prospect altogether displeasing!"

He was gone. I did not allow myself to believe it, even after the
silence had continued long. Even after Ellen returned and, shaking
her head worriedly, put me into bed. Still I lay expectant, shud-
dering; nothing she said or did could calm me. But he did not come
back, not that night nor the next. And then the Duke of Northumberland came and told me I was being sent to Chelsea. "For a
rest," he said. So Ellen and myself, and several dozen servants and

attendants, departed from the house on the Strand.

Chelsea Manor had fallen into my father-in-law's hands, like the rest of the Seymour property. It was no longer Lady Catherine's Dower House, the place where she had fled for peace after the death of King Henry. But it seemed to me as I walked through those familiar halls again that I could hear the rippling loveliness of her laughter. I could see Lord Thomas's face, too, fair and strong, like Edward's—alight with the joy of life. Ghosts. Mocking ghosts. A cruel echo of what was forever lost.

I think it was going back to Chelsea that did it. In that house my beloved Lady Catherine had found new meaning for her life with the Lord Admiral. And there was I, married but still not married, separated both from my husband and from the man I loved. My nerves, taut from the strain of the last three weeks, snapped.

20

Guildford's mother was forced to move to Chelsea to take care of me. I felt her contempt for me, her resentment, and my condition worsened. I became convinced that she was trying to poison me, and was seized with unreasoning terror. Every morsel of food had to be tasted before I would eat; candles were placed about my bed at night to keep back the shadows. At each slight sound I awoke, crying out— sometimes for Ellen, sometimes for Lady Catherine.

"Why does she not come, Ellen? If she knew I was ill, she would come."

"Aye, lass. She might. But yer mither's here. Would ye like to see her?"

"Mother?" I frowned.

"Aye, the Duchess sent for her. She's come this hour on the barge from Sheen."

"I do not think—no, I do not want to see her, Ellen. Please do not let her—"

"*Nonsense!* Whatever do you mean, you do not wish to see me?"

Mama swept in with a rustle of silk skirts, followed by a tall, grave-looking man in a physician's frock. She removed her gloves and placed her hand daintily upon my forehead.

"She is feverish. At least she is not feigning illness. But what a bother, Jane. Now, of all times, when you should bear the blush of a happily married woman!" She laughed as I turned my head away.

"How is Papa?"

"Well. Highly displeased with your behavior, I might add."

"And Katie?—Have you heard from Katie?"

She shrugged. "I warrant she will have no complaints until she is truly husbanded. I have Pembroke's word that will be soon." She eyed me sharply. "*Your* marriage was consummated, I trust?"

"No, Mama." The color rose in my cheeks.

"No? I shall not stand for that! This is Northumberland's doing; he shall have to—"

"Mama—I beg of you. Annul my marriage to Guildford."

"Why?"

"I do not have the feelings for him that I should. I do not love him, Mama."

She regarded me incredulously, then began to laugh. "You truly astound me, daughter. Love! Love is for peasants and fools." The amusement faded from her face. "You are a greater fool than I took you for."

"You do not love Papa, do you? You never did."

"Quite right, my dear. Our marriage was arranged, just as yours was. I was looked upon as a very desirable *parti* as the daughter of Charles Brandon and Princess Mary Tudor. Your father was at the time betrothed to Lady Katherine Fitzalan, daughter of the Earl of Arundel. It was even said he 'loved' her.— So much for your love! When he heard my father would accept his suit, he left Katherine. They say she never recovered from the humiliation. We were married shortly after."

"And you wish," I whispered slowly, "to inflict me with the same sort of marriage? God forbid!"

She struck me then and, white-faced, turned to the physician who hovered nearby. "I charge you to see that Lady Dudley recovers her health. Bleed her if you wish. Do whatever you think is required; but you will be answerable to me! Do you understand?"

"Aye, your Grace."

She turned back to me, her expression void of emotion. "You must get well quickly; everything rests upon it. *You cannot disappoint us this time.*"

I did not disappoint her: I recovered, in spite of the physicians and their evil-smelling potions and their lancets. The ghosts gradually receded and left me in peace. Mama and the Duchess of Northumberland also left, following a violent quarrel with each other.

The human spirit is a wonderful thing. Like a reed bruised and trampled under a careless foot, it will yet struggle to right itself and turn green under the healing sun. I wanted to live because I was only sixteen and all of life was ahead. I could not believe God had finished His work with me. He was my Sun, and I would gather strength as I reached toward Him. All things were possible, I thought, even love.

How sad and strange that as life returned to me, it waned within the sick body of my cousin, the King. By the end of June there was little hope that he would recover. He was hemorrhaging, his limbs were swollen and discolored, and his breathing was labored. My heart ached for him, and yet I could not pray that his agony be prolonged. Northumberland would allow no visitors. He dismissed the royal physicians and hired a woman who claimed she could keep the King alive. There were murmurings of ill-play. A tense expectancy engulfed the land.

Who would be King Edward's successor? By the will of King Henry the Eighth, Princess Mary was to follow Edward, and Princess Elizabeth in the event Mary should die without an heir. Next would be Lady Frances Brandon, my mother, and her heirs. Since Mama as yet had no sons, the royal line—for the first time in history—stretched to an almost endless procession of females.

But would Edward comply with his father's will? He was an earnest Protestant; like me he had sat under the zealous teaching of Reform leaders. To elect the Lady Mary now would be to place the movement in great jeopardy.

Moreover, I could not help thinking that Mary's accession would also put my father-in-law in great danger. His persecution of her priests and intolerance of the Mass—even though he was once himself a Catholic—had won her hatred. He could look for no mercy from her as Edward's heir.

To pass over Princess Mary's hereditary right of monarchy, however, would take the approval of the Council, the Parliament, and the people—and was highly unlikely. Mary was the next rightful Queen. That she had been declared illegitimate by her father made no difference; so had her stepsister Elizabeth. And if one were to be declared ineligible, so would the other by the same token. King Edward appeared to have little choice in his successor.

As my health improved, I was required to return to my husband at Durham House. And it was during those early, sultry days in July that I became Guildford's wife in every sense. What can I say of that time, except that it filled me with feelings and desires I had never known existed? Guildford was surprisingly gentle. I drove from my mind all thoughts except my duty to him, and after my initial fear I found myself responding to his passion with a hunger that shocked and appalled me. Was it wrong to have those feelings? Surely not. But long afterward, as Guildford lay sleeping, I wept, and my tears were both of gladness and of sorrow for something lost.

"It is your duty to remain close to your husband," the Duchess of Northumberland announced. "I am resolved you should stay here."

"But I should much prefer to go back to Chelsea. The air is cooler and far more pleasant, and I have resumed my studies—"

"You need concern yourself with studies no longer, my dear. All that is past." She looked around; we were alone in the library except for the Duke who was writing at his desk.

"You do understand that the King is likely to die at any time?"

"Yes." I was angered by the casualness of her tone. "I do."

"Then you must hold yourself in readiness! When it pleases God to call Edward to Himself, you may be summoned—to take his place."

"That is preposterous!" I gasped, careless of Northumberland's presence. "And treasonous as well! I must ask you not to speak so lightly of so grievous a matter as my cousin's death. Heaven knows he does not deserve it—" Tears pricked my eyes, and my voice wavered. "He wanted so very much to be a good King."

"Aye, but he would never have made another King Henry."

"England could not have borne another!" I said, bitterly defensive. "Our late Majesty might have benefited by some of his son's gentleness."

The Duchess's pale eyes watched me carefully.

"Will you not consent to stay here—with Guildford? He, too, has need of your gentleness. It is not womanly to leave him now."

"I have need of this time alone, my lady. Please. I shall be a better wife for it."

"Let her go." Northumberland's command came just as his wife's face clouded with refusal. "Guildford can forgo the pleasures of his bed for a day or two. And we want to keep our daughter content."

Why did his smile always fill me with dread? I had seen him wear that look as he defeated Papa in game after game of chess—as if the outcome were predestined. He was a man in control of himself, but the few times that his control gave way his rage was terrible. It was said no man could stand before him, and certainly no woman. I returned to Chelsea with a sense of having put off, for a time, a fate with which I must one day come to terms.

21

Shortly after midnight I woke up, listening. At first there was nothing but the chirping of grasshoppers and cicadas outside the window. Then I heard again the sound that had broken my slumber—the voices of two women, one overlaid with a heavy Scottish brogue, raised in argument. I smiled drowsily.

"I'll no allow ye to be wakin' the lass over some triflin' matter that can wait till the mornin'!"

"And I tell you I cannot wait! I have an urgent message for your mistress, and if you will not wake her, I shall!" At this the door of my room burst open and I sat up straight.

"Mary? Is that you?"

The face above the wildly flickering candle was hard to distinguish, but I had at least identified the voice as belonging to my sister-in-law, Mary Sidney.

"Aye, it is, Jane. I am frightfully sorry to be disturbing you, but you know Father. He insisted that I fetch you at once, and one does not argue with the Duke of Northumberland."

"But what is it? What is wrong?"

"Nothing, I do assure you!" The reply came too quickly. "You are to come with me, that is all. To Sion House."

"At this hour of the night? Whatever for, Mary?"

"I cannot tell you, really I cannot. All I know is that we have little time; the barge is waiting. I shall call your maid to help you dress."

I stared after her, astonished, as she hurried to the door. *This is madness,* I thought. Reluctantly I crawled out of bed, and splashed

182

water on my face. Mary was already rummaging through my wardrobe.

"Here, Jane, wear this."

"But—that is my best gown!" I watched with dismay as she pulled out a pale blue silk embroidered with silver and flung it over my bed. "Mary, I insist that you tell me what this is about. I shall not stir from Chelsea until you do."

She looked upset.

"I only know that you are to receive something. Something that was ordered for you by the King."

"The *King?*" I was more startled than ever. "What in heaven's name would the King have for *me?* And why should it be necessary to deliver it to me in the middle of the night?"

"I do not know," she cried in exasperation. "What I do know is that if we delay any longer Father will be furious!"

"I am not going," I said, sitting down abruptly.

"*What?*"

"I—I do not think I feel very well, Mary."

"But you were perfectly fit a few moments ago!"

"Yes, well, it has just come over me." It had truly enough. A strange premonition about this midnight summons had made me limp with fear.

She stared at me, then shook her head reluctantly.

"I am afraid that will not do, Jane. It would not satisfy Father. Now come, let me help you with this gown."

All too swiftly I was dressed, and with a hurried farewell to Ellen we went out into the darkness and down the stone flight of steps to the waiting barge. Silently we slipped out into the river. The stars were very close. I remember looking up at them and shivering, although the night was warm.

Our Father, who art in heaven, hallowed be Thy name. I listened to the steady dip of oars as we left Chelsea farther and farther behind. *Thy kingdom come, Thy will be done on earth, as it is in heaven.*

Mary and I lifted our skirts high and stepped onto the wharf landing. I hesitated, looking up at the great stone mass that was Sion House, looming ghostlike in the moonlight. Mary took my hand and pulled me through the portal.

"Is this supposed to be some sort of jest?"

I turned on Mary angrily. We stood alone in the great hall with no one to receive us and nothing to indicate we were expected

183

except countless burning tapers in sconces along the walls. My voice echoed eerily. "You told me Northumberland was waiting! Where is he?"

"I—I do not know! He said he would be here—"

She looked about nervously, staring at the shadows as if she expected him to emerge.

"Well, I am going back to Chelsea. I do not like this place nor do I care for mysteries."

"No, Jane, wait! You must not go. I am certain Father will be here soon. He would never forgive me if he thought I disobeyed him."

She looked so distressed that I relented. "Very well, do stop tearing that handkerchief into shreds. This is probably our esteemed Duke's idea of testing us; I do not pretend to understand the workings of his mind. You must not let him frighten you so, Mary."

She only shrugged and subsided into an unhappy silence. I paced from one family portrait to another, somewhat depressed by the stern, striking features that stared down at me. Guildford's portrait was not yet among them. I wondered if, someday, our own son's likeness would hang here, and if it would differ from the others. I was so much shorter than Guildford, and fairer. . . . Perhaps I would have only daughters, like Mama. If so, I would love them equally.

The gilt French clock above the fireplace chimed loudly. A quarter of an hour . . . half an hour passed. The tension within me grew. It was absurd to wait any longer.

But just as I turned to go I stiffened, listening.

Mary flew to my side like a bird seeking protection. The clatter of horses and riders shattered the midnight air.

"He has come!" she exclaimed.

Yes, but who were those with him? There was something wrong—very wrong. I felt a coldness take possession of me. I wanted to run, but stood rooted where I was.

The oak doors of the great hall were flung open. Northumberland advanced, splendidly arrayed in black velvet and satin. Behind him I identified various other members of the Privy Council—the Earl of Arundel, Huntingdon, Lord Pembroke—nearly all must be there, I thought dazedly.

Before I could voice my bewilderment I was shocked even

further. The body of men before me were removing their hats, and with a rattle of swords dropped down upon one knee. They were *bowing*—to *me!*

"My lords—*Please!* What does this mean?"

No one answered. Northumberland alone rose and stepped closer. I saw the triumph glittering in his eyes.

"If Your Grace pleases, these noble lords and I shall escort you to the Chamber of State."

Without waiting for my consent, his hand closed firmly on my arm. A shudder ran through me, but I was powerless to pull away. In a trance I moved with him through the adjoining doors.

And there, sinking low in homage as they saw me, were Mama and Papa, the Duchess of Northumberland, my husband, Guildford. The Duke led me past them all to a small dais under a velvet canopy, reserved for royalty.

Dismay loosened my tongue at last. "This place is for His Majesty! You mock me, sir!"

A whisper rippled through the assembly. I looked wildly from Papa to Guildford, back to Northumberland. "What is the matter? Why—why does everyone stare at me so strangely?"

"The King is dead, my lady."

Dead?—Edward?

I gave a little cry that was half moan, half sob. He could not be dead. We had played together. . . .

"God delivered his virtuous soul from a body of pain," Northumberland continued unctuously, insistently. "It was a mercy."

A mercy to die so horribly, so young?

"When—did it happen?"

There was another silence; the Councillors shifted their gaze.

"It was—three days ago, my lady," the Earl of Pembroke admitted finally. "The Council did not want it made known until certain—legal difficulties—concerning the succession were settled."

"But *three days!*" I was astounded. "Was there not already a Statute of Succession passed by Parliament?"

"It was altered," Northumberland cut in. "King Edward instructed me to draw up a new devise some time before his death. It was signed before all who are present. And it was His Majesty's will and pleasure, my lady, to appoint you—his cousin—heiress to the Crown."

"No. . . . *no!*" I buried my face in my hands and burst into tears.

"The Crown is not my right! Princess Mary is the rightful heir!"

Blackness spun through my brain, dizzying, overpowering . . . I clutched blindly for some support and then slipped heavily to the floor.

How long I lay thus I do not know. When I opened my eyes once more, it seemed to me that no one in the room had stirred. There was a deathly quiet.

Dear God, what shall I say? They are waiting for me to accept the Crown, and I cannot. I *cannot!*

And then I heard the words as distinctly as if they had been spoken aloud, the words given long ago to another young girl, Queen Esther: *"Who knoweth whether thou art come to the kingdom for such a time as this?"* Was this God's answer?

All of my life I had studied under the finest tutors in the realm—Aylmer, Coverdale, Catherine Parr—absorbing their great knowledge. I had corresponded with European Reformers and seen the growth of the Protestant movement in England under King Edward and Protector Somerset. Had it all been a preparation for—this? And if it was given to me to offer myself to God's service, had I the right to refuse?

Surrender broke at last through my grief and confusion; I looked up to meet the still-watchful eyes of my family and the Councillors, and got slowly to my feet.

"If it is indeed my duty and right to succeed to the throne," I said steadily, "then God grant me the wisdom to govern this realm to His glory. His sovereign will be done."

There was an audible murmur of relief and approval.

"Aye, God's will be done! *Long live Queen Jane!*"

The lords parted to allow my mother and the Duchess to escort me from the Chamber of State. I was then taken to an elegantly appointed bedchamber and told that I must take what rest I could. It was already close to dawn of the morning of July tenth. On this day, the year of our Lord 1553, King Edward VI would be proclaimed dead . . . and I, Jane, the Queen.

I did not think it would be possible to sleep. But I must have been more tired than I felt, for it seemed only seconds after I closed my eyes that I was awakened; someone had drawn the heavy curtains from my window and I could see the sun streaking the sky.

"Your Highness slept well. I'm glad for it."

The voice was unfamiliar, and so was the chamber. I looked about me, bewildered, and then the memory of the night's events returned. *She is talking to me! I am the Queen!*

A maidservant who appeared not much older than I set a heavily burdened breakfast tray in front of me with a giggle.

"Beggin' my lady's pardon, but you look so surprised like."

I smiled. "I expect I do. I have not been a Queen for very long, you know. It takes a bit of getting used to."

"Aye. Will Your Highness be needin' anything else, then?" She had slipped back into the role of respectful servant; I felt disappointed.

"No—ah, yes. I really do not think I can manage any of this food. You had better take it back with you. And—if my mother has risen, please tell her I should like to see her."

"Aye, mum. The Duchess said I was to let her know just as soon as you'd eaten." The mask slipped once again. "She's been up all night, she and all them lords! Haven't given us servants a minute to breathe downstairs! But we wish you well, my lady."

I was moved. "Thank you."

She dimpled and then, as if frightened by her temerity, bobbed a curtsy and fled. A few moments later Mama swept in with a fluttering retinue of gentlewomen.

"Come, daughter, there is no time to dally in bed! We have a multitude of things to see to before the procession."

Why could she not see, this once, how desperately I needed her smile, her reassurance?

"Procession?" I echoed.

"Of course! The people of London must be introduced to their Queen. They will expect her to look like one." She gestured to a lady-in-waiting. "Here is the gown you will wear. It had to be finished without the usual fittings, but I think it will do."

It was exquisite. I held my breath and fingered the material, a dark green brocade. The waist came to a fashionable point in front with an undergown and turned-back sleeves of silk, studded with countless precious stones—diamonds, emeralds, rubies, and pearls. There was a froth of white lace at the collar and wrist. *White and green*, I thought, *the colors of a Tudor monarch.* . . .

187

Mama signaled the women to remove my nightdress. I winced as their eyes passed over my flesh, wasted by my recent illness. "Mama, please send for Ellen. She should be here."

"Nonsense. As the Queen you will grow used to being attended by strangers."

"All the same," I insisted firmly, "I should like Ellen to attend me as well."

"Oh—as you wish!" she snapped.

The ladies finished lacing and buttoning the bone stays and drew the gown carefully over my head. It fitted snugly.

"Now bring the diamond pendant. And the hood. Quickly!" As they fitted me with the French hood—also of Tudor green, banded with jewels to match those on the gown—I began to realize the preparation that had been made for this day. How long ago, I wondered, did the seamstress begin work on this dress?

One by one the ladies-in-waiting stepped back to admire and exclaim.

"Your Majesty, you must see yourself in the glass!" they urged. Mama frowned, but she did not object as they led me to another room; perhaps she guessed my lack of self-assurance.

"But this does not look like me at all!" I laughed uneasily, shaking my head. "Tell me, Mama. Do I look like a queen?" *Do I please you, Mama? Will the people accept me?* I looked anxiously at her face for approval and was stunned by the expression of bitterness I found there.

"The Crown belongs to me—*me!* I am the daughter of Mary, Queen of France, sister to Henry the Eighth! If Edward chose to disinherit his sisters, Mary and Elizabeth, the right to succeed is *mine!*"

"Then—why did Edward not make you his heir? Why did you accept the devise, Mama?"

"Do you think I had any choice?" she hissed. "Northumberland convinced the King I would waive my right in favor of you and your male issue! That way the Duke knew he could control you through his son. I had to agree. Your father made me see it was the only way for any of us to come to power!"

"I see." *Edward, Edward, what a strait you have put me in!* "What do you want me to do, Mama?"

"Nothing. You are Queen Regnant. Let it remain so. *But do not forget as long as you live to whom you owe that privilege!*"

"I shall not." She suffered me to take her hands. "I shall always remember, I promise you, Mama."

"Let us go, then. Only one last word. Northumberland is your Chief Councillor and will do all that he can to bend you to his will. But you have the power to resist, if you use it wisely. He is still your subject."

I was grateful for her advice and straightened myself proudly as we descended together to the Great Hall. Everyone seemed to be assembled; the busy murmur of voices hushed as we entered, and every eye turned in my direction.

Guildford was the first to reach my side, a wide smile spreading across his handsome features. Then Northumberland took my hand and touched it to his lips.

"Very impressive, my dear," he said softly.

"I am glad you approve, my lord."

"You will please the people. That is what is important. But you are much too short to be seen above the crowds."

A nervous titter escaped me before I could suppress it. He frowned. "I am afraid that little can be done about my brevity, my lord!— Unless I can be set upon a horse!"

"Fit Her Majesty with clogs, three inches in height," he commanded a gentleman near him. "Then escort her to the royal barge. We are to leave for the Tower immediately."

I shall never forget our progress on the river Thames that day. Indeed, what girl of sixteen, presented for the first time to her people as their Queen, would ever forget? It should have been the supreme moment of my life. I had already been proclaimed throughout the city, and the riverbanks were thronged with a colorful pageant of tradesmen, householders, children, slaves. . . . My heart was touched by the destitution I saw, just as it had been six years before when Lady Catherine and I made our way to Hampton Court. How long ago that day seemed. Now I was no longer a child, nor was I without power. I was free to ease some of the misery of the people about me. I would never be accused of indifference.

But there was something wrong. Even as my love expanded and strengthened within me, I saw no answering love displayed from the shores of the river. There were no warm cries of welcome, no "God save the Queen!" on every tongue. I smiled determinedly, lifting my hand, but a feeling of dismay clawed at my heart.

"Papa!" I whispered to my father, standing close by, "What is it? Why do they not cheer?"

"It is nothing; do not let their silence frighten you. They but grieve for King Edward."

The barge drew alongside the Tower wharf. Northumberland jumped off and offered me his hand. I took it, feeling awkward and self-conscious in my high clogs. Even now the people watched impassively as we started toward the gate. How I longed for a reaction! Any reaction.

Mama herself insisted on bearing my train. I blushed with humiliation, and then was even more chagrined as Guildford took the lead a few feet in front of me, stopping every several paces to bow abjectly. If only they would let me appear naturally to the people, without all this affectation and display. Perhaps then they would receive me more willingly.

But the faces, as I passed close by, were not all hostile. There were even some smiles and shy curtsies, and I began to breathe more freely. *Perhaps they are just waiting to see what kind of monarch I shall be. Well, I shall not disappoint them. With God's help we shall have a kingdom that no man shall lament.*

A volley of cannon saluted my arrival inside the gate. Sir John Bridges, the Lieutenant of the Tower, and the Yeomen of the Guard stood at attention in their colorful scarlet and gold dress. The Marquess of Winchester, Lord Treasurer, then dropped to one knee and offered me the Tower keys. I hesitated only for an instant, but it was long enough for my father-in-law to step forward and take the keys from Winchester so that he could present them to me himself. There was a small gasp of surprise from everyone about us. Guildford took my arm, and we proceeded up the small rise, past the Green and the church of St. Peter-ad-Vincula, to the White Tower. I entered the cool stone keep with relief. There would be a few hours, at least, before I would be called upon for any official act. I had smiled until my face ached, and I longed to be rid of some of the heavy outer clothing that had become hotter by the moment under the July sun. If only all these courtiers, pages, noblemen, councillors, and ladies-in-waiting would give me space to grow used to my new home! *Home.* A strange word to apply to this

190

imposing fortress whose walls in some parts were fifteen feet thick. Not at all the sort of place I had imagined for myself as a bride. But I was determined not to think of these things; my stay at the Tower need not be long. After the traditional few weeks I could go to whichever London palace I chose.

The state rooms on the upper floors had been prepared for me; I was surprised at the brightness and the large proportions of the rooms. Great vases of roses and gladioli stood on tables, the floors were strewn with fresh rushes, and handsome tapestries ornamented the walls. I wished that Guildford had not chosen to remain below with the Privy Council; it would have been pleasant to investigate our new quarters together. Rather shyly I peered into the royal bedchamber. There was a sudden rustle of skirts, and I turned.

"Ellen!—Oh, *Ellen!*"

She had dropped into a deep curtsy before me, her plain, weathered face alight with pride. "Your Majesty," she said simply.

I ran and put my arms around her. "I am so glad you are here, Ellen! So much has happened. The King—!"

"Aye, I know." She said nothing for a moment, sharing my grief over Edward's death. "'Twas shocking sudden."

The others had withdrawn; at last I could ask the question that weighed most heavily on my heart without risk of reproach or deception.

"Ellen, was I right?—Tell me. Was it right to accept Edward's crown?"

I believe if there had been any hesitation in her reply, even at that moment I might have turned back. But her words, like her eyes, were firm and steady.

"It was the King's own will that you should take his place. Aye, I ken well ye fear yer father-in-law had more to do with it than was proper. But 'twas the King who put his hand to the plan, because he believed in ye. He believed God could use ye more than his own two sisters.

"Aye, lass, ye did right. Lady Catherine would have been proud of ye this day!"

And, listening to her words, I put all doubts out of my mind.

I was to learn much later that the Council feared Mary's rebellion against King Edward's devise from the very beginning. It was decided amongst themselves not to inform her of Edward's death until she was rendered incapable of doing anything about it. To put it in other terms, she was to be taken and confined until my accession was assured.

Ah, Mary. If only I had known something of Northumberland's diabolical scheme! I might have done something to prevent it. But, guessing the sympathy between us, he kept me in ignorance until it was too late.

On July the seventh, when the news of King Edward's death was as yet unknown, a message was sent to the Princess Mary requesting her to come to Hampton Court at once, as her brother was gravely ill; he had asked to see her one more time.

Mary, of course, was touched. She set off immediately from. Hunsdon, perhaps hoping for a reconciliation with her long-estranged brother. Their religious differences had set them apart, but she had always hoped for a closer relationship with him. This hope was to be cruelly dashed.

Part way to Greenwich she was stopped by a messenger from Sir Nicholas Throckmorton. Horsemen lay in wait to take her captive, he warned. She was riding into a trap; her brother was already dead. Her only course was to flee for safety.

Mary was thrown into a quandary. Should she believe this messenger, who might be in Northumberland's employ? If her brother was not truly dead and she proclaimed herself Queen, she would be liable for treason. But if the message was indeed from Sir Nicholas, she was in great danger. She decided to take his word, and stayed the night in the home of a Master Huddleston, near Cambridge.

Early the next morning she disguised herself as a market woman and set off again. At the top of a small rise she stopped and turned to look back at where she had spent the night. The house was on fire, lighted by Protestants from nearby Cambridge. Those who were with her say a change came over her then—a stiffening of determination that was never to leave her during all of the days of struggle ahead. "Let it blaze!" she said. "I will build Huddleston a better!"

At Kenninghall she rested and wrote a letter to the Privy Council offering a free pardon for their actions if they would acknowledge her as their Queen. In answer they sent messengers to every part of the realm proclaiming me, Lady Jane Grey, Queen Regnant of England and Ireland.

On the evening of the tenth I took my place under the royal canopy of the Presence Chamber, and Winchester brought me the crown jewels. I was alone except for my attendants and Guildford. The other lords had withdrawn to discuss the next move against Mary. I stared at the jewels like one mesmerized, fearful of touching them.

"Your Majesty may try the crown," urged the Lord Treasurer, "to see how it fits."

I shook my head. The huge Black Prince's ruby and the sapphire of Edward the Confessor winked at me like great, knowing eyes. *What right have you*, they seemed to ask, *an untried maid of sixteen, to wear this sacred symbol of the realm? How dare you represent yourself as God's anointed?*

"It—it is much too large, my lord, and too heavy. King Edward fainted under the weight; I know I should."

"Nevertheless, it is the weight all of our sovereign majesties have borne, by God's grace." Still I hesitated, and the Marquess impatiently lifted the crown from its velvet-lined case and placed it on my head. "If Your Majesty will permit me—? The coronation will take place in two weeks; we must have everything prepared." I closed my eyes, trembling, as the full weight of the headpiece sank around my brow. I could feel my husband's eyes upon me and I knew even without looking at him that he was smiling.

"Very good," murmured Winchester. "Our late liege lord was of slight frame, also. I will, of course, have another crown made for Your Majesty's husband."

"My husband?" I looked across at Guildford; he was still smiling. "I know nothing of this."

The Marquess looked embarrassed. "If Your Grace does not require me any longer, perhaps—?"

"Yes. You may go. All of you." I gestured to my attendants. "And take the crown away, also, my lord."

He withdrew, leaving the caskets heaped with masses of gold chains and pendants, bracelets, diamond and emerald necklaces. Guildford waited until everyone was gone and then picked up a necklace with deliberation. "Emeralds. They become you, my love. I remember the night we met you were wearing an emerald."

"Guildford, what does he mean by your crown?"

"Why, the crown you are to present me at Westminster Abbey, love. To make me the King."

"*King?*" I choked on the word. "That is impossible, Guildford! You know that!"

He dropped the necklace into the box and turned to face me. He was no longer smiling. His dark, handsome face was flushed.

"Nothing is impossible to the Queen."

"But it would take an act of Parliament!"

"Then you will persuade the Parliament. Father made you the Queen; he can as easily unmake you if you do not do as you are told."

I caught my breath. "Are you threatening me?"

"You are mine. I will say whatever I wish. Are you not bound to submit to me in all things?"

"We are *both* bound to submit to the laws of the realm, Guildford! I beg of you to be reasonable. I can make you a Duke, if you wish it, but more than that I cannot do."

"I will be King!" he shouted. "*King! Do you hear me?*"

The door crashed behind him. Mrs. Tylney must have been waiting just outside for she hurried in. I sat white-faced, clutching the arms of my chair.

"Does my lady have need of—some salts perhaps?" She regarded me anxiously.

"I should like you to tell Lord Pembroke—and Lord Arundel—that I should like to see them at once, Mrs. Tylney."

While she was gone, I tried to gather my wits about me. How could I dissuade Guildford from this mad scheme? That it was Northumberland's suggestion I had no doubt; I remembered my mother's warning and determined not to let him have his way.

At the same moment that Lords Pembroke and Arundel made their entrance, bowing, the Duchess of Northumberland swept in on her son's arm.

"What mean you by this contempt for your husband, madam?" she demanded without preamble.

"And what mean you by this show of discourtesy for your sovereign!"

I returned her look coolly. With her teeth gritted in rage, she sank into a low curtsy and waited for recognition.

"My lord husband. My lady. I have sent for these my Councillors to make my wishes known to all. There seems to be a misunderstanding. It is not, and never shall be, my will to act on so grave a matter as my husband's coronation without the consent of the people by act of Parliament. It is not my intent to begin my reign by taking on powers that are not mine."

There was an astonished silence. Then— "You ungrateful little chit!" my mother-in-law hissed.

"Did I not tell you, Mama?"

"You will not stay here to be used so cheaply, Guildford. It is a sad day indeed when a wife knows not where her duty lies!"

"Where are you going?"

"To the wharves, madam! To take barge to Sion House."

"No!"

"We shall. And mind you how it will look to the commons when your husband no longer even shares the same habitation!"

With a triumphant nod she lifted her skirts and sailed from the room, Guildford close on her heels.

"My lords!" My voice sounded abnormally loud in the Presence Chamber. Arundel and Pembroke refused to look directly at me; my chin lifted.

"Lord Guildford must not leave the Tower. Whether or not he—chooses to share my bed, as before, his place is by my side. I suggest you make no delay, gentlemen. *Fetch him back!*"

The Duchess and Guildford returned, as of course they had to. But it was a bitter victory. Guildford chose not to forsake my bed, but to avenge himself in the only way that he could. When he took me that night it was with intentional cruelty, and when I cried out he laughed. I shall never forget that laughter. As I lay awake in the dark hours before dawn, I heard its echo, and knew with that sound the passing forever of the light-hearted maid called Jane Grey.

On Sunday morning Master Ridley preached a sermon on my behalf at St. Paul's. I was pleased to think that so eminent a man in Reformed circles would choose to support me, but not pleased that he should denounce Mary and Elizabeth as bastards in the same breath.

"But 'tis law, by Henry the Eighth," Ellen asserted. "Ye shouldna' fash yerself over what is simple truth."

"It is not necessary to humiliate them! My claim for the throne is based solely on King Edward's devise, but the people still love Elizabeth and Mary. I am a stranger to them. It does not seem right or wise to stir the people's anger."

We both fell silent, thinking of the incident on the day when heralds had proclaimed my accession. One in the crowd had shouted, "Lady Mary has the better title!" and for his boldness had been pilloried by his master. Later his ears were cut off.

"If only I could win their trust, and their love, without such violence."

"'Tis not you the people hate, lass! 'Tis the Duke of Northumberland—the 'Bear o' Warwick' they call him. He's never cared tuppence for the commons, and they know it well."

"They fear I shall be his pawn," I murmured. "I must prove that I am strong enough to rule in my own right."

Sir John Cheke, King Edward's former tutor and now one of the Privy Councillors, asked permission that moment to see me.

"You have news, Sir John. I can tell by your frown that it is not good."

"You are right, Majesty. The Council just received Princess Mary's reply to their demand for surrender." His eyes met mine steadily. "She refused."

"She is a brave woman."

"Brave, or merely stubborn, like her father." He shrugged, drawing his hand over his ragged, dark beard. "Perhaps in the end it is the same. But she has reached Framlingham Castle in safety and will no doubt remain there, with her standard raised defiantly over her fortress, until we come to fetch her."

"Why do you suppose she chose Framlingham, Sir John?"

"Because it is best suited for defense. The walls are forty feet high, eight feet thick, and in good repair. The castle stands on a high mound, with a triple moat about it and in excellent view of the coast. If she decides on an escape by sea, she will be able to sight any approaching ships."

"She chose shrewdly," I said. "Oh, Mary! If only we could live together in peace."

"There is not room for two Queens in England, Your Grace."

"Then she has proclaimed herself?"

"Yes. And she has called for an army to defend her title."

Then peace was not possible. What had I done? I did not wish to make war against my cousin, my friend.

"What do you advise me to do, Sir John?"

"The Council has already acted in Your Grace's behalf. Lord Robert Dudley and his brother are advancing on Framlingham this moment with a party of horsemen."

I shrugged, feeling helpless. "Then it is out of my hands."

"As long as it is in God's hands, my lady, we need not fear." His voice was kind.

"Yes. You are right, of course. I shall pray for His will. Thank you, Sir John—for reminding me."

I found myself often in prayer in the days that followed. I tried to keep busy, ordering yards of velvet and fine Holland cloth from the Master of the Wardrobe, planning for the coronation robes and the new gowns I would need. But since I was excluded from all Council business, the news I received was secondhand, and I was never certain of how much I was being told. It made me frustrated and tense. From time to time Papa came with papers for me to sign, and I would question him eagerly.

"Do you not think I should receive the foreign ambassadors, Papa?"

"No. Time enough when you are crowned."

"But are you sure they do not favor the Lady Mary? She is in close touch with the Emperor Charles—"

"Renard and de Scheyve arrived only a few weeks ago from Spain. They will give us no trouble. Nor will de Noailles of France.

They are cautious. They wish only to establish a friendly relationship with England's new monarch."

"Papa, if only there was something I could do!"

He smiled and patted my hand. "Everything is being done, my dear. That is what your ministers are for."

"I am quite sure Mary does not let others do her thinking for her! What if the people choose to support her, Papa, instead of me?"

"They will not," he said with conviction, "of that I am certain. They fear Mary's fanaticism for the Catholic religion and the possibility of her marriage to a foreign prince. England would become a vassal of France or Spain by such a marriage."

"And I am 'safely' married to Guildford Dudley," I said, not without bitterness. "How safe is that, Papa? If I—by some chance—should die, Northumberland's son would reign as King."

He looked startled. "That cannot happen. I swear to you, Jane. As long as I live I will let nothing happen to you."

That night as we sat at dinner a message arrived from Lord Robert Dudley. Their attack had failed. Mary's army now numbered over ten thousand.

The Duchess burst into frightened sobs; the rest of us sat in shocked silence. After a moment Mama spoke.

"What do you propose we do now, my lord Duke?"

"We arm," he replied tersely. "We fortify the Tower with adequate men and artillery for defense. And we attack. Time is crucial. We cannot dally here while Mary gathers more troops."

I shook my head, troubled. "I do not understand why they are rising for her." I turned to the young soldier who had brought the message. "Can you tell me?"

"Aye, Your Majesty, that I can! We heard naught else as we rode through the country but that the Lady Mary promises to make no changes in the religion or laws of the land if she be Queen. 'Tis won many a wavering Protestant to her, to my mind."

"Promises!" spat Northumberland. "She would swear to anything to win them, and have them all saying their rosaries within a fortnight!"

I rose; the others scrambled hastily to their feet. "The Lady Mary is an honest woman, my lord, and clever. I do not fault her for fighting for what she believes to be hers. If we hope for success in our design, we must employ her cleverness and practice honesty with each other. I leave you to your work, gentlemen."

All through the night I lay at Guildford's side and listened to the rumbling of carts, bearing their loads of soldiers and firearms through the Tower gates. We would be well garrisoned, but what of the army that we would need to raise against Mary? Northumberland was right; our hope lay in a quick offensive.

Another thought occurred to me as I reviewed the situation. The Duke of Northumberland would be required to take command of our troops; he was the logical person. That would leave me free of his presence at the Tower. At last! I could truly be in authority without his overbearing influence upon the Council. The people of London would see that I could act as Queen.

The next day was spent in busy preparation. Proclamations of my accession were reissued throughout the kingdom, and an ambassador was sent to Charles V to encourage his support. At length the Council members came for my signature on the commissions; I scanned the list rapidly. Lord Huntingdon, Warwick, Sir John Gates, Northampton. . . . But there was Papa's name—the Duke of Suffolk!

"There has been some mistake, my lords. My father's name is here."

"It is no mistake." Papa stepped forward. "I am to take command."

"But that is impossible! I need you here, Papa. The Duke of Northumberland is quite capable of leading our men."

There were mutters of impatience. "Your Grace, we have discussed the matter at length. The Duke has elected to remain here to govern the Council."

"Your ladyship's father has much influence over the commons," said another. "Northumberland, if the truth be told, lacks somewhat in popular esteem."

I looked about uncertainly at the faces of my Privy Councillors. Who among these stern men could truly be trusted for their loyalty to me? What they said was true, but I could not bear the thought of being left wholly to Northumberland's devices without Papa near. He was the only familiar rock left in a heaving sea. I could depend on him, if no one else.

Slowly I laid the quill upon the list of commissions, unsigned.

"You will please tell my lord Duke that I will not consent to Suffolk's going."

"Jane!"

"Northumberland shall command our army. It is my wish that my father tarry here, with me."

There was a stunned silence. My refusal had evidently not been foreseen. Then, one by one, they left me—Papa last of all. I would not meet his eyes.

Had I made a mistake? Perhaps if I had more fully understood the danger of my position I would have been more hesitant in letting Northumberland go. He and Papa were aware, as I was not, that the Council was unstable, that only the Duke's terrifying personality kept them in hand. I should have been warned when, later that day, two of their number left to join Mary's forces: Sir Edward Hastings and Edmund Peckham, Cofferer to the Household. But I think I would still have deliberately ignored my danger, so great was my fear of Northumberland.

Reports came in from Cheshire, Norfolk, and Devonshire that both peasantry and nobles were rising for Mary. My father-in-law, who had resisted my decision to keep Papa at the Tower, was now forced to accept his commission. He made up his mind to leave at once to rally the counties that were still undecided. But before going he held a great banquet for the Council.

It was a strategic move. He wished to communicate his last warnings and instructions in an atmosphere that was half-comradely and half-threatening. I was not invited to that gathering, but I know what went on from the glowing descriptions given by Guildford. He doted on his father, so I believe I can say every word of his account was accurate.

I can see him standing there so clearly, the proud and powerful Duke encircled by four tall sons, his black eyes sweeping the company of his guests. His eyes held both a challenge and a command, lingering on each face until he was satisfied with what he saw. He waited until the last conversation died away, and then his voice rang out, sovereign and unchallenged.

"My lords! I and our noble company are prepared to hazard our lives for your benefit, as well as for the life of the Queen. We commit our wives and children to your loyalty, without fear that through malice, conspiracy, or dissension you might leave us—your friends—in the briars and betray us! For God would not count you innocent of our blood, nor free you of the sacred oath of allegiance which you *each made to our Queen—who was crowned by your and our enticement, rather than by her own seeking and request.*

"I speak not in distrust; only to remind you that if you mean deceit, *God will revenge it!* I will say no more."

There was a swift murmur of indignation and one rose to protest.

"Your lordship is deceived if you distrust us. Which of us here can wash our hands clean of this matter?"

Northumberland only turned and stared until the younger Councillor's gaze dropped.

"I pray God that it is so. In a few days I will bring back the Lady Mary, like the rebel that she is."

After the dinner my father-in-law came to me in the Presence Chamber and knelt to receive his commission formally.

It was the last time I ever saw him.

Early on the morning of July the fourteenth Northumberland took a barge to Durham House to muster his forces. Our army would consist of three thousand foot soldiers and two thousand on horseback until it could gather strength from adjoining counties. It was a fine, clear day—a good omen, everyone said. But though crowds gathered to see the Duke mounted on his steed, his scarlet cloak flowing boldly around him, there were none to cheer him on his way.

Guildford returned and told me about it, his mouth twisted with bitterness. "I saw him speak to your uncle, Lord Grey. 'Do you see,' he said, 'all who have come to see us march? And not one who will wish us Godspeed!'"

"Your father is a brilliant soldier, Guildford. The people respect him for that."

"Respect! The peasants know not what the word means! They are ruled by their fancies. They hate him."

"Then perhaps they have cause." It was only a murmur, but he heard me.

"You hate him, too! Is that why you sent him out there—to be killed? Sometimes I think you want us all ruined."

"I want God's will to be done, Guildford. More than anything I want that."

"King Edward appointed you his successor. Is that not enough?"

"It was, at first. Now I am not so certain."

He looked disgusted. "My father is at this moment risking his life for you. It would become you to display a little more confidence."

"I owe your father *nothing*, Guildford. He has brought me nothing but unhappiness. I would thank God if I never saw his face again!"

He left me, pale with rage. I sent for Sir John Cheke and began giving him instructions. For the first time I took upon me the business of my office.

It was well that I had it to keep myself occupied. There was little news after Northumberland's departure, and the Council was already showing signs of restlessness. I wrote to Master Ridley and requested that his next sermon at St. Paul's be preached with greater attention to the Scriptures and less to the Lady Mary. The less said about her the better. I also wrote to the Duke of Norfolk, imprisoned ever since Edward's reign, and promised to reinstate him as Earl Marshal if he would pledge me his loyalty.

Perhaps I obtained greatest satisfaction from the discharging of an old debt. Sir William Sharington, the man who had helped to send the Lord Admiral to his death, was still Sheriff of Wiltshire. I dismissed him from his office and appointed another to take his place.

On the evening of the fifteenth we were shaken by the report that many of our army had deserted. Northumberland, now in Cambridge, sent to the Council for reinforcements.

That night I prayed long in the little chapel of St. John the Evangelist. I loved the tall, vaulted ceiling, the stark columns that spoke of the solidarity of hundreds of years. There was a simplicity there, a peacefulness that eluded me in the elaborate chambers of state.

Give ear to my prayer, O God; and hide not Thyself from my supplication. . . . My heart is sore pained within me: and the terrors of death are fallen upon me. . . . And I said, Oh that I had wings like a dove! For then would I fly away, and be at rest. Lo, then would I wander far off, and remain in the wilderness. I would hasten my escape from the windy storm and tempest. . . . Evening, and morning, and at noon, will I pray, and cry aloud: and he shall hear my voice. He hath delivered my soul in peace from the battle that was against me: for there were many with me. . . . Cast thy burden upon the Lord, and he shall sustain thee; He shall never suffer the righteous to be moved.

The words of David's psalm brought healing to my troubled spirit. I knew that whatever the outcome of the battle now waged against me, God had already "delivered my soul in peace."

Another day passed, hot, rainless. Papa came to me, his face drawn and unhappy.

"The eight ships we sent to lie off Yarmouth, to prevent Mary's escape, have surrendered."

"Surrendered?" I could only echo him blankly.

"Aye, without a struggle! It does not fare well for us, daughter."

"I see. What says the Council?"

He shrugged. "They say little. Too little. I distrust their look."

"But they cannot desert us, Papa. They have said themselves they have gone too far!"

"Perhaps." But I could tell that he said it only to comfort me. That night Lord Treasurer Winchester and Lord Pembroke attempted to leave the Tower under cover of darkness. The Yeomen Warders alerted me, and I sent soldiers after them.

"Hereafter the gates will be locked and the keys brought to me every evening. Is that understood?"

"Aye, madam."

Wearily I turned to Ellen after they were gone. "So it has come to this. Our friends have become our prisoners."

"Ye mustna' say that, lass! The pair o' them are cowards, not fit to bide here. Let them go, and good riddance!"

"But my sister is married to Pembroke's son. If I cannot trust him, whom can I trust? Oh, Ellen." I leaned against her, seeking the warmth of her nearness. "Everything is so confused. If the other members of the Council want to leave, I cannot hold them with lock and key."

"Now, lass, this worryin' does ye no good. Yer father and husband will hold the Privy Council together, without ye wearin' yerself thin over it."

Father—Guildford? I wanted to laugh, but something caught in my throat. My dear husband was too concerned over niceties due his rank to worry about the problems of an unstable crown. Only today he had had another argument with the Council over his title. He would be called "Your Grace," he insisted; he would be treated with more respect, and he would dine alone, in state. He obviously still cherished the idea that he would be King. And Papa—well,

Papa was only one man, and not a forceful one.

But time was running out for us all. Northumberland sent another frantic note for fresh troops, to which the Council delayed reply. Word came that Oxford had proclaimed Mary. There was a warrant promising one hundred pounds to any yeoman, five hundred pounds to any gentleman, and a thousand pounds in land to any nobleman who could bring Northumberland in a prisoner to "Queen Mary."

"It was a mistake to send him out there. I knew it!"

Mama, who had said little to me these past few days and kept to her own chambers, now divided her anger equally between Papa and me. "You are a fool, Henry! If they take him, we are lost."

"The Council has decided to respond to his request for troops. Pembroke and Arundel will leave with men at first light."

"*Pembroke!* Papa, he tried to desert us! You cannot put the men in his charge!"

"He has as much to lose as we do. You forget; he is related to us by marriage."

"Please do not trust him, Papa."

"I forbid you to listen to anything else she says, Henry! We are in this trouble because you did not go in the first place. Arundel and Pembroke will serve as well as any of the others."

Her words proved ironically true. The lords of the Privy Council approached me on the following morning, the eighteenth, with the request to make a special visit to the French ambassador, de Noailles. Their purpose was to enlist his aid and support, they said, since it did not appear that our cause would be won as quickly as hoped. Foolishly, I gave my consent.

Cecil, Paget, Winchester, Arundel, Pembroke—they all went, and they did not return. I learned later that they met first at Baynard's Castle to pass a resolution in favor of Mary. Then they sent off a demand for Northumberland's surrender. The bells began to ring all over London. Mary was proclaimed in the streets.

I heard the bells from where I sat under my royal canopy. I was in the Presence Chamber, I remember, awaiting one of the guardsmen's wives who had asked me to stand as the godmother of her child. The child was named after me.

"Papa, is something wrong?"

He was standing at the door, not moving, just staring at me as though in a trance.

"The bells are ringing. Do you hear them ring, Jane?"

"Yes, I do. Papa, *please!* Tell me what has happened!"

He came nearer, and I saw there were tears on his cheeks. I had never seen Papa cry before.

Slowly he reached for the green velvet canopy above my head. There was a tearing sound and the draperies dropped to the floor.

"It is over," he said. "You must put off your royal robes and be content with a private life."

"Oh, Papa!"

I flung my arms around his neck. A great tide of relief washed over me and then ebbed, leaving me clean.

"I put them off much more willingly than I put them on!" I said at last. "I have erred. I have confused obedience to the will of God with obedience to you and Mama. Now I willingly relinquish the Crown." I removed my robe and laid it across the chair.

"May I go home now, Papa?"

The question seemed to shatter his last self-control. "Home?" He groaned and turned his face away in anguish. "God forgive me!"

"Where are you going? Wait, Papa! Please do not leave!"

"I must. Must—go—to proclaim the Lady Mary—Queen. God save us, Jane!"

He was gone. "God save us," I whispered. "Farewell, Papa."

I went to my chambers and told my attendants what had happened. They wept, although I tried to persuade them there was no cause for grief. Ellen alone seemed to understand.

Mama did not come as I expected, nor did Guildford or the Duchess. Not knowing what else to do, I waited quietly in my rooms. Someone would come for me, eventually, and until then I would be content. My nine days' reign was at an end.

24

It never occurred to me that the Tower which had received me
as Queen Regnant of England and Ireland would now become my
prison. I suppose I was naïve to believe that it was all truly over,
that I would be free to return to Sion or Sheen or Chelsea and take
up life again as though those nine troubled days had never been.
I saw no reason why I should be held. Had I not willingly given
up all claim to the throne? Indeed, the Council could swear that it
had never been my ambition. Northumberland would admit the
same.

Northumberland. . . . I know now what befell him, and can
even feel some pity for the agony he must have endured while his
troops deserted by the hundreds. The replacements that he sent for
never arrived. While he waited in Cambridge, he sought to convince the university dons to declare for him. The Vice-Chancellor,
Dr. Sandys, agreed to preach a sermon in my behalf at Great St.
Mary's, but it was too late. Northumberland himself tore down his
written proclamation, flung a fistful of coins to the surrounding
citizens, and cried, "Long live Queen Mary!" Shortly after, he was
arrested by the Earl of Arundel. It was said that when he was
brought back to London he could hardly be saved from the hatred
of the crowds. Verbally abused, pelted with refuse from the streets,
my proud father-in-law reaped the contempt he had sown.

When the guards came for me at last, they told me that
Guildford had been removed already to Beauchamp Tower. Papa
was arrested at Sheen and brought back to join him. Mama and the
Duchess were under guard.

"And shall I stay here also, until Queen Mary comes?" I asked.

They shook their heads. I was to be conducted to the lodgings of the Gentleman-Gaoler, facing the Green. I was to be permitted three attendants and a page, if I desired. And I must leave immediately.

There was not time to gather all my things. Most of my belongings could be sent after me, so I chose only a few dresses, writing materials, and of course my books. Ellen would come with me and Elizabeth Tylney. My ladies-in-waiting fluttered around me and sobbed, begging me to take them with me, making the farewells more difficult. In the end I selected a Mrs. Jacob, a cheerful young woman not much older than myself. Her husband was a sailor who spent long months at sea, and her unflagging good spirits had often been able to lift my own.

Together our small party descended from the royal chambers and stepped outside into the sun. I felt no sadness in leaving the White Tower. I had never belonged there and had never fully accepted it as my right. Halberdiers guarded either side of me as I walked past the Beauchamp Tower. I thought, *Papa is there—so is Guildford,* and shuddered. It was a grim building, lichen-covered and brooding. I wondered if they could see me walking past, and what their thoughts were. The guards quickened their steps as if they feared I would make some move of communication.

My own lodgings were much less forbidding. The house sat on one end of a large rectangle of grass and flowers, directly opposite the Chapel of St. Peter-ad-Vincula. It was a neat, half-timbered dwelling of fairly recent construction, having been built to suit the fancy of Queen Anne Boleyn.

I paused for a moment before entering. This was where I was to spend—how much of my life?—God alone knew. I was suddenly loathe to go inside.

"Lady Dudley?"

A short, fat little man appeared suddenly at the open doorway; beside him stood a woman who was undoubtedly his wife. She examined me rudely, and I heard an indignant indrawn breath from Ellen behind me.

"I be Master Partridge, the Gentleman-Gaoler, my lady. Me and me mistress are pleased to welcome you." He waited while his wife dropped an almost imperceptible curtsy. I suppressed a laugh at the aptness of the man's name to his person, round and well-fed. But the bright, darting eyes were kind. Unlike his wife's, I thought. "Your quarters be on the second floor. If you'll follow me?"

The door closed behind us. Master Partridge led the way up a narrow flight of stairs, and we found ourselves in a modest sitting room of sorts, dominated by a fire-blackened hearth, a bench and two chairs, and a small table. A chamber for the servants branched off this main room and, further along the passage, another bedchamber that boasted a carved oak door.

"That's your room," said the gaoler's wife with peculiar emphasis. "Maybe you'd like me to show it to you?" She opened the door without pausing for a reply and stood aside for me to pass. There was nothing extraordinary about the room; it was, in fact, quite unornamented except for a coffer for clothing, a narrow bed, and a writing desk by the window. Stark, but clean enough, although I suspected Ellen and Annie Jacob would insist on a thorough scrubbing. Mistress Partridge watched me narrowly, waiting for criticism.

"I don't suppose you think it's good enough for the likes of you?"

"But I do, Mistress Partridge. I think I shall be quite comfortable for the short time I am here."

"Aye." She chortled unpleasantly. "There was another one didn't think she'd be here long either! Mistress Anne."

"Anne Boleyn?"

"Aye. This was her room. She used to stand at that very window, lookin' out."

I opened the leaded pane casement, almost against my will. "'Tis a pleasant view. I do not wonder that she found enjoyment in it."

"Ah, but she didn't look for enjoyment! She could see them buildin' her scaffold down there on the Green." She leaned closer, as though relishing my look of horror. "That's where they cut off her pretty head!"

"*Get out!*" Mrs. Tylney, her face white with anger, brushed into the room with a rustle of skirts. "Leave this room at once, do you hear? And do not come again unless you are summoned."

The woman shrugged insolently, then flounced to the door. "I take no orders from prisoners! You and your fine lady just remember that. You're not queen any more, *Mistress Dudley!*"

209

"What a horrid woman." Mrs. Tylney shut the door and moved to put her arms around me. I laid my cheek against the lavender-scented silk of her gown and closed my eyes, ashamed to discover I was trembling.

"She said—she said this was her room. Queen Anne's."

"I know, my dear—I know. Don't let it upset you. It was a long time ago—before you were born. Our Gentleman-Gaoler's wife probably wasn't even here then."

"Do you think so? Do you think she just made it up—about Anne standing at this window?"

"I'm sure of it!"

She smiled and gave me her handkerchief. 'We'll have a lot to do to make these—surroundings—" she gestured, "more habitable. But first we shall have a cup of tea. I'll ask Mrs. Jacob to make some for us."

She left, and I turned to study the room more carefully. It looked so—empty. Desolate. I tried to throw off my depression. It was the twenty-fifth day of July; Mary would undoubtedly reach the Tower in another week—perhaps two. And then I would be able to talk with her. Surely I could bear my confinement until then. I went once again to the window and looked down on the Green. There was nothing there—nothing but green grass and flowers. I would not let Mistress Partridge frighten me with her ghoulish tales again. I left the casement open to air the room and went to join the others.

The next day the Lieutenant of the Tower, Sir John Bridges, came to see me. Our positions had reversed since last we met; the ruler was now subject to his greater authority. He bowed, removing his velvet cap, and straightened, a broad-shouldered, black-bearded giant who might have overwhelmed me if it were not for the gentleness in his face. He looked ill-at-ease standing there, and I offered him a chair.

"No, Lady Dudley. I cannot tarry. I come but to see if you require anything."

"I lack nothing but my freedom, Sir John, and I trust by God's grace to have that soon restored."

He nodded. "So shall it please the Queen. I shall leave you to the care of Master Partridge then. He and his wife will provide your fare, and I doubt not that they will be pleased to ask you often to their board below."

I stiffened. "I think not."

"Ah, you have met Mistress Partridge! Her meat is sweeter than her tongue, I do assure you. Perhaps you will change your mind."

"Sir John—can you tell me anything of my parents or my husband?" He hesitated, and I urged him anxiously. "Are they well and comfortable?"

"Perhaps I can relieve your mind; I see no harm in it. Your ladyship's mother, the Duchess of Suffolk, was released today. The Duchess of Northumberland is also at liberty; there is word that they are on their way now to the Queen at Newhall."

"Oh—Ellen!—Mrs. Tylney! Did you hear that?" I turned to them, my face glowing. "This is wonderful news!"

"Aye, lass, so it is."

"Does Papa know? Do you think I might write and tell him and my husband, Sir John?"

"I'm sorry. You are not allowed to communicate with them."

"Oh. I understand, of course." He started toward the door, and I touched his arm. "I do appreciate your telling me, Sir John."

"You are quite welcome, Lady Dudley. Farewell."

His visit had cheered me considerably. I had had no expectation of Mama's release, and the news that she was already setting out to petition Mary strengthened my hope. Mama was a single-minded woman—more than a match for my cousin, I was certain.

"Well! Master Lieutenant appears to be a decent sort," observed Mrs. Tylney, "Quite mannerly, in fact. I expect he will see that Master Partridge spends his shillings where he should."

"You mean *our* shillings," I corrected dryly. The Gentleman-Gaoler's wife had already advised me of the "supplement" I would have to pay if I expected edible provisions. "I only hope Papa and Guildford do not suffer want. I should not complain, I suppose."

"Ah, lass, 'tis only those too poor to bribe their keepers who suffer. And it willna' be for long, will it?"

"No! It will not be long now. Perhaps even sooner than we thought."

The days crawled by. I spent most of them reading, thankful that I had brought books to occupy my mind. Although the weather continued to be fair, I was not permitted to walk outside, and I watched wistfully the activities of those below my window. How lightly we esteem our liberties until they are withdrawn! Was it only a year ago that I had wandered in my gentle Leicestershire valley, unbridled by man's physical or political lust? I felt so much older than my sixteen years—and tired. Tired of death and the things that happened to people when they set power—and wealth—above all natural affection.

I still loved Edward Seymour; I probably always would. But I did not deceive myself that we could someday be united. I would strive to be a loyal wife to Guildford, for this was my duty. But it was not easy. My actions I could control, but my thoughts? They reared like renegade horses and kicked down the careful enclosures of my mind. And during those times that they ran wild and free I did not believe it possible to bear the rest of life without Edward.

On the last day of July I saw my father. He was walking across the courtyard in the company of his valet and two warders, who, curiously, did not have the appearance of guarding him, but rather serving as an escort. He strode purposefully toward the gates, and it suddenly occurred to me that he was leaving. In a moment more he would be out of sight.

Frantically I flung open the casement and leaned far out, willing him to see me. *"Papa!* I am here, Papa! *Look up!"* For a terrible moment I did not think he had heard me. Then he stopped. He raised his eyes as if he had to force himself to do so—as if he had known all along I was there but was unwilling to acknowledge that it was so. And his eyes met mine.

I shall never forget that look. It held suffering such as I had never before seen in a human countenance. Suffering and shame. It was a look I had only seen in the dark, pleading eyes of a dog, begging for forgiveness. "Papa!" I knew the tears were streaming down my face. "You are going!—Godspeed, Papa! We shall meet again soon!"

He nodded his head slowly. The slumped shoulders lifted slightly, becoming firmer, more determined. He lifted his hand and then was gone.

He was free! The realization made me dizzy; for a moment I

clung to the sill in support. Mama's entreaty of Queen Mary had been a success! Any moment I, too, would receive my freedom. I ran to tell the others.

But though we waited through the next hour, and the next, nothing happened. Impatiently I sent a page for the Lieutenant of the Tower. After a long interval he came.

"He has been released!—I saw him!"

Sir John nodded. "Your father—yes. The order came this noon from the Queen. He has been pardoned."

"And was there—no other instruction, Sir John?" He knew what I meant. I watched him take a cloth from his pocket and carefully wipe the perspiration from his brow. My heart sank, even before he spoke.

"No, my lady. I am sorry."

I turned away. "Would you care for some ale, Sir John? The day is very warm." He nodded, and I sent Annie Jacob to fetch a mug from below.

"I expect the Queen will wait, then, until she comes to the Tower. I should have expected that. We must talk together, she and I. There is so much to explain."

He did not reply, and I went on with a little laugh. "Mama will be quite put out that she could not manage to have me freed at once along with Papa. She is very persuasive."

"Aye, my lady, she is indeed, from what I've heard."

"You know, then, what happened? Please tell me, Sir John. I should like very much to know."

He looked as though he regretted his admission and, accepting the ale from Annie, ran his finger thoughtfully around the rim of the mug.

"No one ever thought she'd see the Queen. The Duchess of Northumberland was turned away, and well she might be! There'll be no mercy for her husband."

"But she gave an audience to Mama?" I prompted.

"She did." Again that hesitation. "By all accounts your ladyship's mother prevailed most pitifully upon Her Majesty, using the argument that the Duke, your father, was ill and would die in the dampness of a cell. She said, moreover, that your father's present condition was caused by Northumberland's evil attempt to poison him."

"*Poison!*" I was astonished. Papa had been in good health on the day of his arrest. The story must have been fabricated to win Mary's sympathy. "Did Her Majesty demand no proof?"

"Aye. Lady Suffolk claimed that the apothecary who served the Duke of Northumberland is now dead by his own hand."

"Is this true?"

"The man is dead, my lady."

How strange—how very strange.

"And by what persuasion did my mother seek my pardon?"

"She—she did not use—any, my lady."

There was a long silence. A storm of feelings broke against my mind—incredulity, shock, anger. *She hates me*, I thought. *She does not care how long I stay here.* With sudden, bitter clarity I recalled my attempts to win her affection through the years. She had been like a goddess; whimsical, sometimes cruel, but always inviting my devotion. If only I could ride well enough—sing, converse, surpass my peers in learning—I had believed I might win a bit of her approval in return. But I never did. Not even when I nursed her during the plague, not even when I became the Queen. And this was her ultimate rejection.

The Lieutenant sighed and excused himself. Absently I watched him go. He was a good man really. Strict in his duty, but kind. In some ways he reminded me of Papa.

Dear Papa. I thought of the way he had looked at me earlier, lifting his hand in a kind of pledge. He would not forget me, I was sure of it. And in a few days Mary herself would arrive.

214

25

How glorious was Mary's triumphal entry into her capital city!
How sweetly she must have savored the victory of being received, at
last, as Queen, rightful heiress to her father's and brother's throne
and dominions. She was now thirty-eight; the years had not been
kind. She had known separation from her mother at fifteen and
unjust rejection by her father. She had experienced poverty, ill-
health, and desperate loneliness. Three times her betrothal agree-
ments had been dissolved. And, the final humiliation, her Crown
had been taken and given to another,—to me, her cousin.

On August the fifth, Mary took up her residence at the Tower.
I had been awake since dawn, unable to sleep. Would it be my last
day in these lodgings built to shelter the unhappy Anne Boleyn?
Could I truly expect forgiveness for the wrong I had done? But
Mary was merciful. She had demonstrated that in the free pardon
to my mother and father and to the Duchess of Northumberland. If
we could only talk, as we had that Christmas at Clerkenwell,
openly and without interference, she would understand.

The shouts of the crowd, the wild pealing of bells, and the cannon fire heralded her approach long before she reached the Tower
gates. The Green was alive with soldiers, officers of the Tower
and their families, pages, courtiers, and state officials. Annie
went below to join the throng; Mrs. Tylney, Ellen, and I took up
our places at the open windows. Each of us, I know, were thinking
of that other day, not four weeks ago, when a different Queen was
received.

Suddenly I started. There, on the far side of the courtyard

closest to the chapel of St. Peter-ad-Vincula, stood Edward's mother, the Duchess of Somerset. With a dawning horror I remembered that she had been imprisoned since the Protector's execution over eighteen months ago. There, too, was the old Duke of Norfolk, still under sentence of death by King Henry the Eighth. I had offered to restore him to his office of Earl Marshal if he would swear loyalty to me, but he had not answered. . . .

"Will ye look at all the clergy drawn up there, happy as ye please! 'Tis the Bishop of Durham, and Winchester—"

"Yes, Stephen Gardiner. He lost his bishopric for opposing King Edward's reforms. I'll wager he'll get it back soon enough now," Mrs. Tylney said grimly.

"Who is that other person, the young man beside Gardiner? I do not recall him."

"Ye wouldna', lass. That's Lord Courtenay, the Earl of Devonshire's heir. The puir lad's been here since he was ten—over twenty years ago!"

Twenty years! "How—*horrible!*" I whispered. To spend one's whole youth imprisoned here. No one deserved that. No one.

There was a sudden fanfare of trumpets. The prisoners knelt, and the rest of the company sank low in reverence. The Queen was passing through the gates.

I had a clear view of her, sitting proudly erect on a small white mare. She was resplendent in a rich, violet-colored gown, and although she was never beautiful, one could not deny her dignity. On her horse she looked taller than she was—a step above clogs, I thought wryly. The masses of people in the courtyard went wild with enthusiasm.

"God save the Queen! Long live Queen Mary!"

No suspicion, no silent accusation. She was their undisputed ruler.

Breathlessly I waited for her to look up, to notice me, but she did not. She paused almost underneath my window, then proceeded up the sloping path toward the White Tower. And then she saw the other prisoners. She called for a man to help her dismount, and the tumult of the crowds fell away. What would be their new monarch's first command? I watched her extend her arms in a gesture encompassing them all. In the still air her voice carried clearly.

"You are my prisoners!" she cried, and, overcome by emotion,

216

covered her face with her hands. Then she raised them one by one to their feet, kissed them, and set them free.

The excitement of the watchers exploded around her. Their voices rose in a crescendo as she moved with her entourage toward the Tower steps, turned to smile and raise her hand at the top, and then disappeared inside.

The scene had held all of the elements of a drama. I was glad for Mary; it was her supreme moment. The fact that I had had no part in it did not disturb me. She had pardoned the others—Protestant and Catholic, male and female, without provision. I knew that my offense had been more personal and might require the payment of a fine or public apology. But that I would, eventually, receive my liberty there now seemed no doubt. I could be content to wait.

Partly to fill the interim with a useful occupation, and partly to satisfy a need to begin my defense, I decided to prepare a letter for Mary. In it I would set down the details of the past months since my marriage to Guildford, omitting nothing. Her judgment I did not fear; it was the Councillors and foreign ambassadors around her whom I mistrusted. I would not make Northumberland's error of leaving my fortunes in their hands.

On August eighth my cousin, King Edward VI, was laid to rest in Westminster Abbey. A peculiar phrase, "laid to rest." I am sure that it refers to the body and not to the soul, the true spirit of a person, for rest came to Edward the moment he closed his eyes in death. It was an escape from all that he had dreaded in the monarchy—the struggle to attain to his father's brilliance, the forsaking of his essentially quiet nature. But it was more than a flight from all these things; it was an escape to something far better. An escape to eternal life with God.

Why, then, should I feel such sorrow? Perhaps it was the close intertwining of our lives, begun the same month and the same year. We had shared the grace of Lady Catherine's life; we had known some of the same tutors—and we had both dreamed of England as a Protestant nation. Now one of us was dead. Was the dream dead, too? Would I be given another chance to keep a part of it alive?

Edward's funeral raised doubts in some minds about Mary's future attitude toward religious tolerance. True, she had sent out two proclamations promising liberty of worship to all, but the second had added that the religion of the land would be settled by "common consent," meaning an act of Parliament. For most of the nobles, who changed their "faith" as they did their garments to suit every new monarch's taste, it was not of serious concern. The Privy Council had even gone so far as to order a man pilloried for petitioning for the protection of Reformers. But it was the Queen's own behavior that most troubled the citizens. She had pointedly refused to attend her brother's funeral ceremony at Westminster Abbey, which was conducted by the Archbishop of Canterbury according to the rites of the Church of England. Instead, she had remained at the Tower and attended a Requiem sung in the Chapel of St. John. Even more ominous was her instruction to the Lord Mayor of London forbidding the open reading of Scripture in the churches, except by her permission.

With the dawn of each new day I waited tensely for a summons. The account of my reign was finished; I sent it by a page to Mary, and then, to occupy my mind, turned to other things—writing short bits of verse, memorizing Scripture passages, attempting again the Hebrew I had begun to learn last year. Surely, surely something would happen soon! I longed for the simple pleasure of walking out of doors, of standing, even for a few moments, under the summer sky. I thought I would go mad, waiting.

And then I heard: Lady Mary was leaving the Tower precincts for Richmond Palace. She would not see me, at least not yet. Sir John Bridges brought me the news.

"But why?" I cried, tears of frustration overflowing. "I thought—surely—she would have allowed me an audience before this!"

The Lieutenant shrugged unhappily. "In truth, my lady, we had all looked to see you freed—especially after your father and the other prisoners—" His voice trailed off.

"What is to be done, then, Sir John? I need you to advise me."

"The trial for the Duke of Northumberland will be held in a few days—on the eighteenth. There is little question that he will be condemned; the Council could not decide otherwise without appearing disloyal to the Queen. Perhaps—with his execution—everyone will be satisfied that there has been adequate retribution."

Mrs. Tylney, who had been listening without comment, now

218

spoke sharply. "Do some press for punishment of Lady Jane?"

"Yes," he admitted after a moment. "The Spanish ambassador, Simon Renard, is one. But they say the Queen will not listen, that she believes you are guiltless."

"Then why does she not let me go?" I demanded passionately. "Do you know, I think I would rather die than to be left here, forgotten, year after year—like Lord Courtenay. I could not bear that."

"Be assured you are not forgotten, my lady! There are many—more than you know—who wish you well. I pray you do not lose courage."

I was touched by his warmth. "Thank you, Sir John."

"I have other words that may please you. You are to be permitted the freedom of the Green, to take exercise whenever you wish. Lord Guildford is also to be given greater privileges."

"That *is* good news. Poor Guildford. He is with his father and his brothers, is he not? At least the trial will be over soon."

As the Lieutenant indicated, the judgment passed on the Duke of Northumberland was almost predetermined. Sir John was present at the trial and later gave me an account of it; and I am sure, although my father-in-law was most certainly guilty, the trial could not be called a fair one. He began his defense by questioning the court on two points: whether a man could be charged with treason if he had acted under the authority of the Council and the Seal of England; and, secondly, if the persons who acted with him could be his judges and pass sentence upon him at his trial!

The Council must have felt some discomfort at that. They only replied, however, that the seal he acted under was not the seal of the lawful Queen, but the seal of a usurper. And if the persons that he referred to had not been charged with treason, and it was the Queen's pleasure to honor them, then they had every right to preside over his trial.

He must have known then that it was no use. With a great show of humility he confessed he was guilty and threw himself upon the mercy of the court. And then Sir John said he added something—something that I cannot explain unless it was to make some amends for the wrong he had done.

"I wish," he said, "to make it known that whatever I myself deserve, the Lady Jane not only did not aspire to the Crown, but she was by force made to accept it."

He ended by declaring that he was prepared for death and that he only hoped his children would be treated with mercy.

The Duke and ten of his chief officers were sentenced to be executed on the twenty-second of August. But even toward her most determined enemies Mary felt compassion; when Northumberland swore to renounce Protestantism and asked to see a priest, she wavered in her condemnation. The Duke wrote to the Earl of Arundel begging for life—even if it were "the life of a dog." It was to no avail. Eight of the officers were pardoned, but three—Sir John Gates, Sir Thomas Palmer, and my father-in-law—were led to the scaffold on Tower Hill.

What must Guildford have endured that morning as he said farewell? Grief, hatred of his father for bringing this punishment upon himself and upon us all, terror for his own safety? I never found out. But I hope there was some forgiveness, for his soul's rest. He had once loved his father. . . .

Lieutenant Bridges conducted the Duke to the scaffold. The crowd pressed in on all sides, making their progress difficult. *"Death to the traitor!"* they screamed. One old woman struggled up, waving a rust-stained handkerchief. "Behold the blood of the 'Good Duke,' revenged this day!" The hatred of the mob redoubled; I could hear their frenzied cries from my room, even with the windows closed against them.

Northumberland met Sir John Gates at the foot of the platform. "Sir John, may God have mercy upon us," he said, "for this day shall end both our lives. I pray you will forgive me in whatever way I have offended, and I forgive you with all my heart, although you and your Council were great reason for my offenses."

"I forgive you, my lord," the Lieutenant heard Sir John reply, "as I would be forgiven. Yet you and your authority were the original cause of it altogether. The Lord pardon you, and I pray you will forgive me."

My father-in-law then ascended the steps. He stood at the railing, looking down at the people who awaited his death, and began to deliver his prepared speech. He spoke of his great sin in supporting the "false religion." He was now a Christian, he said, although for the last sixteen years he had lived in error.

"I beseech you all to bear me witness that I die in the true Catholic faith."

He repeated a few psalms in Latin, then laid his head upon the block.

So ended the life of John Dudley, Duke of Northumberland. The triangle was complete: the Lord Admiral, the Duke of Somerset, and Northumberland. Each man had played his unique part, yet their fates were identical. Was it over now—the grasping ambition, the violence? I prayed God that it was so, that Mary's reign would mark the beginning of a lasting peace.

26

The unpleasant business of execution completed, all attention now focused on the Queen's approaching coronation. The Council found themselves confronted with an embarrassingly empty exchequer with which to pay for the event. The Queen, however, insisted that no expense should be spared. The result? A loan of twenty thousand pounds was made by London citizens to crown their Queen. And I, her prisoner, was made to pay most dearly.

When Annie announced one afternoon that the Marquess of Winchester was waiting to see me in the sitting room, I was startled. It was obviously no social call; Winchester had been among the first to desert his place on my Council. He was not likely to chance Mary's disfavor by consorting with me now.

"Good day, my lord. What fair wind brings you to my humble lodgings? Perhaps you wish to bring a word of solace and hope to the prisoner?"

He colored; I suppressed my amusement. He was flanked by two sturdily built Yeomen of the Guard whom I took to be his protection.

"I am here by the Queen's command," he said stiffly. "Whether the wind be fair or foul, I leave to you. If you choose to be open with us—"

"I have never used deceit, my lord."

"Then you will assist us in our duty?"

I lifted my shoulders. "If it is in my power."

"Good." He looked around him, surveying the room carefully. "You have removed your belongings from the White Tower? They are all here, I suppose."

"No. Only a small part. I had not the means—or the time—to take everything. We left rather—suddenly." What could be the purpose to such a question? The Lord Treasurer considered my reply for a moment and then looked toward Ellen and Mrs. Tylney, who stood at a discreet distance.

"You attended your mistress, did you not?"

"Aye, we did, and a shame it was the way my lady's things had to be carted here by those guardsmen! Turned the chests upside down on the way, I'll wager, *and* dropped them by the look of those gowns—"

"My good woman, I am not interested in the condition of Lady Dudley's gowns. What I should like to know is what you took with you beside the gowns."

"I canna see what concern that is of yours!"

"Ellen," I interceded, "perhaps the Lord Treasurer has good reason for his interest."

"I do indeed, madam!"

"Very well. There were shoes, of course, linen, candles, a hat, books, materials for writing, a clock, some pictures. My lord, there are some personal items—keepsakes, actually—that I should like very much to have here, if you could—"

"I shall see to it. You did not—ah—mention your jewels." He smiled, and I did not like the look of that smile. His words, meant to be casual, belied his expression.

"I myself carried my lady's jewel coffer," Mrs. Tylney stated with dignity.

"Ah! Your ladyship will have no objection if I examine the contents of that coffer?"

"I do object, my lord—most strenuously." My voice hardened. "Perhaps you will give me the courtesy of disclosing your mission."

"But of course. Her Majesty, upon making a thorough inventory of the state jewels, has discovered that there are several very valuable pieces missing. They were last in your possession; I myself delivered them to you in the Chamber of State." He hesitated. Did he remember, as I did, the moment he set the Crown Imperial upon my head, overruling my objection?

"We think it therefore reasonable to conclude that you still have them. Either you or Lord Dudley would have had no difficulty retaining them as you left the Tower."

Indignation made me catch my breath. "That is absurd! Neither of us kept anything belonging to the Crown."

"I am afraid I must insist on conducting a search. The Queen—"

"*Make your search!* You shall find nothing."

The two men with Winchester began, at his nod, to look in all the possible hiding places within the rooms. Mrs. Tylney went into my bedchamber to fetch the jewelry coffer, her back set in a straight line.

"Every one of those jewels are my property," I told the Lord Treasurer as he pored over the contents of the box. "That brooch—it belonged to Queen Catherine Parr."

"Very pretty—very pretty indeed." His fingers lingered over the delicate ruby and pearl necklace Mary had given me at Clerkenwell. Then he picked up a pendant. It was not a particularly striking piece; the emerald that hung from the gold chain was but a small one. But I felt my heart turn over. I had not worn the necklace since my betrothal.

"We have found nothing of value, m'lord."

"And does that surprise ye, lads?" Ellen, who was regarding the two men with an expression threatening enough to intimidate a ravening wolf, whipped off the top of a kettle hanging above the fire. "Would ye no like to pass yer gormy fingers through the stew to see what's hidden in it?"

"I suppose you have already visited my husband with this preposterous charge." I tore my eyes away from the emerald, now returned to its place.

"I have."

"And found nothing, of course?"

He shrugged. "I am satisfied the jewels are not within your lodgings. But you could have had them secreted elsewhere."

"I find it difficult to believe my cousin has any part in this slander against me. She would not do this!"

"Since you refuse to produce the jewels, my lady, I have no choice but to claim all that you have of any worth in the name of the Crown." He closed the coffer and lifted it under his arm.

"In the name of heaven, man, *have mercy!*"

Mrs. Tylney, more thoroughly distressed than I had ever seen her, flung herself at the Lord Treasurer's feet.

"You leave my lady without means to support herself here! All her money is in that chest! We need food—!"

"Master Partridge is paid to buy your meat. The Queen will see that you each get an allowance."

"Must you take it—all, then?" *Not the brooch, not Edward's emerald. Please, God. Not that!* "If I could but have one thing. Just the—emerald—my lord." They were all looking at me, but I did not care. *"Please."*

For an instant I saw pity in his face. Then the hardness returned, and I knew I could expect nothing from him, or from any of the Councillors.

"I am sorry, madam."

Long after he had gone we sat there, shaken, not daring to express aloud the fear that gripped us all. Was this unlooked-for violation a reflection of the Queen's mistrust? Or had Winchester taken it upon himself, hoping for her approval?

"Well, then!" Ellen gathered her determination around her like a cloak. "We may no be havin' the fine feasts of Bradgate or Sheen, but we'll fare well enough. Aye! We'll manage fine."

"He—he said we should have an allowance," Mrs. Tylney said faintly.

They were concerned about the kind of board Mistress Partridge might choose to provide if she were not given her money. Strange. My own thoughts had left the future and were turning toward the past . . . toward a hard, green stone that had once lain against my breast, afire with my love.

Mary's coronation must have been all that she could have wished. As the first female to ascend the throne since ancient times, there were new precedents to be set. Some of the old traditions—like the wearing of spurs and sword—were to remain, but at least she would be spared the royal title of *King*, enforced by other governments for their monarchs regardless of sex.

The ceremony at Westminster Abbey was to take place on October the first, but following custom Mary took up residence in the White Tower three days before. I did not see her arrive; there was so much confusion with members of her household swarming about the courtyard (my own outside privileges were temporarily withdrawn) that I caught only a glimpse of her train. *Perhaps,* I thought, *she will see me now.* But I did not feel very hopeful; Mary would be distracted by preparations for the coronation, and it was not likely she would spare time for the one who had nearly usurped her place. On the twenty-ninth we learned she had created fifteen knights of the Order of the Bath. These men would keep vigil in the Chapel of St. John all night before the coronation.

It is to the Princess Elizabeth, invited by her sister to take part in the festivities, that I owe most of my information about this time. She wrote to me soon after under an assumed name, and I was deeply grateful for the gesture. I knew that her every move was under observation and any communication to me could be interpreted as treason. I have, of course, since destroyed the letter; but from her vivid coloring of detail I could almost see the spectacle unfold.

The grand procession, which took place the day before the coronation, wound from the Tower through Fenchurch and Gracechurch streets, past Cheapside and St. Paul's, and finally through Temple Bar to Whitehall Palace. Here Mary was to rest until the next morning. It was about three o'clock on the thirtieth when she set out from the Tower fortress. Her gown was deep blue velvet trimmed with ermine, and she sat upon a litter strapped to six majestic horses. Above her dark, plain face was set a golden coronet, sparkling from the light of countless precious stones. It must have been very heavy for her; Elizabeth said that she put her hand up to it now and then, as if to support its weight.

Preceding Mary's litter rode a royal escort of foreign ambassadors and five hundred other gentlemen, including the Lord Mayor who bore the scepter. Immediately behind the Queen came Elizabeth herself and King Henry the Eighth's only living widow, Lady Anne of Cleves. Each of them wore robes of silver cloth set off magnificently by the red velvet lining of the chariot in which they rode. Next, in order of their degree with those of highest rank leading the way, rode seventy of Mary's female attendants, all dressed in cloaks of crimson velvet over gowns of gold or silver cloth. In the rear came the royal guard and gentlemen-at-arms.

All along the route were arranged small performances to honor the Queen—orations, musical entertainments, the presentation of a thousand marks from the alderman at Cheapside.

It was near evening when the company at last reached Whitehall. Mary had a severe headache and retired almost immediately. She was up early the next morning, however, and appeared fully recovered when she took the barge to the Palace of Westminster. Here she was robed and at eleven o'clock started for the Abbey. Her scarlet train was borne by the Duchess of Norfolk, and immediately behind her walked Elizabeth and Lady Anne of Cleves. At the Abbey she was met by Bishop Gardiner (Mrs. Tylney's prediction about him had proved quite correct) and ten other bishops vested in gold robes and miters and bearing crosses. As the choir began singing, the bishops censed her and sprinkled holy water, then took their places in the procession.

Elizabeth was particular to note that it was Stephen Gardiner, the Bishop of Winchester, and not the Archbishop of Canterbury, who officiated at the coronation. The archbishop was in prison for supporting Protestantism. Would this act bring the misfortune promised by legend to the ruler he did not crown?

At the altar Mary was conducted to St. Edward's Chair and presented to the assembly:

> *Sirs—here present is Mary, rightful and undoubted inheritrix, by the laws of God and man, to the Crown and royal dignity of this realm of England, France, and Ireland. And you shall understand that this day is appointed by all the peers of the land for the consecration, unction, and coronation of the said most excellent Princess Mary. Will you serve at this time, and give your wills and assent to the same consecration, unction, and coronation?*

The people responded with a "Yea! God save Queen Mary!"

She then mounted the steps to the high altar and lay prostrate as prayers were said for her protection. The Bishop of Chichester preached a lengthy sermon after which Gardiner read the coronation oaths. Mary swore to observe them as long as she lived and prostrated herself again as the choir sang the Litany.

After the anointing, Mary retired briefly to be robed in white taffeta, with a mantle of purple edged with ermine. Elizabeth said that when she returned a sigh of approval went up from the gathering. With dignity the Queen offered up her sword and seated herself near the altar where Bishop Gardiner approached with three crowns: St. Edward's Crown, the Imperial Crown of the Realm of England, and a crown particularly designed for her. All but the last was rested only briefly upon her head with a fanfare of trumpets; then a ring was slipped onto her marriage finger. One by one various peers stepped forward with the rest of the regalia—the bracelets of gold, the spurs, the orb and scepter, St. Edward's staff, and the golden chalice—until she was fully appareled. Gardiner led her to St. Edward's Chair and then knelt with representative nobles to declare his loyalty.

I knew it was the custom at the coronation ceremony to read a general pardon of prisoners; I had even dared to believe that Mary might, in the impulse of that moment, grant my release. But it was not to be. There were so many exceptions to the general pardon, said Elizabeth, that it might as well have been forgotten. It was a sore disappointment.

After Bishop Gardiner celebrated Mass, Mary's regalia was taken away and offered upon the altar. Then she withdrew to exchange her royal robe for a processional train of purple velvet, covered by an exquisite mantle of white silk and gold. With her specially made crown still upon her head, she left the Abbey for Westminster Hall.

According to Elizabeth, the ceremonial banquet that followed there was almost as lengthy as the coronation, and possibly more dramatic. Particularly the time-honored moment when the Queen's Champion flung his challenge to the guests:

> *If there be any manner of man, of whatever estate, degree, or condition, who will say that our sovereign lady, Queen Mary the first, this day here present, is* not *the rightful and undoubted inheritrix to the Imperial Crown of this realm of England—and that of right she ought* not *to be crowned Queen—I say he lieth like a false traitor, and that I am ready to maintain the same with him while I have breath in my body, either now at this time, or any other time it shall please the Queen's Highness to appoint. And therefore I cast him my gage!*

There was a moment's tense silence as the knight threw down his gauntlet. Would any, indeed, be rash enough to pick it up? The moment passed. Mary smilingly drank a toast to her champion and sent him the gold cup. There were more speeches, more toasts, and, at long last, the banquet itself (Elizabeth declared that if they had been made to wait another minute they all would have perished of hunger).

It was late in the evening when the company took their barges back to Whitehall, where yet another reception awaited. The festivities lasted far into the next morning.

Thus Mary was crowned. It was final; there were none who would challenge the right of an anointed Queen. Yet I felt a small worry nagging at the back of my mind. Would she be the Queen everyone had looked for? I prayed that England would prosper under her hand.

27

It truly appeared, a few days later when Parliament was opened, as if a new reign of mercy might have begun. The cruel laws that had choked England's spirit were dying. The taxes imposed by Northumberland, the punishments of King Henry the Eighth, would soon be only a memory. It was hard to comprehend how a civilized country such as ours could have so long tolerated such injustice as the death sentence for trivial theft—for stealing a hawk's egg or for taking a horse across the border into Scotland. Thousands were executed on the gibbet during Henry's reign. The country was perishing from self-inflicted wounds. Perhaps now it could heal.

The Queen's first act was to void King Henry's act of divorce from her mother, Catherine of Aragon. Now, at last, Mary was freed from the stigma of illegitimacy and her mother's name was restored. I devoutly hoped it would give her peace. The great pity of the act was that in order to shift the disgrace from Mary it had to be placed upon Elizabeth. Her mother, Anne Boleyn, was no longer recognized as the legal wife of King Henry. I could imagine Eliza's fury.

The second act of Parliament was a bill of attainder against Guildford and me. John Bridges brought me the news. Our trial was to take place on November the thirteenth. I think he dreaded telling me, but it was something I had been expecting.

"I am relieved, actually," I told him. "One way or another the matter will be settled."

"Yes. I can understand that."

"Sir John, what do you think my chances are?"

"How do you intend to plead?"

The question surprised me. "I shall plead guilty, of course."

"You but obeyed the will of King Edward."

"It was wrong to obey it. I know that now. My cousin and I were both influenced by Northumberland."

The Lieutenant sighed. "Even if you should be legally convicted, there is little doubt but that you will be pardoned."

"I want to know—I want to know how the sentence will read. So that I shall not be startled. It will be death. I know that. But by what means?"

His brow furrowed. "Lady Jane—"

"*Please*. It would be a kindness."

"According to the law, if a woman commits high treason against her sovereign or petty treason by killing her husband, she will be sentenced to be beheaded or burned alive, at the Queen's pleasure."

I closed my eyes for a moment and took a deep breath.

"Thank you."

"You do understand—in your case the punishment will most certainly be waived."

I took his hand and pressed it. "Dear Lieutenant Bridges, you are a good friend. You will be there?"

"I will indeed. There will be nothing secretive about this trial. If I may say so, my lady, you have the sympathy of the people—and of the Queen herself. Do not be afraid."

The dawn of the appointed day was dark and wet, a forerunner of winter. When Ellen shook me awake, I thrust my feet out of the warm covers into the chill air and stood shivering before the fire; she returned a moment later with a bowl of porridge and a steaming mug. She planked them down on the table and commanded me to eat.

"I really could not, Ellen—"

"It doesna' concern me whether ye can or no. Ye'll no be wastin' good food! Now—sit."

I could perceive that this was one of those times when objection was futile; I sat.

"I wonder if he has changed at all," I said, lifting the spoon absently to my mouth.

"Lord Guildford?"

"He has had a more difficult time of it than I. Mistress Partridge told me there are rats in Beauchamp Tower—and it is fearfully damp. The moisture runs off the walls."

"Ye've not gone believin' that hag?"

"We have to be grateful for her food, Ellen. She *is* a good cook."

"And a grand gossip! Ye can be certain that whatever ye might have told her has by now been published to every willin' ear from here to Hampton Court!"

"Still, some of what she says must be true. I should not like to think he has been suffering."

Her face softened. "Aye, well, ye'll be the judge of that soon enough. Ye've bin parted nigh to three months; it isn't natural for a man and his lass."

Three months. . . . It seemed more like three years within these walls. But Ellen had mistaken pity for affection. This separation, after the final horrors of our marriage bed, had almost been a relief. I turned away and picked up the deep blue velvet gown that lay upon the chest. "Do you think this color will be suitable? I should not like to wear black—"

"And why should ye, I ask? Ye're not in mournin'! The blue will look bonny."

"I wish—I would like to appear the best that I can. Do you think Mrs. Tylney might be persuaded to dress my hair, as she did on my wedding day?"

"Aye."

The word sounded muffled. As she reached for my tray, I took her hands in mine and kissed them.

"Ellen, you are not afraid of what will happen today, are you? Sir John told me what I might expect, and he said no matter what sentence is passed I shall be pardoned. The trial is only a formality."

"Aye, aye, I'm no afeared of that. But it willna' be easy—the crowds gapin' at ye and sayin' heaven knows what manner of things. 'Tis no place for a gentle lass."

"It will be over soon. We must keep telling ourselves that."

I did not have long to wait before Sir John arrived. As Annie

232

went to open the door, Mrs. Tylney came and put her arms around me. Her cheek was soft and wet. I knew she had been crying.

"Lo, I am with you always," she quoted, "even unto the end of the world."

"God *is* with me, Mrs. Tylney," I replied softly.

Ellen fixed the lieutenant with a stern look. "Ye'll see that the lass suffers no harm?" He nodded. "Mind that ye do. I'll be makin' oatcakes for tea today, so dinna' tarry bringin' her back!"

I saw him at once. He was standing within a small circle of guards, his face turned expectantly toward the door from which I came. When he saw me, he smiled and started forward to greet me.

"Lord Dudley! You will please remain here until the lieutenant gives command!"

The smile disappeared; a familiar dark flush rose in his neck.

"Lord Dudley may advance. The prisoners will proceed to the Guildhall together," announced Sir John.

For a moment after Guildford took my hands we did not speak. He looked at my face searchingly.

"You are well? You seem—smaller than I remember," he said finally.

I laughed. "You are not used to seeing me without clogs. I am quite well. And you, Guildford? How have you fared?"

"Poorly since that wretched Winchester confiscated every penny I had. But I have not starved. I suppose he took your money too?"

"Yes. And the jewels. He said that it was in payment for the lost state jewels."

His fist clenched and unclenched. "He shall pay for that! I swear it!"

My attention was diverted by the opening of the Tower gates. There, drawn up in rank upon rank of astonishing numbers was an escort of soldiers.

"There must be three or four hundred of them!" I gasped. "Are they all for us?"

"Perhaps they expect some sort of riot," he replied, not too assuringly.

The lieutenant motioned for us to begin walking, and we passed through the gates. At once a great mass of people surged forward, trying to catch sight of us, and the halberdiers had all they could do to hold them off.

"God save you, Lady Jane! Good fortune to you!"

Everywhere we saw fluttering handkerchiefs, curtsying women, men respectfully waving their caps. . . . I blinked disbelievingly; they were wishing us well!

"They do not hate us, Guildford! They do not—hate us."

"They never hated you. It was my father they would not accept. Now he is dead, they can let their feelings show."

His voice was thick with bitterness. I wanted to say something but felt at a loss.

"Your father fared much better, did he not? Less than a week in prison."

"Yes."

"Tell me, what sort of man is it who can leave his daughter to rot in prison when he was responsible for putting her there?"

"Guildford—"

"You will not defend him surely? What possible excuse could he have for such a wretched, cowardly—"

"No! I tell you, Guildford, I will not let you speak about Papa like that. If he was ill, he would have died in the Tower. And he was only a—a pawn—of Northumberland."

"Ah, how simple it is to blame it all on my father! Your parents were never motivated by ambition, were they?"

"We should not argue like this, Guildford," I said suddenly. "There is so little time."

He drew a hand over his eyes and sighed. "You are right, of course. And I promised myself, all during those weeks in prison, that I would only ask your pardon. I have been beastly to you, Jane. I used you as if you had no mind or feelings of your own. How you must hate me!"

"I do not—hate you, Guildford."

"But you do not even like me. I suppose it is too much to hope that you ever shall."

"We never really got to know each other, did we? Perhaps—if we had the chance to start over, God would give us something to build upon."

"I love you, Jane. What a fool I have been not to know it before now! God *must* give us another chance!"

His dark face was earnest, and its pallor made it handsomer

234

than ever. Why then did I feel so unmoved by what he said?

We were drawing near the arched stone entrance to the Guildhall. I looked up at its bleak aspect and a shudder ran through my body that was not from the cold.

What am I doing here? I thought, panic enveloping me. *Why am I, Jane Grey, being tried for high treason? Oh, God, stand by me!*

The guards halted. All at once there was no time for last words, for the kind of farewell that we should have taken.

"Do not lose courage, Jane!" Guildford cried as the lieutenant took my arm. "Fare you well—until it pleases God to bring us together again."

He gave me a half-desperate smile. The soldiers led him inside to a chamber to await a separate trial; I followed Sir John into a narrow passageway that opened into a large, vaulted room filled with people. On two sides were galleries containing members of the nobility and wealthy citizens. Ahead, on a dais, sat Justice Morgan and the twenty-five lords of the Privy Council. Upon my entrance the murmur of conversation fell away. Everyone leaned forward; I felt small beads of perspiration break out on my forehead, and lifted my head proudly. I would not be made to feel as if I were some common felon. I was not the Queen, but I was still the eldest daughter of the Duke and Duchess of Suffolk, and fourth heir to the throne of England in my own right.

My judges stared down at me—Arundel, Pembroke, the Marquess of Winchester—all of the men who had once owned me as their sovereign. I saw no compassion in their faces, no sign of recognition. *How can you do this to me, you who brought me to this moment?*

"The accused will approach the bar to hear the reading of the charges against her."

The trial was short, and probably a disappointment to those who had paid for a place in the galleries. I offered no impassioned defense for my actions. All of the charges were quite true, and just as true was the fact that the Councillors knew the reasons for them. If I were to be pardoned, it would be by Mary, whom I had wronged, and not these men.

"The accused will hear the decision of the court."

I waited, not daring to hope.

"It is with the unanimous consent of the court that the prisoner, Lady Jane Grey, spouse of Guildford Dudley, is declared guilty of the charge of high treason against Her Royal Majesty,

235

Queen Mary the First; and that according to the law of this realm she shall be executed, by burning or beheading, on the day that the Queen shall appoint."

A roar of excited voices burst from the galleries around me. My vision wavered for a moment, then steadied. I was not going to faint. Sir John had prepared me for this sentence. Why, then, did it now sound so—*insupportable?* It was not going to happen to me. Everyone said so.

Justice Morgan dismissed me from the court. I turned, almost stumbling in my haste to be gone. I could not breathe any longer in that room; everyone was watching me, pitying me. I did not want their pity.

At the doors of the Guildhall I paused. A low, keening wail arose, and I saw what everyone else in that crowd of London citizens saw: the blade of the halberdiers's axes were turned toward me. It was the signal of death.

I felt the lieutenant grip my arm and hurry me down the steps, through the crowd, to the waiting escort. All around me the faces of the people—angry, distressed—blurred. *They care,* I thought wonderingly. *It really matters to them what happens to me.*

"I want to stop and tell them it is all right," I told Sir John. Reluctantly he paused, and I began to speak, but my voice did not carry more than a few feet in the uproar. We moved on more quickly.

It seemed like a thousand years had passed when we reached the sanctuary of the Gentleman-Gaoler's lodging. The guard was dismissed; wearily I began climbing the steps to the second story. The lieutenant's kindness and concern reached out.

"Are you all right?"

"Yes, truly I am."

"I am sorry you had to go through this. But now you see how the hearts of the people lie with you."

"I cannot say what that means to me, Sir John. If they understand, then so will my cousin."

"You shall know as soon as the Queen makes a decision."

"Thank you—for everything. I am sure the worst is over now. Adieu, my friend."

For many days I heard nothing. Then, four days before

Christmas, Lord Northampton and Sir Henry Gates—close confederates of Northumberland—were pardoned and released. Mary sent word that I was to be given freedom to walk as far as Tower Hill if I wished. Sir John confided that Guildford's privileges were also extended. It would not be long, he said, before we received a pardon.

But why the delay? Now that release was imminent the waiting seemed harder than ever to bear.

"The Queen's had a grand lot on her mind," Ellen soothed. "They say she's been verra ill. And then there's the matter of her marriage."

Yes—her marriage. I smiled to myself every time I thought of it. Cousin Mary had made it plain that she was not going to be pushed about by her advisers. After a humiliating lifetime of having everything decided for her, she was making her own decision on this most vital matter. When an anxious Parliament dispatched a delegation to extract a promise that she would never marry a stranger or foreigner, she refused. Her predecessors had married whom they chose, she told them, and so would she.

Sir John related that she had sent that very evening for the Spanish ambassador, Simon Renard, and led him into her chapel. There she knelt before the altar and made a solemn vow: while she lived she would marry no man but Prince Philip of Spain.

For a time the engagement was kept secret. When it was finally made known, all England was aghast. That the Queen would marry a Catholic had been an inevitability; the young Edward Courtenay or Cardinal Pole, who had never taken priest's orders and could therefore marry, were the obvious candidates. But marriage to a man who was not only a Catholic but a foreign prince and son of the all-powerful Emperor Charles the First? Even many of the Catholic members of Parliament were opposed. Mary would yield her scepter with her virginity! England would become a petty vassalage of Spain. It was impossible for anyone to conceive of a Queen reigning successfully independent of her husband.

"But why not?" I demanded of Mrs. Tylney and Ellen. "Mary's grandmother—Isabella of Castile—is an excellent example; two independent countries can be ruled separately by two sovereigns married to each other. Both countries can benefit."

"Aye—if Queen Mary is strong enough to hold her own."

"She is. I know she is. No matter how badly she wants to wed

Prince Philip, she would do nothing to endanger England."

"It will not be easy to convince Parliament of that," said Mrs. Tylney.

"Cousin Mary is a determined woman. She will not give in. And I for one hope she does not!"

As Parliament continued to resist her decision, however, Mary solved the problem by dissolving Parliament. Plans for the marriage treaty with Spain went ahead.

It was at this same time that I received a visitor from the Queen, and I understood at last the reason for the delay in my pardon. Mary wanted to convert me before she released me. She would not be satisfied until I became a Catholic.

"There is a Doctor Feckenham here to see you, mistress," Mrs. Jacob's voice, sounding clearly in the cold morning air of my bedchamber, held a note of disapproval. I laid down the quill with which I had been writing a letter to my parents.

"Feckenham? I do not think I know him. Did he say who he was, Annie?"

"No, he didn't, and he didn't have to! I can tell a priest when I see one!"

Why would a priest be calling here? I wondered.

"Thank you, Annie. Tell him I shall be with him in a moment."

John Feckenham was indeed a priest; in fact he was Mary's private chaplain. When he told me this, I betrayed my amusement.

"I know that a sovereign sends his personal physician to attend his friends, but I have never heard of one sending his confessor."

He was unperturbed. "Perhaps it is the greater evidence of concern to attend to the soul's need."

"There is no such need here. You may tell Her Majesty that I thank her, but my soul is in splendid health."

"In your own estimate, perhaps. You would not object if I examine the state of it myself?"

"To what purpose? I believe in the doctrines of the Reformation; to me this is good health, to you it is illness. We should never agree."

"I am here, my lady, by command of the Queen—"

"So you have already said."

"And I shall remain here and return as many times as it is

necessary to achieve my purpose, whether or not you are opposed to it."

"You cannot hope to convert me? Mary knows well that such hope is vain."

"You are young. Her Majesty believes it is possible to turn you from error."

"This is absurd!" My amusement had suddenly vanished. "I would like you to go now."

"Very well. I will call again tomorrow. Meanwhile, think upon your condition, and pray that God will enlighten your darkness."

He bowed slightly and was gone.

"How *dare* he? How dare Mary presume upon my privacy like this? I shall write to her immediately. I will tell her that I will not countenance this man's visits!"

"Aye, lass, a fine idea!"

"I wonder—" Mrs. Tylney looked thoughtful. "If the Queen has determined that you shall hear the priest, why not let him come and say what he has to say?"

"Listen to him? I could never pretend to agree with what he says!"

"No, you needn't. But Her Majesty will at least be satisfied that she has done her duty toward you. I think when she is convinced of that she will let you go."

Ellen frowned. "I dinna' like it, Elizabeth Tylney!"

"I cannot say I do either," I admitted. "But if it will shorten my stay in these lodgings, I can put up with a dozen priests!"

But I was determined to make my position clear from the start. When Dr. Feckenham returned the next day, I informed him that I would lose my life rather than turn to Catholicism. He only smiled.

"I wonder," he said.

"Wonder what?"

"If you are really as prepared to die as you think. It takes a certain kind of person to become a martyr. Someone older, usually, who has participated in life long enough to tire of its uncertainties. Or someone proud or obsessed, hoping for a share of glory."

"To die for God is a holy thing!"

"Life itself is holy. God does not need the death of anyone, least of all a young woman of—what is it, seventeen?"

I shrugged. "There really is no use in debating what I would or would not do, is there, doctor? I intend to live. That is, if I can endure these wretched dialogues!"

Something glittered in his eyes that might have been laughter. "Where do you plan to go when you are released?"

"I do not know. To Sion, perhaps, or Bradgate, if Papa will allow it. That is what I should like above all things—to return to Bradgate, to live quietly as if nothing had ever happened."

"Do you think that kind of life would appeal to Lord Guildford?"

"Guildford?" Confusion must have crossed my face, for he saw it. "You have not overlooked your husband's wishes? For of course you would stay in London if that is what he chose."

"Of—course."

"Tell me, Lady Jane, do you love Guildford Dudley?"

I gasped. "You dare ask such a question of me?"

"Is it so unusual? Wives are commanded by God to love and honor their husbands. And you say that you are a follower of scriptural teaching."

"I am, but—"

"Perhaps I should ask a question that is more to the point. What are your feelings for Lord Edward Seymour?"

Color flooded my face; I rose, trembling.

"You forget your place, Doctor Feckenham!"

"My child, my only wish is that you see yourself without the fetters of self-deception. We have all sinned, but we all have access to God's mercy if we but confess our sin. I will gladly hear your confession—"

"I have already confessed my sins—to God Himself! I need no intermediary."

"A priest holds the place of God on earth; he is *alter Christus*—another Christ. Whoever confesses to him receives the forgiveness of God. Lady Jane, I know that you were formerly betrothed to Lord Edward; I know that you violently opposed your forced marriage to Guildford Dudley. It was all in your letter to the Queen—even the details of your unhappy married life."

"She—showed you all of that? Oh, Mary—!"

"I am her confessor," he said gently. "The Queen is a compassionate woman; she understands your feelings. But the fact remains that it is adultery to harbor love for a man other than your husband—"

"It is not like that at all! God knows I have asked Him to make me stop loving Edward. And I shall try to be a good wife to Guildford."

"But you cannot, do you not see? My child—"

"Do not call me your child," I said sharply. "God is my Father, and my earthly parent I love dearly. You are only an intruder, and one I am finding it increasingly difficult to tolerate!"

"That is a sin."

"If it is, I shall pray God to forgive me. Good day, Doctor Feckenham."

Ellen, who had been hovering near all this time, opened the door with grim satisfaction.

"I expect ye'll no be comin' back?"

"Oh, yes," he replied calmly. "I shall be back."

28

I was not the only one with whom Queen Mary was having difficulty conforming to her wishes. Public sentiment against her marriage to Philip had grown alarmingly; Lieutenant Bridges, by now a familiar visitor at our lodgings, came one January afternoon with the news.

"I'm afraid this whole issue may erupt into something very serious indeed," he confided worriedly.

"You think there may be some kind of—action—against the Queen?"

"It is possible. There are several factions who believe she has shown a blatant disregard for the welfare of England. A few days ago Count Egmont, a Spanish ambassador, arrived in Kent to conclude the marriage treaty. The locals nearly tore him apart. They took him for Prince Philip."

"How dreadful! Mary must have been humiliated. What did she say to the ambassador when she saw him?"

"Her Majesty apologized, but she was most tactful. They say she told him it wasn't becoming for a virgin to discuss her intentions, but she must leave it to her ministers. And then she looked down at her coronation ring and added that it must always be remembered that her realm was her first husband and nothing would make her violate the pledge she had made to her people at her coronation."

"What a lovely way of expressing it. Surely no one could fear her intentions after such a statement."

Sir John continued to look gloomy. "The articles of the marriage contract will soon be concluded, and of course much depends on how they read. Yet—" he hesitated.

"Yes?"

"It is not simply the marriage that is at issue. There is the Queen's religion. Many joined her against Northumberland only because she promised to allow free worship. But she has already repealed most of the laws passed by King Edward to encourage the New Religion. The Mass has been reestablished everywhere, even at St. Paul's, and Reform leaders are being thrown into prison. Latimer, Ridley, Hooper, Coverdale—"

"Not Dr. Coverdale?"

"Aye, and there will be more to follow if they do not convert. There are many clergy, like Harding, who would sooner change their frocks than lose their freedom."

I felt anger leap within me at the name of my old tutor. Dr. Harding had ever seemed to me despicable, but this evidence of faithlessness was beyond endurance. I would write to him. I would tell him exactly what I thought of such betrayal of all he had professed. Perhaps he could be urged to take a more manly action.

"Even the Catholics are disturbed by Mary's desire to reunite the Church with the Pope. She says a woman cannot be Supreme Head of the Church like her father was. There are thousands in England—Catholic and Protestant—who oppose her. Many of them would see a Protestant throne restored."

"Protestant? But that would mean—Elizabeth." I caught my breath.

"You understand these are only rumors—and not likely to amount to anything. But even if rumors were ever to reach the Queen's ear—"

"I know, Princess Elizabeth would be imprisoned immediately. They are already on uneasy terms with each other." I shook my head. "There is some reason you are telling me all of this. It is not like you to be so—indiscreet—with such information!"

He got up and walked to the window. It was a raw, bone-chilling day that threatened a storm, and he could not have found very much in the dismal scene to engross him; but it seemed an unbearably long time before he replied.

"I felt you must know there is one other who has been proposed to take the place of the Queen. She, too, is Protestant, youthful, with a powerful attraction to the people that was recently demonstrated. She was queen once—an uncrowned queen."

I was on my feet at once, protesting. "That is not true. You know it is not!"

His face was inscrutable. "You have heard nothing about this?"

"I have not! I swear it! Sir John, you must believe me!"

"What I believe is of no consequence. And as yet I have no evidence that this rumor has reached the Queen. Pray that it does not."

"There must be some truth to this rumor, or you would not have troubled to mention it. You wanted to gauge my reaction, did you not? You are a friend, Sir John, but I have not forgotten that you are the Queen's loyal officer."

"Try to understand. I had to be certain."

"No one who truly desired my good fortune would ever suggest such an idea, Sir John. If my cousin heard of it, I do not think she would spare me. Be assured that my family will lay your rumor to rest."

"It relieves me to hear that." His face relaxed. "Thank you, Lady Jane."

"I am glad you were candid. Queen Mary's welfare—and successful marriage—are in my prayers always. Please let me know when the articles of the treaty are settled. I shall be most interested."

"I will, my lady."

It was not the lieutenant who brought me word, however, but the indefatigable Dr. Feckenham. It was the third week of January, and against everyone's advice I had elected to take a walk in the light powdering of snow that had fallen during the afternoon. It was so fresh, so lovely. The harsh outlines of the buildings were softened so that I could almost pretend I was in my valley, with the rose-hued towers of Bradgate rising above me. I closed my eyes and felt the flakes melt against my uplifted face. It was good to be alone. Sometimes, living within those walls with the same dear but unchanging faces, I felt that I would go mad. I wondered how much longer it would be before I would see my family again, know how they fared. Letters were few. I was sure the prison officials kept them from me. All I knew of Katie was that she had been expelled from Baynard's Castle when I was imprisoned, her unconsummated marriage to Lord Pembroke's son annulled. It was hard to think of them all going about their normal lives at Sheen. Did they ever think of me? Ever wonder what I was doing?

If Miles Coverdale were with me this moment, I told myself, *he would remind me of his little sparrow, and how it learned to sing and accept its confinement. But how hard it is, my friend. How very hard!*

Without warning a vision of Edward, fair and laughing, came to me, and the longing to see him and touch him became so intense I almost cried out.

"It appears this weather pleases you, my lady. Not many would forsake their fires on such an evening."

I came back to reality sharply; the priest's approach had been so silent I had not been aware of him.

"The fire will feel all the more welcome after the cold; like freedom after confinement."

"Or like the warmth of the true church after heresy?"

"You never give up, do you, Doctor Feckenham?"

"Stubbornness is no sin if it will save a soul from destruction."

I sighed. "Can we never talk of anything else?"

"Is there something particular you would like to discuss?" He fell in step beside me. "I must admit that my acquaintance with subjects of interest to young women is somewhat limited. Dress fashions, for instance, are—"

"I should like to know if a date has been set for the Queen's marriage," I said promptly. "You must know. You are very close to her."

"No one is close to the Lady Mary. However, I am pleased to be able to report that the marriage document is at last signed and sealed. As soon as the deputation returns to Spain and arrangements are made, the ceremony will be performed by proxy."

"And how do the articles read? Have they been published?"

"Yes. Queen Mary and Prince Philip are to rule their own dominions, with Philip having only the honorary title of King of England. Any child of Mary will succeed to her title as well as inherit a good deal of property from Philip, which will forever thereafter belong to England. The Queen will never leave the realm without her own consent. If she dies without issue, all connection between England and her husband will cease; if Philip dies first, she is to receive sixty thousand ducats a year. The Prince may never involve England with the Emperor's wars, nor may he claim any part of Mary's income, her ships, or the crown jewels."

"What about the Spaniards who will be permitted to live in England? We shall not be overrun?"

"There will be no foreign army allowed, nor can Spaniards hold any office in our government. Even most of Prince Philip's servants must be English."

"That will be hard on him, but I suppose it is the only way."

"Indeed, the prince will receive few benefits from this agreement."

"Do you think it will be accepted by the commons?"

"Why not? In any case, the marriage will take place. I have never seen a woman more determined on a matter!"

"Of course, Mary and Philip are both devoted Catholics—"

He gave a little laugh. "So that is what bothers you!"

"Not only me," I said, and noticed that his smile faded.

"The Protestant heretics in this country are not so numerous that they need be feared, God be thanked. Those who strayed from the Mother Church during King Edward's reign will be led back to her embrace."

"Led, or *pushed?* Will you go back to the torturings and burnings of Mary's father, King Henry, as a means of persuasion? Or perhaps there will be a repetition of the Spanish Inquisition. The Six Articles make it a capital offense to preach, speak, or write against the dogma of the Catholic church. Such intolerance does not lie lightly on men's hearts."

"Men, like children, sometimes require the rod to bring them to obedience. It is for their own good."

"But men cannot be treated like children, Doctor Feckenham. They have been known to snatch the rod away and turn it upon the one who threatens them with punishment!"

He stopped walking to scan my face. "That is a very strong statement, Lady Jane. I trust it does not indicate a rebellious heart toward Her Majesty's authority."

I shook my head. "No, I am surrendered to the fact that it is God's will for my cousin to be on the throne. Only—for her own sake—I wish she might study tolerance toward the Reformers."

"It is never a kindness to tolerate error, especially when that error is blasphemous to God!"

It was getting dark. The wind rose and shifted some of the snow from the buildings, and the Tower resumed the bleak aspect of a fortress. I shivered and drew my cloak more snugly about my shoulders.

"I am going inside, if you will excuse me. It is so very cold." He did not reply, only stood watching silently as I turned toward my lodgings. He made no move to follow me.

How very odd that on that same evening the Spanish delegation was alerted to a plot against their lives. Without stopping to take leave of Queen Mary, they slipped away from the palace and made their escape to Gravesend, where their ship stood at anchor.

It was not a moment too soon. The rebellion that Lieutenant Bridges dreaded had broken out all over England. The people did not want Philip for their King. They would fight the treaty and, if necessary, Mary herself before bowing to it.

"I vow, the whole city's taken leave of its wits!"

"Or come to them at last!" Ellen and Annie struggled in and flung themselves onto the bench near the fire. "Never seen the like! Soldiers everywhere. 'Tisn't safe for a body to be out in the streets!"

"You oughtn't to have gone," Mrs. Tylney scolded. "You *would* insist on going to the market yourself, instead of letting Mistress Partridge buy our bread and cheese."

"Trust *that* woman with our precious allotment from the Queen? I've a wee bit more sense than that, Elizabeth Tylney!"

"Come, warm yourselves, and tell us the news," I urged.

"The trouble appears to be comin' from more directions than one. Sir Peter Carew has already taken over the city and castle at Exeter. They say he means to put the Princess Elizabeth on the throne!"

I paled. "Elizabeth is in terrible danger, then. If Carew should fail—"

"There's another uprising, in Kent. Wyat's the leader of the rebels there."

"Sir Thomas Wyat, the poet's son?" Mrs. Tylney looked puzzled. "I thought he was a Catholic. Surely he isn't fighting to make Elizabeth queen?"

"'Tis said he only wants to stop Lady Mary from weddin'

Prince Philip! He's dead set against Spaniards; somethin' about his father bein' an ambassador over there and nearly gettin' himself caught in the Inquisition."

"I remember meeting Thomas Wyat," I said. "It was at Court. He could not be over twenty-three now."

"Well, the lad may not have many years, but he has a fierce number of supporters. They say the Queen's sendin' a large party against him—"

"And your father is to take command!" Annie interrupted excitedly.

"Papa? She is sending *Papa* to Kent?" I looked at her disbelievingly and then started crying, for no reason, I suppose, except that I was happy. "Do you realize what this means? She *trusts* Papa! She might have chosen any lord on the Council to defend her, but she chose him!"

"'Tis almost over, lass," Ellen said softly. "Your father will put the rebels down, and the Queen will set you free."

I managed an unsteady smile. "Perhaps we are rushing things a bit. There *is* the matter of routing Wyat."

"Ah, a wee trifle, hardly worth the mentionin'. The Duke will have the matter in hand in no time."

"Ellen, I do not think we ought to minimize the gravity of the situation." Mrs. Tylney tried to look severe but failed. "However, I must say it all does look very hopeful. We must all pray that the Duke will have little difficulty in Kent."

"Meanwhile I'll put the water on to boil. It doesna' look like we'll be needin' to stretch our bread and cheese much longer."

I think we were all rather lightheaded that night. We stayed by the fire into the late evening, telling tales, reading aloud, just talking. When a knock sounded at our door, Annie got up impatiently.

"Who is there?"

"John Bridges, Lieutenant of the Tower!"

I rose hastily as he entered and held out my hands. "Sir John. How good of you to drop in. You are just in time for a late cup of tea—"

"I'm afraid I cannot accept your offer, Lady Jane." The lieutenant's dark features looked drawn. I felt a stirring of uneasiness.

"Well, you shall at least warm yourself by the fire. Find a place for Sir John, Annie. The night is bitter."

"For a moment, then." He moved to the hearth, extending his hands toward its warmth. "The Queen has ordered a mustering of all soldiers; I must see to the Tower guard."

"The insurrections—are very serious?"

"Far worse than anyone envisioned. They are spreading like fire from one coast to the other."

"Sir John, they said the Queen has commissioned Papa to deal with Wyat. Can you tell me anything more?"

There was a closed expression on his face; he did not answer.

"What is it?" I whispered. "Why do you look at me like that? Has—something happened to Papa?"

"Happened? I suppose ambition 'happens' to a man, like an illness. And he is sometimes never cured.

"Your father has left London, Lady Jane, but not to lead the Queen's army against Wyat. He and his brothers, Sir Thomas and Sir John Grey, have taken horse to Leicestershire. And through every hamlet and village they have passed they have proclaimed you Queen of England."

I swayed, and Ellen's arm went around me.

"You are—quite certain?"

"I am."

Into the silence the flames crackled and sputtered. It was the end. I saw my hope evaporate with my father's last impossible act of defiance. And then, unbelievably, I heard Annie laugh.

"What are we all standing here for like it was the end of the world? It's good news, isn't it? Lady Jane's father has turned the Queen's misfortune into gain. We should rejoice!"

"Annie Jacob, you're mad!"

"Am I, then? Is it not a proud thing for the Duke of Suffolk to proclaim her ladyship? There's more than one who has had his fill of a papist Queen and will wish him Godspeed!"

"You forget yourself, Annie!"

"He canna' succeed—"

"No? Then why looks Master Lieutenant so pale?" she demanded triumphantly.

We all looked at him; he did indeed look unhappy.

"I shall tell you why. I have come to regard my acquaintance with Lady Jane as somewhat more than that between a gaoler and his prisoner. I have, in fact, become quite fond of her." Sweat glistened on Sir John's forehead; he burst out angrily: "If she were

249

my daughter, and I were responsible for putting her in this prison, then I should do nothing—*nothing!*—that might imperil her life further! The Duke of Suffolk is utterly consumed by a selfish greed for power. I feel nothing but *contempt* for such a man!"

Ellen released my arm and stepped in front of me.

"Sir John, you'd best be goin' now. Whether or no the lass's father has done wisely, I willna' be the judge. But ye have no right to speak of him that way in front of her. He's still her father; she owes him respect."

"Lady Jane," he said evenly, "owes him *nothing.*"

He turned on his heel and walked to the door. "I have never wished ill upon you; but as God is my witness, I shall do everything in my power to defend the Queen's Majesty and bring all who rebel against her to punishment."

He was gone. I felt bereft of a great friendship, just as I was beginning to understand the full measure of it. For a long moment we stared at one another in a kind of shock—Annie, hopeful, a smile of anticipation trembling on her lips; Mrs. Tylney, wary; Ellen, carefully impassive. I knew she was waiting to see how I would react.

Oh, Papa, what have you done? If you fail this time, we shall both die! If you succeed. . . . Oh, Papa! I love you, but I cannot accept the Crown of England again. Not even for you.

During the next few days we lived in the motionless center of a world that rocked in battle. We knew nothing, heard nothing, and feared even to ask. Ellen braved the city's marketplaces several times in an attempt to gather reports, but they were so diverse, so contradictory, that it was nearly impossible to separate gossip from fact. What she did manage to learn was that the old Duke of Norfolk, along with five hundred trained men commanded by Captain Brett, was making for Kent in Papa's place. Sir Peter Carew's stand in Devon appeared to be losing ground; some of his men were already deserting. As for Papa, we knew only that an army led by the Earl of Huntingdon had been sent to make his arrest.

"If only I could go out and do something instead of sitting here waiting for news!"

"Yes, it is difficult to be confined inside again. Why don't you work on your Greek for a while? It will distract your mind."

"Mrs. Tylney, how can I possibly concentrate on Greek? And how can you go on embroidering when the whole kingdom is falling around us? Tomorrow will be the first of February. Surely someone has news of Papa by now. Why do they not tell us? I must know. I cannot endure this uncertainty!"

Mrs. Tylney stood, folded her sewing into a neat pile, and asked Annie to fetch her cloak.

"Where are you going?"

"Into the city. I will find out anything there is to know."

"But—it is raining and miserable. And there are too many soldiers in the streets! It is not safe; you cannot go alone."

"She won't be alone, mistress." Annie was slipping on her own cloak, white-faced but cheerful.

"No." I shook my head. "Now that I consider more carefully, I am sure we would have heard anything of importance; Mistress Partridge would have taken great delight in bearing us tidings, whether good or ill. We shall all just have to wait here and—"

I stopped. Above the howling wind and rain we could hear the sounds of men shouting, the clattering of horses on stone, then the pounding of the heavy door below us.

Annie ran to the window and looked down. "It is Master Bridges, mistress!"

"See him up then. Quickly, Annie."

A cold hand of fear gripped my heart. Sir John had brought news—of what? Papa's victory in raising the north counties in my name? Or his defeat? I closed my eyes, suddenly not wanting to know. *Dear God, teach me obedience to Your will.*

"Lady Jane?"

Sir John stood before me. I had to open my eyes, look up into his face. And when I saw the pity there, I knew.

"Was Papa—hurt, Sir John?"

"No. Huntingdon met him near Coventry; there was a skirmish, and he and your uncles fled. They are still hiding somewhere in the countryside."

I looked around the room. Ellen and the others had withdrawn into the next chamber.

"So." I moistened my dry lips with my tongue. "The dream is over. I fear the Queen will not pardon him again."

"I am sorry, my lady."

"He is not—evil—Sir John. I know what you think, but he is not. He just had to—to prove something to himself—and to Mama, I think."

Sir John studied his hands; he did not speak.

"I should like to talk to him. I would so much like to—" I covered my face and a great sob racked my body. "Oh, Sir John! *Why?* Why did he have to do this, when I was going to be freed? Everyone said it was just a matter of time. If Papa had only—left things—*alone!*"

Without a word the great man drew me against the warm thickness of his uniform. How long I rested there, weeping, I do not know. When I straightened at last, I felt utterly exhausted.

"When they find him—will they bring him here?"

"Yes."

"Thank you, Sir John. I think I would like to be alone now."

With a bow he left the room; I could hear his heavy tread on the stairway, then the opening and shutting of the Gentleman-Gaoler's door.

Within twenty-four hours Father and his brothers were arrested. The rebellion in Devon was also over. Sir Peter Carew was rumored to be on his way to seek asylum in France. Only Wyat was left, and there did not seem any possibility that he could escape when the others had not. And yet—the Duke of Norfolk's attempt to disperse Wyat's forces had been unsuccessful. Captain Brett, a secret follower of Wyat, deserted to his side at Rochester with three-quarters of his army and the artillery. Sir Thomas now had fifteen thousand followers. He was demanding the surrender of the Queen and her Council and was advancing toward London. The city was seized by terror.

Mary must have been very certain of herself to have remained at her residence in Whitehall. The palace, outside the walls of the city proper, had no defense except its gates. Yet she refused to move and only rode from Whitehall to inspect the city's fortifications before Wyat's arrival. There was another purpose to this visit: she wanted to show herself to the people, to measure the strength of their support. To this end she was received at the Guildhall by the Lord Mayor (who, they say, wore a complete suit of armor under his robe), and with her scepter in hand addressed the throng. I wish I might have been there. Dr. Feckenham recorded the speech, however, and I believe this to be a faithful rendering of it.

I have come in my own person to tell you what you already see and know; I mean the traitorous assembling of the Kentish rebels against us. Their pretense (as they say) is to resist a marriage between us and the Prince of Spain. Of all their plots and ill-contrived articles you have been informed. By their own answers, however, the marriage is found to be the least of their quarrel, for swerving from their former demands, they now arrogantly require the governance of our person, the keeping of our town, and the placing of our Councillors!

253

What I am, loving subjects, you right well know: your Queen, to whom, at my coronation, you promised allegiance and obedience. I was then wedded to the realm, and the espousal ring which I have here on my finger has never, and shall never, be left off. That I am the rightful and true inheritor of the English crown I take all Christendom to witness! My father (as you all know) possessed the same regal estate; to him you were always loving subjects. Therefore I doubt not that you will show yourselves so to me, his daughter; not suffering any rebel, especially so presumptuous a one as this Wyat, to usurp the government of our person.

And I say this on the word of a prince: I cannot tell how naturally a mother loves her children, for I never had any. But if subjects may be loved as a mother does her child, then assure yourselves that I, your sovereign, do as earnestly love you. I cannot but think that you love me in return; and thus, bound, in concord, we shall be able to give these rebels a speedy overthrow!

Now, concerning my intended marriage. I am neither so desirous of wedding, nor so wedded to my will, that I needs must have a husband. Hitherto I have lived a virgin, and I doubt not with God's grace I can live so still! But if, as my ancestors have done, it should please God that I should leave you a successor, I trust you would rejoice, as I know it would be to your comfort. Yet—if I thought this marriage would endanger any of you, or the royal estate of this realm—I would never consent thereto nor marry while I lived! On the word of a Queen I assure you that if the marriage does not appear before the high court of Parliament, nobility, and commons for the benefit of the whole realm, then I will abstain.

Therefore, my subjects, lift up your hearts like true men! Stand fast with your lawful sovereign against these rebels, and fear them not! For I do not, I assure you! I leave with you Lord Howard and Lord Winchester, my treasurer, to assist the Lord Mayor in the safeguarding of the city from spoil and sack, which is the aim of the rebellious crew. That is all. God bless you!

The citizens, overcome with admiration, cheered wildly as Mary mounted her horse and turned again toward Whitehall Palace.

"God save Queen Mary! God save Prince Philip of Spain!"

She smiled at them, and I knew what pride and happiness must have welled inside her. At last she could be sure of the loyalty of the people—for her and for Philip. At Whitehall she set her energies for the stand against Wyat.

Sir Thomas's first plan to strike the city from the river was diverted because of the heavy fortifications. The rebels succeeded in getting only as far as Bishop Gardiner's house, and took great pleasure in making a ruin of it, ripping out even the leaves of the books in his library. Most unfortunately for Queen Mary, however, the repulse of Wyat's forces from the city meant that they found their way around it to her residence all the quicker. Because he could not be quite certain if the Queen was at St. James Palace or Whitehall, Wyat divided his men between the two places in a three-way assault: one divison against St. James Palace, one to the rear of Whitehall, and the last group, led by himself, attacking the front gate.

At two o'clock in the morning of February sixth the alarm went up by a rebel deserter that Wyat would reach Whitehall in two hours. The palace erupted in panic: barricades were erected, a tight guard placed around Mary, while her female attendants began moaning and wringing their hands in terror. In the midst of all this Mary herself remained calm, and when Bishop Gardiner implored her on his knees to leave Whitehall and take the boat he had provided for her, she refused. She would not set an example of cowardice, she told him, and if Pembroke, her general, and Lord Clinton proved true to their posts, she would not desert hers.

Meanwhile Lord Courtenay, who had been sent to repel Wyat's division, was turning out to be an unhappy choice. At the first sign of danger he turned and ran back to Whitehall and, throwing himself down before the Queen, cried out that the battle had broken. Mary, related Dr. Feckenham, looked down at him in scorn.

"Such is the fond opinion of those who dare not go near enough to see the truth of the trial!" she said. "I shall myself go into battle and either see the end of this or die with the men brave enough to fight for me! Those who dare not fight may fall to prayers."

The guards attempting to defend the rear of the residence were encountering the fiercest part of the battle. Even as Mary watched them from the gatehouse, she saw her infantry break and scatter. It

255

was then that she ran down into the courtyard and took a stand between two of her gentlemen-at-arms. It was a mad and courageous thing to do, and it gave the men about her the courage that they needed. Lord Pembroke made a final, desperate charge—and broke the strength of the rebels. They turned and fled, stumbling over the bodies of their fellows. Sir Thomas Wyat, turned back from Ludgate and cut off from the rest of his army, surrendered on Fleet Street.

The third and last rebellion against the Spanish wedding was broken. No one else would dare to resist.

30

It was the morning after Wyat's arrest. I woke early, listening to the stillness; there was nothing except the harsh cry of a raven outside the window. I had grown quite used to these glossy-winged predators that fluttered about the Tower courtyard as if drawn by it. Why was it only this morning that I remembered they were the omen of death?

Ellen came bustling in to draw the curtains and prod the coal ashes into a bit of flame, muttering all the while about the dampness of the river and its effect on her bones.

"Praise be the rain's stopped for the time bein'. It's glad I'll be to see the end o' this winter."

"Do you think it *will* end, Ellen?"

She stopped poking and looked at me hard. "And why shouldn't it? Spring follows winter as surely as morn follows night."

"Sometimes I can close my eyes and see it all so clearly— Bradgate's orchards dripping wet and shiny after the rain, the snowdrops and bluebells flowering under the trees and hedges. How green the valley was in the springtime, Ellen! Like the earth was newly planted. And how the linnets and sparrows sang! One could think their hearts would break for joy. Oh, Ellen, I do so want to see and smell and hear it all again! I do not think I could bear it not to."

"Ye will. Ye *will*, lass."

Through the diamond-paned window I could see that the raven was gone, swallowed by the mist. I relaxed a little and began to think about Papa, and what Mother would do without him. How odd that I could consider them both so calmly now. The blind anger, the resentment were mostly gone. All I felt was an inexplicable peace, an assurance that somehow "all things would work together for good."

The morning passed quietly, almost happily after the tense days of waiting. When Dr. Feckenham came to see me that afternoon, I felt no surprise.

"The streets are still unsafe," he told us, his fine, dark eyes clouded with pain I could not remember seeing there before. "Disloyal Londoners are being hanged from their own doorposts as a warning. There are crying children, women in mourning everywhere. Even at court there is distrust; the Queen's person is watched day and night. Her advisors—the Privy Councillors and foreigh ambassadors—warn her she must move swiftly and harshly to eliminate any future trouble."

"That means—Princess Elizabeth will be imprisoned, does it not?"

"Yes. And—" He sighed heavily, running a hand through unkempt hair. "This morning, only a few hours ago, the Queen rode to Temple Bar. Some of the worst of the fighting went on there; the ground is still soaked with the blood of her men. She signed a warrant there for your death. You and Lord Guildford are to be executed on the ninth of February. In two days."

The shock was complete. Annie, groaning, fell to her knees. Mrs. Tylney and Ellen stood rooted, staring at him uncomprehendingly.

Suddenly I felt far removed from that scene. I was back in my bedchamber in Bradgate with my parents standing over me announcing that I was to marry Guildford Dudley instead of Edward. I thought the world had come to an end that day. But it had not. It went on and, after a fashion, so did I. Now I realized I was being released from the obligation of going on.

They were all waiting for me to speak; there was a hard knot of tears in my throat, and I wondered how I would be able to make them understand that the shadow which had lurked behind each day of my imprisonment was not the hideous thing I had thought it to be. I was going home after all! Not to Sion or Chelsea Manor or even to my beloved Bradgate. But *home*. All pain and loneliness, fear and bewilderment would be forever left behind in the prison of mortality.

There was but one trial left for me to face. I had to know how I was to die.

"Dr. Feckenham, how did the Queen say—how are we to—"

"The sentence is beheading, on Tower Hill."

"Thank God! I could not bear—the other." The deaths of Anne Askew and the others who had gone to the stake were vivid in my mind. At least my ordeal would be over quickly.

"Oh—*my lady!*" A choked, grief-stricken cry tore suddenly into the silence. Cool, self-controlled Mrs. Tylney, who never lost her poise, ran and wrapped her arms around me, rocking me as though I were her dying child. "*No! No! I won't let this happen to you! It cannot!*"

"Please!" I struggled to free myself from her grasp. "*Please,* Mrs. Tylney!" I felt her terror lap over me, drowning me. I had to get away. . . . And then I was freed. Ellen had moved between us, a safe, thick wall of separation.

"Stop it! Stop yer hysterical wailin' this verra minute, Elizabeth Tylney! The lass has no need of yer tears, so if it's that yer after ye can take yerself elsewhere!"

John Feckenham spoke, quiet but authoritative. "Lady Jane, if I might have a few words with you in private?"

"Whatever you have to say can be said in front of these women, sir. But if you would seek to turn me toward your persuasion, I beg you not to. There is too little time now to waste in argument."

"You will not hear me?"

"I have heard you! And I would fain listen to a higher Voice that tells me to hold fast to my faith."

"Is it the same voice that told you to accept the throne? Because that was high treason, and the only one whispering in your ear was Satan!"

I winced. "I sought God's will, but I had no clear direction. I truly believed it was the right thing."

"But you were wrong, were you not?" Gently he took my hands, forcing me to look at him. "If it was possible to confuse God's will then, is it not possible that you are wrong again? You are seventeen, too young to take upon yourself this matter of your soul. You must trust me." I wanted to look away, but I could not. His black eyes held mine, probing, relentless. I was frightened.

"I will return as quickly as I can," he said abruptly.

"Where—where are you going?"

He did not answer, only smiled, and strode toward the door. If I had known his mission, I would have stopped him.

The four of us were left with a curious sense of being cast adrift into deep waters. The routine duties, the little things we had taken up to fill each day, seemed suddenly pointless. I had two days to live, or, as some might say, to prepare myself to die. But had I not already lived the life that was given to me here on earth? And was I not prepared to die, by God's grace? What, then, does one do with two days suspended between heaven and earth?

I thought of my family and, with a guilty pang, Guildford. How selfish to be so consumed with my own fate and to have given so little thought to him. What must he be feeling at this moment? *"We shall not have that chance to begin again now,"* I whispered. *"We must believe that God has chosen rightly."*

Two days—too much and too little time to write down all of my thoughts, but I would try. I would tell each member of my family what they had meant to me, ask forgiveness for the things in which I had failed, and grant forgiveness as well, as honestly as I could. If only I could see them all once more! Even for a few moments.

"I shall need to write some letters," I said aloud. I started toward my chamber, then turned back. "Annie, do you think you could make some of your special meat pies for dinner? It would be a treat for us."

Annie got hurriedly to her feet, wiping her eyes with the corner of her apron. "Aye, mistress! I'd be most happy to."

"And make a fine mess of it, like as not!" Ellen snatched a kettle from the hearth. "I'd best give ye a hand with it." Annie, for once, submitted without argument.

I got to the door of my chamber before looking back once more. Mrs. Tylney sat hunched by the fire, her face grey and old-looking.

"Mrs. Tylney, would you mind very much sitting with me while I write? I should like to have your company."

Slowly she raised her head and nodded. "If you wish it," she said, in something of her old voice. "If you think I may be of help."

When Dr. Feckenham did not return by early evening, we all assumed he had changed his mind. Ellen was vocal in her satisfaction.

"It couldna' please me more to have seen the last of that priest! How he looks after the Queen's soul, with all his slaverin' after yours, I dinna ken. *She's* the one to be needin' confession!"

I smiled. "I should be very sorry to lose Doctor Feckenham's friendship, for all his persistent efforts to convert me. But perhaps he is convinced at last that my case is hopeless."

At that moment we heard a loud hammering on the door below. Ellen groaned. "That's him, I'll be bound. I knew we'd not be like to be rid of him!"

Dr. Feckenham burst into the room, brushing past an indignant Annie who had gone to open the door. I saw his face alight with triumph.

"I have news! From the Queen!"

Mrs. Tylney rose. Unconsciously my hands gripped the arms of my chair.

"What news?"

"She has consented to extend your sentence for three more days! She believes there is a hope you will recant, Lady Jane. She is most gracious, and most eager to give you every chance."

I shook my head dazedly, not knowing whether to laugh or cry.

"But that is not all of it! Lady Mary definitely said that she *might revoke your sentence entirely* once you have forsaken the heresy of the New Learning! Think of it! You have only to say you will—"

"*No!*"

He stopped his excited pacing and searched my face. "You do not believe me. But I would not give you a false hope. You have my word—"

"Of course I believe you. It is not that. But I cannot give you a false hope either. I will not be converted, Doctor Feckenham; not in three days, not in three hundred days. You must tell my cousin that."

"But—"

"You should not have gone to her. It was—wrong." I put my hands over my face so he would not see my tears. "Why will you not leave me alone?"

"Because I cannot. Not in all conscience. I do not think you

261

are sure of what you claim, Lady Jane, not if it were put to the test."

"Will ye no leave off worryin' the lass! Ye've said what ye've come to say. Now go back to yer mistress and tell her Lady Jane will have none of her favors!"

"Is that what you want?"

I nodded, unable to speak.

"Very well. Good-by, then." He paused a moment, then strode through the open door and down the stairs. I was sorry to see him go thus. He had tried, after all, to do what he thought was the right thing. But I simply did not have the strength to thank him. *Or was it that I was afraid he was right?—That my faith might, if put to the test, yield to the desire to stay alive at all costs?* The question tortured me long after he had gone.

31

It is the eleventh day of February. I have nearly completed the journal of my experiences begun four days ago when I learned that my execution was to be postponed. I have been grateful for the labor, for it has helped to fill the long hours which might otherwise have held too much temptation. My spirit, it is true, is ready to embrace the eternal life that will come hereafter, but my flesh is weak and shudders at the approach of its ordeal. Dear God! It was so much easier before, to die for my wrong against the Queen. Now I must die for my faith. I have not the courage of the martyrs; and yet, how can I deny what my Lord has taught? "I am the Life." Without the Life—there is no living.

The quietness of these days has been unbroken, except for yesterday's interview. When Dr. Feckenham arrived with Lieutenant Bridges I was surprised, for the priest had not returned to my lodgings after I told him of my wish to refuse the Queen's offer. My request to leave the execution date on the ninth was denied, and I supposed that Dr. Feckenham had at last abandoned his futile endeavor to persuade me of my error.

In the forenoon, however, a large party of horsemen rode into the Tower courtyard, dismounted, and went into the Chapel of St. Peter. When we saw Dr. Feckenham detach himself from the group and join the lieutenant, then make his way toward the Gentleman-Gaoler's lodging, we were nonplused. What could this visit mean? Annie went to greet them while Ellen, grumbling, straightened up the sitting room. Hastily I smoothed my dress. I was aware that the pale shade of green brocade made a flattering contrast to the red-gold hair visible underneath my hood. Strange that my vanity should survive even now, with death so very near.

"It is good of you to come, Doctor Feckenham, Sir John. I know you have business elsewhere, so I shall not ask you to stay longer than you can."

"Our business concerns you." Dr. Feckenham pressed my hands briefly and released them. "It gladdens me to see you in good spirits, Lady Jane. If only you could assure me that your soul is in like healthful condition. I and my brothers have come today to reason with you one last time."

"Master Feckenham—!" I was dismayed. "I have come to regard you—in spite of our great differences—as a friend. Why, then, do you persist in haranguing me with your doctrine? Leave me to these last few hours without controversy, I beg of you."

"If your faith be true, it will stand the test of debate."

"My faith has already withstood the test of flames! It does not need my poor eloquence."

"You will not consent to the meeting? You do not have to, you know," said Sir John quietly. I turned to him in despair.

"But do you not see? If I refuse to make a public witness, the Lady Mary may say—and rightfully—that I dared not subject my faith to the arguments of these men. The Scripture instructs us to be ready always to give an answer to every man who asks, a reason for the hope that is within us. I must obey that command, Sir John, or I will doubt myself."

He shrugged. "You are seventeen. The men you face are several times that and well-practiced in dealing with heretics against the Catholic church. There are nobles as well as the priests. They are here because they expect you to be humiliated."

Ellen, who had until now remained discreetly silent, could no longer restrain her agitation.

"Listen to him, lass. 'Tis true! They're only after trickin' ye into sayin' somethin' ye dinna mean to say!"

Was it a trick? If so, I could not hope to stand against these clever lords and priests. I would fail, and in failing disappoint Master Aylmer, Dr. Coverdale, all the Reformers in the kingdom who watched me now. I hesitated, looking from one to the other. And then the cool voice of Elizabeth Tylney cut through my indecision.

" *'God hath chosen the weak things of this world to confound the*

264

mighty.' It is true—if you go alone, you will fail. But *with God,* all things are possible!"

I nodded slowly, then went to fetch my cloak.

I had never guessed what an ordeal it would be to stand before those men as they began asking questions. They were hard and relentless, probing ceaselessly for every vulnerable point in which to drive their doctrine. It was worse than the trial at Guildhall—far worse, for then I stood only in peril of my mortal life. In the Chapel of St. Peter-ad-Vincula on that bleak day in February it was my soul for which I fought.

I planned at first to counter their questions with my own, to outwit their strategy, but it was a mistake. They were far too quick and knowledgeable not to forsee my arguments. So after that I confined myself to answering as simply as I could. As the hours wore through the afternoon, it was all I could do to remain alert.

"What is required of a Christian?"

"That he should believe in God the Father, the Son, and the Holy Ghost, three Persons and one God."

"What? Is there nothing else required of a Christian than to believe in Him?"

"Yes. We must love Him with all our heart, and all our soul, and with all our mind, and our neighbor as ourself."

"Why, then, faith neither justifies nor saves."

"Yes, truly, as Saint Paul says, faith alone justifies."

"Saint Paul says, 'If I have all faith without love, it is nothing.'"

"That is true," I affirmed. "For how can I love him whom I trust not? Or how can I trust him whom I do not love? Faith and love go together."

"How shall we love our neighbor?"

"To love our neighbor is to feed the hungry, to clothe the naked, and to give drink to the thirsty, and to do to him as we would do to ourselves."

"Then it is necessary to salvation to do good works also. It is not sufficient only to believe!"

"I deny that! And I affirm that faith *alone* can save. It is right for a Christian who follows his Master Christ to do good works, but we may not say that they profit to our salvation. For when we have done all, we are still unprofitable servants, and only faith in Christ's blood saves us."

"How many sacraments are there?"

"Two—the sacrament of baptism and the sacrament of the Lord's Supper."

"No, there are seven."

"By what Scripture find you that?" I challenged.

"Well, we will talk of that in a moment. But what is signified by your two sacraments?"

"By the rite of baptism I am washed with water, and that washing is a token to me that I am the child of God. The sacrament of the Lord's Supper offered to me is a seal and testimony that I am, by the blood of Christ which He shed for me on the cross, made partaker of the everlasting Kingdom."

"What do you receive in that sacrament? Do you not receive the very body and blood of Christ?"

"No, surely I do not! I think that at the Supper I receive neither flesh nor blood, but bread and wine. The bread, when it is broken, and wine, when it is drunk, put me in remembrance that for my sins the body of Christ was broken and His blood shed on the cross."

"Did not Christ speak these words, 'Take, eat, this is My body'? Do you require any plainer words? Does He not *say* it is His body?"

"I grant that He said so, and so also did He say, 'I am the Vine; I am the Door,'—but He is never a physical door or vine. Does not Saint Paul say, 'He calleth things that are not, as though they were'? God forbid that I should say that I eat the very natural body and blood of Christ! For either I should lose my redemption, or there were two bodies or two Christs. One body was tormented on the cross, and if the disciples ate another body, He had two. Or if His body were eaten, then it was not broken upon the cross."

"Why?" my inquisitors demanded. "Is it not as possible that Christ, by His power could make His body both to be eaten and broken, as to be born of a woman without seed of man, and to walk upon the sea having a body, and other such miracles as He wrought by His power only?"

"Yes, if God would have done any miracles at His supper, He might have done so. But I say that He wished to do no other thing than to break His body and shed His blood on the cross for our sins!

"Answer me this, sirs," I continued. "Where was Christ when He said, 'Take, eat; this is my body'? Was He not at the table when He said it? He was at that time alive, and did not suffer until the next day. What did He take but bread? What did He break but bread? And what did He give His disciples but bread? Yet all this time He Himself was alive and with His disciples, or else they were deceived."

"You ground your faith upon such authors as say and unsay both in a breath, and not upon the church, to whom you ought to give credit!"

"No, I ground my faith on *God's Word,* and not upon the church. For if the church is a good church, the faith of the church must be tried by God's Word, and not God's Word by the church. It is an evil church, and not the spouse of Christ but the spouse of the devil, that alters the Lord's Supper and both takes from it and adds to it. Shall I believe this church? God forbid."

Their questioning did not go on much longer after that. The men were clearly convinced that I was lost and that they should waste no more of their time. I was given leave to go, and Sir John opened the door.

"Lady Jane—"

Dr. Feckenham's voice, heavy with disappointment, stopped me. "I am sorry for you, for I am certain we two shall never again meet after this life."

"It is true that we shall never meet, Doctor Feckenham, unless God changes your heart. For I am sure that unless you repent and turn to Him, you are lost. I pray that in His mercy He will send you His Holy Spirit. He has given you His great gift of utterance; if only it would please Him also to open the eyes of your heart."

Our eyes met.

"Lady Jane, I should like you to permit me to accompany you—to the scaffold. I know you have requested a minister, but the Queen has forbidden it. By my word I shall not trouble you more."

I nodded, my throat full of tears, and quickly followed Sir John out of the chapel. The air was cold and clean. I breathed deeply, feeling a great sense of sorrow and relief.

"Was it very difficult?"

"Yes, and no. Little was said that has not been said before. The biggest contention is always transubstantiation—whether the bread and wine is Christ's real flesh. How many hundreds—

thousands!—have perished because they refused to subscribe to the church's doctrine? It must grieve God, for the really important issue—that Christ died for our sin and rose that we might have eternal life—is often neglected."

"Perhaps now Feckenham will leave you in peace."

"Yes, he will. He is a good man, Sir John." I gave a little laugh. "I never thought to hear myself say that about a priest! I grew up believing they were all corrupt, self-indulgent, ignorant men, but I was wrong. I have met one who is none of those things."

We were passing by the center of the Green where there was a small bustle of activity. Several men were taking timber off a cart and others were pounding together some of the pieces.

"What are they doing, Sir John?"

"My lady—I have something I must tell you. You and Lord Guildford will not be permitted to—die together. There is a great deal of public sentiment against your execution. The Privy Council is afraid your appearance together might provoke a riot of some kind. Lord Guildford will go alone to Tower Hill."

"So—this is where I am to die. They are building a scaffold—*for me!*"

I was frozen by a sick horror. Sir John took my arm, but I could not move or tear my eyes from the place. It was real. I, Jane Grey, would be executed in two days. "Like Anne Boleyn," I whispered, "and Catherine Howard. They both died here, too, did they not? Mistress Partridge was right."

"Lord Guildford has asked to see you; I am sure the Queen will grant permission." He waited, I suppose to hear my assent. I shook my head.

"I—do not know. I must think."

"Of course." He watched me with concern, and his hand tightened on my arm. "Let us go in now, Lady Jane. You are tired. Come."

That was last evening. I slept little and woke early to the sound of hammering. Now this day, too, is gone: my last full day upon earth. The journal is nearly complete, my letters written. I have just read over what I have written to Katie within my Greek New Testament, and it seems lifeless and dull, not at all what I wanted to say. Ah, Katie, my lovely, lighthearted sister. . . . Have you changed at all? What will become of you? My words to you are serious, because I have learned that life is serious and must not be treated as an end in itself: *Live still to die, that you, by death, may purchase eternal life. . . . And as touching my death, rejoice as I do, good sister, that by losing a mortal life I shall win an immortal one. . . . Fare you well.*

I have no letter for Mama. I wrote a dozen and tore them up; the words would not come. And, somehow, I do not think she would expect a last message. My life ended for her when they put me in this prison and her dream of royalty was destroyed. I have no bitterness left. It is she who must live with whatever it is that drives her to seek satisfaction at such great cost. Does she remember, I wonder, those weeks at Richmond Palace when she lay ill? She said she had everything to live for and nothing to die for. My prayer to heaven is that Mama, and my sister, will find that One who alone makes life worth living and death worth dying.

For Papa, two letters—one in the little prayer book that I shall take with me tomorrow, the other the lieutenant has promised to deliver this night. Poor Papa—I hear he blames himself for my death. He must not. . . . *If I may without offense rejoice in my own mishaps, it seems in this I can count myself blessed; for washing my hands in my innocence, my guiltless blood may cry before the Lord. . . . And yet I must acknowledge that in seeming to consent to what happened I grievously offended the Queen and her laws. . . . To you, my father, my death seems woeful; to me there is nothing that can be more welcome than to go to that heavenly throne of all joy and pleasure with Christ our Savior, in whose steadfast faith—if it is lawful for the daughter to write so to her father—the Lord continue to strengthen you, that at the last we may meet in heaven. Jane.*

32

The first thing that came to me as I opened my eyes this morning was a promise: *Be thou faithful unto death, and I will give thee a crown of life.* It is the twelfth of February, 1554, my coronation day.

I and my good friends—Ellen, Annie, Mrs. Tylney—gathered at dawn to break our fast together for the last time. How close we have drawn during these last seven months. My eyes lingered on each face, remembering the moments we had shared, and rested finally upon Ellen. *Dear Ellen.* Her hair, once black and bonny, is now silvery under the white mob cap; odd, I never noticed when it changed. She has ever been the same to me, my beloved nurse and companion for sixteen years. It will be hardest to leave Ellen behind.

The sweetness of our communion was broken unexpectedly by the intrusion of Mistress Partridge. Mrs. Tylney rose angrily and demanded to know her errand.

"I should have thought that I had a right to the upper half of me own lodgings whenever I choose! Master Partridge is gaoler here. Besides, I come to tell the lady there's some gentlewomen below waitin' to see her!"

"Gentlewomen?" I exchanged a puzzled look with Ellen.

"Aye, from the Queen they are."

"And why are they here? Ye know, don't ye, woman?"

She gave Ellen a smug look. "I guess there ain't much that goes on I don't know about." Her eyes slid over to me. "They be the matrons sent to make examination of my lady—to see if she be with child."

270

"What?"

"The Queen's heard rumors. It seems she don't fancy havin' a baby's blood on her hands."

"But it is not true!" I cried. "You know it is not!"

She shrugged. "I'm only the Queen's servant, ma'am. How can I say what I don't know to be true?"

"Why should I hide it?"

"Heretics are a queer lot; they might take it in their heads to do almost anything."

"You—*evil*—woman. *You* started the rumors yourself. *Why?*"

She did not answer, only smiled at me in a way I found particularly loathsome. Then she went to the door and summoned the women.

I had to submit to the examination. I had no choice; Mary would, I knew, insist on this evidence to answer any future accusations. It was the ultimate violation of my privacy. As I laid myself upon my bed, Mistress Partridge stood over me gloatingly; she would not be moved, not even by Ellen's most violent threats. The women began their task and I closed my eyes tightly, trying to force my mind from what was happening. Once, when their clumsy hands forced a startled cry of pain, I thought I heard a low sound of laughter. Ellen moved beside me and took my hand.

At last they were finished; I lay still, bruised and humiliated, unwilling to open my eyes until the women had gone.

"Well, now, I fancy Her Majesty will be right pleased the rumors have come to naught. A pity it is for *you*, my lady—a babe might have spared your life! *Unhand me*, you foul scotswoman! I'll see you're reported to the Queen!"

"If ye and this pack of women are no out of this house in the blink of an eye, ye'll no be in condition to report anythin' to the Queen!—Do ye ken that, Mistress Partridge?"

The woman nodded.

"Away, then! And dinna' let me set eyes on ye agin!"

Alone once more, Annie and Ellen helped me into a warm black gown. I then went to the window and waited for Guildford to appear. I had decided there should be no last interview with him. What would such a meeting accomplish, except to distress us both? Before the trial we had said so much that was important, without tears, and looking forward instead of back. This was what I felt we must do now. Sir John said Guildford was often given to tears; I

271

knew I could not be strong enough for us both, if he should lose control in front of me. Therefore, I sent a message telling him I thought it best that we waited until we saw each other on the other side of death.

Dr. Feckenham joined me just as Guildford emerged from Beauchamp Tower with the lieutenant and two guards. Guildford looked thin, even from a distance, and I saw with a pang that the shoulders beneath his black cape were slumped. If only Mary would have granted him the slender comfort of a minister. It seemed so little to give. . . . And it appeared that others thought the same. Sir John Throckmorton, Sir Anthony Browne, and half a dozen other gentlemen—all Protestants—were waiting to accompany him to the outer gate. Surrounded thus I saw little of him until, at the gate, Lieutenant Bridges delivered him up to Sir Thomas Offley, the Sheriff of London. *Dear God,* I prayed as he disappeared from sight, *give him the strength to endure this final trial!*

The others sought to draw me away from the window. They wished to spare me the sight of what I myself must shortly undergo. But some force I could not explain held me there, waiting, and in what seemed only a few moments we heard the rattle of a handcart over rough stones.

The wagon passed directly beneath my window. I saw him—or, rather, that which was the mangled corpse of him who had been my husband—flung upon the straw. Beside him was a bloody cloth covering what must surely be his severed head.

"Oh, Guildford—Guildford!"

I reeled, fighting a desperate desire to be sick. Was this the end of us, then—this atrocity, this less than human thing? What had we done—what had either of us done—to deserve this?

They took his body out of the cart and carried it into the Chapel of St. Peter-ad-Vincula. A crowd began to swell around the wooden platform erected on the Green. *He that is faithful unto death. . . . Dear Father, do not let me fail You!*

They will be coming for me now. Have I left anything undone? I look around my little chamber and think it strange that soon all trace of me shall be swept from it.

There is a ring of boots upon the stair. Ellen clasps her hands in an effort not to cry. Mrs. Tylney and Annie weep openly. There is agony in the eyes of the priest. Soon it will be over. Soon I shall see the smile of my Bridegroom.

It is enough. I must deliver this record to my Ellen's keeping. I shall close it and look once more upon the lines I have written upon the wall of my chamber as my last testament.

Deo juvante, nil nocet. . . . malus;
Et non juvante, nil juvat labor gravis,
Post tenebris, spero lucem.

While God assists us, envy bites in vain;
If God forsakes us, fruitless all our pain.
I hope for light after the darkness.

Jane Dudley

Epilogue

My name is Ellen. You will know me as the companion of my mistress, Lady Jane, whose life ended at the Tower of London on the twelfth of February, 1554. That was fourteen years ago. My own death is now very near, and I wish, before I die, to make the record complete.

How clearly that winter day remains in my memory. It might have been only yesterday that Elizabeth Tylney, the priest, and I followed Lady Jane and the Lieutenant of the Tower down the stairs of Master Partridge's lodgings. As we started toward the center of the Green, I saw the lass put one hand on the lieutenant's arm; in the other she held her prayer book which she read on the way. Elizabeth and I, a few feet behind, wept to see how like a bairn she looked beside him.

At the scaffold we mounted the steps and saw the headsman standing there in his scarlet robes and mask. Lady Jane turned to Sir John to ask if she could give the speech she had readied. He nodded, and she went to the rail. A great hush fell over the people. There were many there; priests, grand lords and ladies from Queen Mary's household, and even women and children who lived there at the Tower. But she looked at them all without showing any fear, and when she spoke her voice was clear and strong. Even in my grief I was proud of her.

"Good people," she said, "I have come here to die, and by law I am condemned. My offense against the Queen's Highness was only in consenting to the devices of others, which is now deemed treason. But it was never of my seeking, but by the counsel of those who should have had more understanding of things than I, who knew little of the law, and much less of the titles of the Crown. Of their procurement and the desire for them I wash my hands in innocency before God and in the face of all of you good people this day."

She stopped, then struggled to go on.

"I pray you all bear me witness that I die a true Christian, and that I look to be saved by no other means than by the mercy of God, in the blood of His only Son, Jesus Christ. And I confess that when I did know the Word of God, I neglected it, and loved myself and the world; therefore this plague is justly and worthily happened to me for my sins. And yet, I thank God for His goodness, that He has given me time to repent.

"And now, good people, *while I am alive*, I pray you assist me with your prayers."

She did not seem sure what she must do then. More than a few about the scaffold were weeping. She looked up at Doctor Feckenham and asked if she should say a psalm. He said yes, and together they knelt. Somehow I knew she would choose the fifty-first.

Have mercy upon me, O God, according to thy lovingkindness. . . . For I acknowledge my transgressions: and my sin is ever before me. Against the, thee only, have I sinned, and done this evil in thy sight. . . . Create in me a clean heart, O God; and renew a right spirit within me. Cast me not away from thy presence; and take not thy holy spirit from me. Restore unto me the joy of thy salvation; and uphold me. . . . For the sacrifices of God are a broken spirit: a broken and a contrite heart, O God, thou wilt not despise. . . .

They got up then, hand in hand, and stood looking at one another. I never thought to see a grown man—not to say a priest—weep, but this one came as close to it as I will ever see. It was plain he had no hope for her soul, and that she knew it. For the first time I felt pity for the man. He was without the consolation that I had that I would see my mistress again.

"I pray that God will reward you for your kindness to me," she told him. Then, with a spark of her old humor, she added, "Although I must say, it was more unwelcome to me than my instant death is terrible!" On an impulse she reached up and kissed him.

Sir John took a step forward, and she gave him her prayer

book, thanking him well for his good and thoughtful help during the past months. She removed her gloves and handed them to Elizabeth, and then began to unfasten the neck of her gown. It was I who should have helped her then—I, who swore to myself I would do nothing to make these moments more difficult!—but I could not. The lass's gentleness undid me so I did not even see the executioner start to unbutton her gown or I should have made him sorry for it! It was Elizabeth who went at last and removed the collar so that her poor shoulders were bare and exposed to the raw wind.

The headsman knelt in front of her, as was the custom, and asked her forgiveness. She gave it, and he stood aside, requiring her to stand upon the straw. Now she could see the block and the ax, and I felt the shudder that then went through her as if it were my own self.

"I pray you—dispatch me quickly!" she said, and knelt upon the straw. "Will you take it off before I lay down?"

"No, madam," he replied.

She took the handkerchief from Elizabeth and tied it herself around her eyes. Then she reached forward for the block. It was not there—it was further than she thought, and panic overcame her. She cried out, *"Where is it? What shall I do?"*

Every last soul of us stood frozen. None of us could bring ourselves to help her toward her death. And while we watched her, she scrabbled all around her in the straw, hunting.

She cried out again, and it was enough to tear the heart from a body— *"Please, someone, tell me where it is!"*

At last a stranger moved from somewhere below the platform, came up the stairs, and put her hand on the block. Quickly she laid her head down in the carved hollow, then spread out her arms.

"Lord, into Thy hands I commend my spirit."

And it was over. . . .

For us who had to go on living with the memory, it has been harder. Elizabeth Tylney is dead now, taken in a plague of the pox. Annie Jacob is back with her seafaring husband. She comes to visit me now and again with her two fine sons.

As for Doctor Feckenham, he was made Dean of St. Paul's just after Lady Jane's death; and the last I knew, John Bridges was still

Lieutenant of the Tower. Many are gone now who had a part in my lady's death. Judge Morgan, who sentenced her, went raving mad soon after, and they say he kept calling her name, begging her to leave him, until he died. But it is Queen Mary who truly bears the guilt of that execution. Her reign was an unlucky one—for her and her subjects. Prince Philip never loved her, and she never had the child she longed for; after a few years he went back to Spain. The Protestants never knew such persecution as under Mary. The fires were rekindled and hundreds like Latimer and Ridley went to the stake. When the Queen died in 1558 there were few to mourn her passing.

But I'm glad the lass was spared the grief of her father's execution on Tower Hill, less than a fortnight after her own. Lord Thomas Grey, her uncle, was beheaded on April the twenty-fifth. The Princess Elizabeth was imprisoned for many months in the same Tower prison as Lord Guildford's brother, Robert Dudley. They became great friends at that time, and now that she is Queen she has made him Earl of Leicester and her favorite courtier.

It is well, too, that my lady did not see her mother's remarriage to Adrian Stokes, the secretary. They were an ill-suited couple, and I do not know what satisfaction they took in the match. In any event Lady Francis died within a few years.

As for young Katie's fate, Lady Jane's heart would have been broken. At the beginning of Elizabeth's reign, Lady Katherine came to me and told me she was going to marry Lord Edward Seymour. They were both alone and both seeking some kind of consolation within their circumstances. But when Elizabeth found out about the marriage, and that Lady Katherine, who was then heir-presumptive, was to have a child, she and Edward were sent to prison. There she bore her child, and, sometime later, a second. After seven more years in an unspeakable dungeon, she died of a fever.

I have not forgotten what my lady asked me to do before she died.

"Ellen," she said, "will you go back one more time to Bradgate, in the spring of the year, and look at it all again for me? Will you promise me that?"

And I have done so. The manor is falling into disrepair now, and the gardens and orchards, once Leicestershire's pride, go untended. But the valley is still beautiful. I shall tell her so when I see her. But somehow I think the lass has other valleys now, valleys even brighter and bonnier than Bradgate. For God has wiped the tears from her eyes, and there will be no more sorrow, or pain, or death for her ever again.

It should be noted that the Scripture passages quoted are from the 1611 or King James Version of the Bible instead of the earlier Great Bible of King Henry VIII which would probably have been used by Lady Jane and her contemporaries. The texts, however, do not differ essentially.

Because I believe one cannot improve on the dramatic force of what actually occurred, I have endeavored to adhere closely to all known facts, occasionally using direct quotations from speeches or letters to lend a more authentic note.

Lady Jane Grey was neither saintly victim or covetous villain; she was a young girl capable of stumbling into the usual pitfalls found in human experience. The overriding truimph of her story lies in her faith, so magnificently declared just before her execution, that nothing, "neither death, nor life, nor angels, nor principalities, nor powers, nor things present, nor things to come, nor height, nor depth, nor any other creature, shall be able to separate us from the love of God, which is in Christ Jesus our Lord."

There alone lies her glory, and her crown.

Bibliography

Augustine, Saint. *The Confessions of St. Augustine.* Translated by Warner. New York: New American Library, 1963.

Bartlett, David W. *The Life of Lady Jane Grey.* Philadelphia: Porter and Coates, n.d.

Chapman, Hester W. *Lady Jane Grey.* Boston: Little, Brown and Co., 1962.

Davey, Richard. *The Nine Days' Queen: Lady Jane Grey and Her Times.* London: Methuen and Co., 1910.

Guest, M. J. *A Handbook of English History.* New York: Macmillan, 1898.

Malvern, Gladys. *The World of Lady Jane Grey.* New York: Vanguard Press, 1964.

Nichols, John G., ed. *The Chronicle of Queen Jane and of Two Years of Queen Mary.* London: J. B. Nichols and Son, n.d.

Plato. *Five Great Dialogues: Apology, Crito, Phaedo, Symposium, Republic.* Translated by B. Jowett. Roslyn, New York: Walter J. Black, Inc., 1942.

Pollard, A. F. *England Under Protector Somerset.* New York: Russell and Russell, 1966.

Strickland, Agnes. *Lives of the Queens of England.* Vols. 2 and 3. Philadelphia: Lippincott, 1893.

Vance, Marguerite. *Lady Jane Grey, Reluctant Queen.* New York: Dutton, 1952.

Williams, Neville. *Henry VIII and His Court.* New York: Macmillan, 1971.

Principal Characters

Lady Jane Grey

Henry Grey / Marquess of Dorset / Duke of Suffolk - Jane's father

Frances Brandon / Marchioness of Dorset / Duchess of Suffolk - Jane's mother

Katherine Grey - Jane's sister

Thomas Seymour - the Lord High Admiral & Jane's guardian

Catherine Parr - widow of Henry VIII

Edward Seymour / Duke of Somerset - the Lord Protector & Thomas's brother

Lady Margery - mother of Thomas & Edward Seymour

Edward Seymour / Earl of Hertford - son of Edward Seymour

King Edward VI - son and heir of Henry VIII

Lady Mary - daughter of Henry VIII

Princess Elizabeth - daughter of Henry VIII

John Dudley / Earl of Warwick / Duke of Northumberland - member of King Edward's Council

Guildford Dudley - his son

Ellen - Jane's nurse and attendant

Annie Jacob
Elizabeth Tylney } Jane's Attendants

Sir John Bridges - Lieutenant of London Tower

Doctor John Feckenham - Mary's priest